An Archaeology of Institutional Confinement

The Hyde Park Barracks, 1848–1886

Peter Davies, Penny Crook and Tim Murray

Studies in Australasian Historical Archaeology
Volume 4

Australasian Society for Historical Archaeology

SYDNEY UNIVERSITY PRESS

Published 2013 by SYDNEY UNIVERSITY PRESS
University of Sydney Library
sydney.edu.au/sup
In association with the Australasian Society for Historical Archaeology
asha.org.au

© Peter Davies, Penny Crook and Tim Murray 2013
© Australasian Society for Historical Archaeology 2013
Adapted from *An Archaeology of Institutional Refuge: The Material Culture of the Hyde Park Barracks, Sydney, 1848–1886* by Penny Crook and Tim Murray © Penny Crook and Tim Murray 2006

Reproduction and Communication for Other Purposes

Except as permitted under the Copyright Act, no part of this edition may be reproduced, stored in a retrieval system, or communicated in any form or by any means without prior written permission. All requests for reproduction or communication should be made to the Australasian Society for Historical Archaeology at the address below:

Australasian Society for Historical Archaeology Inc.
PO Box 2497
North Parramatta NSW 1750
Australia

secretary@asha.org.au

National Library of Australia Cataloguing-in-Publication entry

Author: Davies, Peter, 1968– author.
Title: An archaeology of institutional confinement: the Hyde Park Barracks, 1848–1886 / Peter Davies, Penny Crook, Tim Murray.

ISBN: 9781920899790 (paperback)

Series: Studies in Australasian historical archaeology; v.4.

Notes: Includes bibliographical references and index.

Subjects: Hyde Park Barracks (Sydney, NSW)
 Women's shelters--New South Wales--Sydney.
 Women--Institutional care--New South Wales--Sydney.
 Women immigrants--New South Wales--Sydney.
 Material culture--New South Wales--Sydney.
 Sydney (NSW)--Social life and customs--1788–1900.

Other Authors/Contributors:
 Crook, Penny, author, Murray, Tim, 1955- author.

Dewey Number:
 362.8398099441

AUSTRALASIAN SOCIETY FOR HISTORICAL ARCHAEOLOGY EDITORIAL BOARD

Professor Eleanor Conlin Casella, University of Manchester, UK
Dr Mary Casey, Director, Casey & Lowe Pty Ltd, Sydney, NSW
Emeritus Professor Graham Connah, Australian National University, ACT
Dr Martin Gibbs, Senior Lecturer, University of Sydney, NSW
Dr Michael Given, Senior Lecturer, University of Glasgow, UK
Dr Grace Karskens, Associate Professor, University of New South Wales, Sydney, NSW
Dr Tracy Ireland, Assistant Professor, University of Canberra, ACT
Dr Susan Lawrence, Associate Professor, La Trobe University, Melbourne, VIC
Professor Jane Lydon, Future Fellow, University of Western Australia, WA
Professor Tim Murray, Dean, Humanities and Social Sciences, La Trobe University, Melbourne, VIC
Professor Charles Orser, New York State Museum and Illinois State University, USA
Dr Caroline Phillips, Honorary Research Fellow, University of Auckland, New Zealand
Dr Jon Prangnell, Senior Lecturer, University of Queensland, Brisbane, QLD
Dr Neville Ritchie, Waikato Conservancy, Department of Conservation, Hamilton, New Zealand
Dr Ian W. G. Smith, Associate Professor, University of Otago, New Zealand
Dr Iain Stuart, Principal, JCIS Consultants, Sydney, NSW

MONOGRAPH EDITORS

Dr Martin Gibbs
Dr Peter Davies

ABOUT THE SERIES

The *Studies in Australasian Historical Archaeology* series is designed to make the results of high-quality research in historical archaeology available to archaeologists, other researchers, students and the public. A particular aim of the series is to ensure that the data from these studies are also made available, either within the volumes or in associated websites, to facilitate opportunities for inter-site comparison and critical evaluation of analytical methods and interpretations. Future releases in the series will include edited and revised versions of Australasian higher-degree theses, major consultancy projects and academic research, and commissioned studies on other topics of interest.

CONTENTS

List of Figures	vii
List of Tables	x
Abbreviations	xi
Acknowledgements	xii
Preamble	xiii

1 Introduction ... 1
   The Hyde Park Barracks: A Brief History ... 1
   Architecture of the Hyde Park Barracks ... 6
      Modifications and renovations ... 8
   Writing about the Barracks ... 9

2 The Underfloor Assemblage of the Hyde Park Barracks ... 11
   Architectural Context: The Subfloor Cavities ... 11
   Processes of Deposition: Accidental Loss, Rats and Concealment ... 13
   Recovery of the Underfloor Assemblage ... 14
   Summary of the Underfloor Assemblage ... 15
   The Stairwell Landing on Level 3 ... 18
   History of the Collection ... 19

3 Charity and Immigration in 19th-Century NSW ... 23
   Government Welfare ... 25
      Female immigrants ... 26
      Irish female orphans ... 27

4 The Workings of an Institution ... 29
   Room Use ... 30
   The Matron ... 31
   The Inmates ... 32
   Asylum Work ... 35
   Control ... 36
   Sanitation ... 38
   Medicine ... 41
   Death and Burial ... 43
   Visitors and Special Occasions ... 44
   Official and Administrative Records ... 46

5 Daily Life in the Asylum ... 47
   Communal Meals ... 47
   Smoking ... 48
   Sewing, Craft and Fancy Work ... 55

Fancy work	57
Hat-making	59
Leather-working and shoe repair	59
Mending and makeshift tooling	60
Textiles	61
Cotton prints	63
Clothing	65
Religious Instruction and Private Devotion	70
Advice to the dejected: Religious Tracts at the Hyde Park Barracks	71
Rosaries and devotional medals	74
Sectarian division	75
Religious faith among the Asylum inmates	76
Printed Matter: Literature and Reading	77
6 Private Lives	**79**
The Applewhaite-Hicks Family	79
Hicks Family Quarters and Artefact Assemblage	84
Lucy Hicks	85
Marked Goods: Ownership and Identification	87
Ephemera and Keepsakes	88
Children at the Hyde Park Barracks	90
7 The Archaeology of 19th-Century Institutions	**93**
Life at the Hyde Park Barracks	94
Daily labour	95
'Making do': Institutional Consumption and Private Adaptation	96
Improvement and spirituality	97
Concluding Remarks	98
Appendices	**99**
1. Institutional occupants of the Hyde Park Barracks	99
2. Inmates from the Destitute Asylum	100
3. Artefact fragment counts from excavated deposits in Level 1 of the main building and peripheral areas	103
References	**105**
Index	**116**

FIGURES

1.1	Plan of Hyde Park Barracks, adapted from Freycinet's 1819 plan, Commissioner Bigge's 1822 plan, and S. L. Harris' 1824 plan.	2
1.2	Location of Hyde Park Barracks in relation to Sydney streets and landmarks.	3
1.3	View of the Royal Mint and Hyde Park Barracks taken from the steeple of St James' Church c.1871, with The Domain, Woolloomooloo and Potts Point in the distance.	5
1.4	General view of Hyde Park Barracks main building.	7
1.5	Detail of Level 1 window.	7
1.6	Simplified plan of Hyde Park Barracks, about 1870.	9
2.1	Cavity spaces between the joists below the floor on Level 3, looking east. Note the stack of floor boards on the scaffold at left.	11
2.2	Minimum dates for joist groups on Levels 2 and 3 of the main building based on ceiling modifications.	12
2.3	Floor cavity on Level 3.	14
2.4	Plan of Level 2 and Level 3 showing joist groups (in large figures) and joist spaces.	15
2.5	The surviving landing on Level 3.	18
2.6	Location of excavation trenches; '4' = Stage 1 excavations (1980); 'A2/6' = Stage 2 excavations (1981).	20
3.1	Sydney Benevolent Asylum, 1861.	24
3.2	White cotton fragment with ink hand-writing, possibly part of a name-tag.	27
4.1	Schematic plan of room functions and numbers.	30
4.2	Bone lice-comb from the Hyde Park Asylum.	41
4.3	Hyde Park Asylum Dispensary Label for Alice Fry on a dark olive-green gin or schnapps bottle. Alice Fry died on 5 February 1868, aged 56 years, of a uterine tumour.	42
4.4	Hyde Park Asylum Dispensary Label for 'F Cunningham' on a gin or schnapps bottle. Francis Cunningham was part of the first intake of inmates in 1862.	42
4.5	Wooden disc with hand-written identification: 'The Ointment / Mrs Harris'.	42
4.6	Daily average of inmate numbers at the Hyde Park Asylum, and annual death-rate.	43
5.1	Well preserved and heavily stained clay pipe from Level 3 with wad of tobacco stuck in bowl.	49
5.2	Hardened string matches from Level 3.	51
5.3	Heavily used pipe bowl made by P. Mclean of Dundee. The cross-hatched heart served as a match strike.	51
5.4	Matchbox from tobacconist Thomas Saywell of Park Street in Sydney.	52
5.5	Matchbox from Swedish manufacturer Björneborgs Tändsticksfabricks.	52
5.6	Matchbox made in Lidkoping in Sweden between 1880 and 1890. The original design dates from 1851–1860 and was made in Finland by Lemminkainen.	52
5.7	Heavily stained stem fragment ground down to form new mouthpiece, with tooth marks.	54
5.8	Shortened and reworked stem with tooth marks around new mouthpiece.	54

List of Figures

5.9	Fluted bowl with bandaged stem of dark woven fabric.	55
5.10	Short pipe stem with bandage of coarse thread over hardened gum or resin.	55
5.11	Pipe stem with bandage of coarse thread over cardboard.	55
5.12	Stained pipe with bandaged stem.	55
5.13	Clay pipe stem modified into possible chalk stick.	55
5.14	Curved pipe stem made by B. Jacobs of London, with mouthpiece edged with metal band.	55
5.15	Small copper alloy thimble inscribed 'FROM A FRIEND'.	56
5.16	Needle packet from H. Milward & Sons.	56
5.17	Handmade pin cushion.	57
5.18	Three wooden cotton reels from the northern dormitory on Level 3.	57
5.19	Wooden cotton reel with remnant brown thread.	57
5.20	Lid from bone cotton barrel.	57
5.21	Bone handle of needlework tool.	58
5.22	Brown velvet embroidered with flower and leaf design.	58
5.23	Plain cotton fragment decorated in broderie anglaise from the Hicks apartments on Level 2. This technique was widely used for baby clothes, dolls' clothes and underwear in the 19th century.	58
5.24	Band of plaited palm fibre.	59
5.25	Leather shoe heel with square nail holes.	59
5.26	Roll of leather for shoe repair.	60
5.27	Shoe repaired with cotton insert).	60
5.28	Plain cotton structural offcut hem.	60
5.29	Makeshift tatting shuttle, possibly crafted from a discarded matchbox.	61
5.30	Makeshift thread reel made from piece of folded cardboard.	61
5.31	Makeshift thread reel made from folded newspaper.	61
5.32	Paper offcut used as pin packet.	61
5.33	Hand sewn leather knife sheath from the stair landing on Level 3.	61
5.34	Roughly made wooden clothes peg.	61
5.35	Scrap of fine cotton with manufacturer's stamp in black ink.	62
5.36	Purple cotton prints from Levels 2 and 3.	64
5.37	Blue woollen sock.	65
5.38	Remains of cotton cuff and sleeve with blue geometric prints.	65
5.39	Cotton bodice in purple print and modified with plain calico sleeves.	66
5.40	Cotton apron with hand-made lace trim; button and tie remnant preserved at waist.	66
5.41	Hand sewn bonnet with ruffle around face.	66
5.42	Dining room at Newington Women's Asylum, around 1890.	67
5.43	Inmates in yard at Newington Women's Asylum, around 1890.	67
5.44	Copper alloy belt buckle with central lozenge and four leaf motif.	68
5.45	Plain cotton glove with elastic wrist band.	68
5.46	Open weave brown ribbon with blue loops on selvage and hand sewn floral motif.	68
5.47	Card backing for a packet of hooks-and-eyes.	68
5.48	Heading carefully torn from religious tract.	73
5.49	*The Economy of Human Life*, originally written by the 4th Earl of Chesterfield.	73
5.50	Rat-chewed Catholic prayer book.	74
5.51	Fragment from the Scots–Gaelic Book of Common Prayer.	74
5.52	Title page of moralizing tract, 'Self Help'.	74
5.53	Devotional medal, obverse and reverse.	75

List of Figures

5.54	Large print religious tract from the Level 3 stair landing.	77
5.55	Fragment of large print religious text for the poorly sighted.	77
5.56	Uncut broadsheet of the front page of the *Sydney Morning Herald* issued on Saturday 4 February 1871.	78
5.57	Sawtooth cuts on edge of newsprint.	78
6.1	Scenes from the Hiring Room at the Hyde Park Barracks Immigration Depot.	83
6.2	Remains of letter probably written to William Hicks.	84
6.3	Remains of letter probably written by Lucy Hicks.	85
6.4	Government form regarding medical comforts to immigrants arriving on the *General Caulfield* in August 1865.	89
6.5	Flask bottle with silk strap.	89
6.6	Shellcraft cover of a pocket album, possibly of photographs or postcards. The spine (UF3339) is marked 'FORGET ME NOT'.	89
6.7	Remains of handwritten list, possibly a list of personal possessions.	90
6.8	Gilt-brass brooch with three pink glass gems.	90
6.9	Wooden toy blocks with traces of illustrated paper.	91
6.10	Miniature pedestal fruit bowl from doll house set.	91
6.11	Printed cardboard toy figure.	91
6.12	Small bone domino, probably handmade.	92
6.13	Infant cotton bodice with decorated bands at sleeves, waist and neck.	92

TABLES

2.1	Summary of Hyde Park Barracks artefact assemblage.	15
2.2	Summary count of artefact fragments by joist group and room number.	16
2.3	Artefact fragment counts in the main building of the Hyde Park Barracks.	17
2.4	Outline of projects affecting the Hyde Park Barracks collection and its catalogue.	19
4.1	Fragments of pharmaceutical items in the main building.	43
5.1	Distribution of cutlery items on Level 2 and Level 3.	47
5.2	Fragments of all smoking items from specific areas at the Hyde Park Barracks.	49
5.3	Clay pipe makers and distributors represented at the Hyde Park Barracks.	50
5.4	Level 2 clay tobacco pipe minimum object count, based on mouthpiece and bowl/shank representation.	51
5.5	Level 3 clay tobacco pipe minimum object count, based on mouthpiece and bowl/shank representation.	51
5.6	Matchbox brands recovered from underfloor spaces.	52
5.7	Glazed clay pipe mouthpiece colours from Levels 2 and 3.	53
5.8	Staining and discoloration on clay pipe bowls from Levels 1 and 3.	53
5.9	Sewing equipment from all three levels of the main Barracks building (fragment count).	56
5.10	Needlework tools.	58
5.11	Shoe pieces and leather offcuts.	59
5.12	Shape of textile offcuts from Levels 2 and 3.	60
5.13	Textile types from Levels 2 and 3.	62
5.14	Cotton textile print colours.	63
5.15	Garment remains, components and accessories recovered from the underfloor collection.	66
5.16	Button forms and materials from Level 2.	69
5.17	Button forms and materials from Level 3.	69
5.18	Fragments of dateable newsprint from Levels 2 and 3 of the main Barracks building.	78
6.1	Artefacts marked with the names individual inmates, immigrants and other unknown persons.	88
6.2	Bead materials.	90
6.3	The children of Matron Lucy Hicks, formerly Lucy Applewhaite.	91
6.4	Child-related artefacts.	91
6.5	Slate writing equipment.	92

ABBREVIATIONS

JG	Joist Group
JS	Joist Space
MNV	Minimum Number of Vessels
SMH	*Sydney Morning Herald*
UF	Underflooor
UG	Underground
SRNSW	State Records NSW

ACKNOWLEDGEMENTS

This book is the result of two collaborative projects between the Historic Houses Trust of New South Wales and Professor Tim Murray of the Archaeology Program at La Trobe University in Melbourne, that were supported by two Australian Research Council grants. We gratefully acknowledge the help of various people and institutions during the life of this project. In the first place we thank senior executives of the Historic Houses Trust of New South Wales, including Peter Watts, Helen Temple, Sue Hunt and Kate Clark, who recognised the importance of the Hyde Park Barracks archaeological collection and have offered unstinting support over the years. Caroline Lorentz, Mark Viner and Dayn Cooper provided invaluable administrative support. Gary Crockett, curator of the Hyde Park Barracks Museum, has been untiring in his management of the artefact database, preparing boxes of artefacts for despatch to La Trobe University, and patiently answering endless questions about the collection.

Our work has built on the previous efforts of many archaeologists, historians and other specialists, including the original excavators and cataloguers at the Hyde Park Barracks led by Patricia Burritt, Wendy Thorp and Dana Mider during multiple phases of work. We also acknowledge the more recent work that has contributed substantially to the preparation of this volume, including substantive research by Bridget Berry and Joy Hughes; Laila Ellmoos (Project Historian, Exploring the Archaeology of the Modern City project who prepared a history of the Barracks building which was adapted for this book); and Sophie Pullar, who catalogued many thousands of artefacts from the Barracks collection in 2003–2004.

Graham Connah kindly donated copies of early archaeological reports on the Hyde Park Barracks, and Annika Korsgaard provided scans of Barracks-related material. Daniel Percival made available a copy of his thesis on the Supreme Court site in Sydney and Jon Prangnell dug out his thesis on the Peel Island Lazaret. Alex Thorn assisted with the collection of archival material. Librarians at the Caroline Simpson Research Library, Historic Houses Trust of NSW, provided access to obscure materials and helped with research queries. The State Library of NSW provided permission to publish images from their collections. Staff and students in the Archaeology Program at La Trobe University, and the Department of Archaeology at the University of Sydney offered valuable feedback and ideas at different stages of the project. Specialist artefact advice came from various individuals, including Jerry Bell, Richard Cosgrove, Kris Courtney, Gary Crockett, Ian Evans, Jillian Garvey, Denis Gojak, Susan Lawrence and Linda Young. Susan Bridekirk did a splendid subeditorial job on the text.

We also appreciate the support of the Australasian Society of Historical Archaeology for agreeing to publish this book in the Society's Monograph Series.

PREAMBLE

This is a book about an extraordinary archaeological collection that represents a globally significant testimony to the lives of convicts, and women both immigrant and destitute, who came to Australia during the 19th century. The collection was excavated in 1980 and 1981 at the site of Sydney's Hyde Park Barracks. Of the 113,606 individual items found, 70% (80,037) were retrieved from under the floorboards of the second and third floors of the main Barracks building, and this book presents the analysis of this larger proportion of the total assemblage. It is the largest, most comprehensive, and best-preserved archaeological assemblage derived from any 19th-century institution in the world.

Concealed for up to 160 years in the cavities between floorboards and ceilings, this underfloor assemblage is of world significance because it is a unique archaeological record of institutional confinement, especially of women. Of course there are other prisons and asylums scattered around the globe, but none have the richness, variety and scale of the Hyde Park Barracks assemblage. The dry conditions preserved a wide range of fragile materials, such as paper, textiles and other organic products that rarely occur in regular subsurface archaeological contexts.

This book demonstrates one of the great strengths of historical archaeology and the fundamentals of its fascination — we know when this underfloor assemblage was created and who made it. And we can link the artefacts to the occupants of the buildings.

The underfloor assemblage dates specifically to the 40 year period, 1848–1886, during which a female Immigration Depot and a Government Asylum for Infirm and Destitute Women occupied the second and third floors of the Barracks. While this means that there were thousands of women who lived on these floors at one time or another, for different periods of time, from days to years, there was also one woman, and her family, who lived there the longest of them all. And for 24 years she had a significant impact on the residents — the one time matron of both of these government institutions — Lucy Applewhaite-Hicks.

Most of the items in the collection from under the floorboards were used by and belonged to working-class women: young female migrants, Irish orphans, sick and old destitute women, many of whose names we will never know, and women for whom we have few, or no historical records. Some of the women can be identified, some are described in newspapers and government reports, and by evangelical visitors and doctors. So while there are accounts of their public lives, the assemblage gives us some evidence of their private lives in the depot and asylum. In some cases the analysis of the assemblage provides us with evidence for an alternative view of the dire Dickensian institution — and one that was more humane. This makes the collection even more special — for here is in many cases the only record we have of their lives at the Barracks. Many of these women were the ancestors of modern Australians. Some of them had been convicts, some migrated to Australia as prospective wives and mothers — as the new colony's 'life blood'. But all of them, in some way or another, participated in the founding of a new nation. Others became outsiders — the old and sick who had nowhere else to go and no one else to care for them, but they had the colonial government's alternative to the Victorian institution or workhouse — the Asylum.

As an employee, a government appointment and a middle-class woman there are many descriptions of Matron Lucy Applewhaite-Hicks, and many historical records in which she appears. In some her opinions are recorded verbatim, in others she is described by others and castigated. She was a public person. But as with the working-class women from the depot and asylum, analysis of the underfloor assemblage, and the documentary records, provides us with evidence for an alternative view of her, and with new evidence of her private and family life.

1
INTRODUCTION

The Hyde Park Barracks is a landmark building of early colonial Sydney. Best known for its fine Georgian architecture and its association with convicts, the Barracks has a complex history of occupation and modification, and a rich archaeological legacy. It is the Barracks' archaeological collection that is the focus of this book. When the last convicts were removed in 1848, the building entered a new phase, becoming, among other things, an Immigration Depot for young female migrants arriving from the United Kingdom, and from 1862, an Asylum for infirm and destitute women. These two groups of women occupied the Barracks until 1886, and over the years they lost, discarded and sometimes concealed large quantities of debris and personal items in subfloor cavities. This material includes an extensive array of sewing equipment, clothing pieces, religious items, medicinal bottles, and literally thousands of textile offcuts and paper scraps, along with numerous other objects. These artefacts provide a unique opportunity to explore the lives of these women and their place in Australian society.

The assemblage recovered from the Hyde Park Barracks is significant as one of the largest, most comprehensive and best preserved archaeological assemblages derived from any 19th-century institution anywhere in the world. The bulk of the collection was excavated in 1980 and 1981, with around 70% coming from underfloor spaces of the main building and dating to the Depot and Asylum period (1848–1886). The collection has the capacity to tell us much about the history of women in the 19th century, specifically in relation to destitute asylums and their English counterparts — the workhouse — and, to a lesser extent, the experience of female immigration in the mid-19th century.

The collection has been the focus of dozens of archaeological studies since its recovery three decades ago, but many of these have struggled to come to terms with the size, complexity and meanings of the material. In 2001 the underfloor collection became the focus of a detailed archaeological assessment as part of the Exploring the Archaeology of the Modern City (EAMC) project, a joint investigation between the Historic Houses Trust (HHT) of New South Wales, the Archaeology Program at La Trobe University and the Australian Research Council (Crook et al. 2003). This work identified the great potential of the collection, and an adjunct project was launched in partnership with the Historic Houses Trust to expand and upgrade the original artefact catalogues. The result was the first substantive monograph on the Barracks to describe the archaeology of the underfloor collection and place it within the context of archaeologies of the 19th century, institutionalisation, consumption and migration (Crook and Murray 2006). In 2008 Davies and Murray began further work to complete the re-cataloguing and contextual analysis of artefacts, and create a consistent database for the underfloor collection.

Our aim in this book is to build on Crook and Murray's previous work and to present a detailed account of the archaeological material and its many meanings within the context of an archaeology of refuge. The unusual nature of the assemblage, however, requires a novel approach, with large quantities of items rarely encountered in conventional archaeological contexts here taking centre stage. For this reason our approach is a holistic one, integrating empirical data about the artefacts with interpretations of spatial context and historical evidence about the Barracks complex and its various occupants. Our focus is primarily on the underfloor collection, that is, material recovered from subfloor cavities on Levels 2 and 3 of the main building, for what it reveals about the lives, relationships and experiences of institutional women in 19th-century Sydney.

THE HYDE PARK BARRACKS: A BRIEF HISTORY

The Hyde Park Barracks was built under instruction from Governor Lachlan Macquarie between 1817 and 1819 to provide secure accommodation for male government-assigned convicts who, until that time, roamed Sydney's streets after their day's work and were responsible for their own lodgings.[1] Macquarie

---

[1] The first convict barracks in Australia was the Castle Hill Government Farm, built at Baulkham Hills near Parramatta in 1803. Excavation of the site in 2005 revealed the foundations of a large stone building, but little in the way of associated artefacts (Wilson and Douglas 2005). Following the Castle Hill uprising in 1804, when a group of mainly Irish convicts rebelled unsuccessfully against the authorities, no further convict barracks were built until 1817, when construction of the Hyde Park Barracks commenced. Around 1819, the Carters' Barracks, at the south end of George Street, were also built to lodge convicts, with up to 180 men employed at making and hauling bricks. Two treadmills were installed in the complex by 1824 (Evans 1983:96–97; Hirst 1983:63; Kerr 1984:53; Macquarie 1925 [1822]:686).

1. Introduction

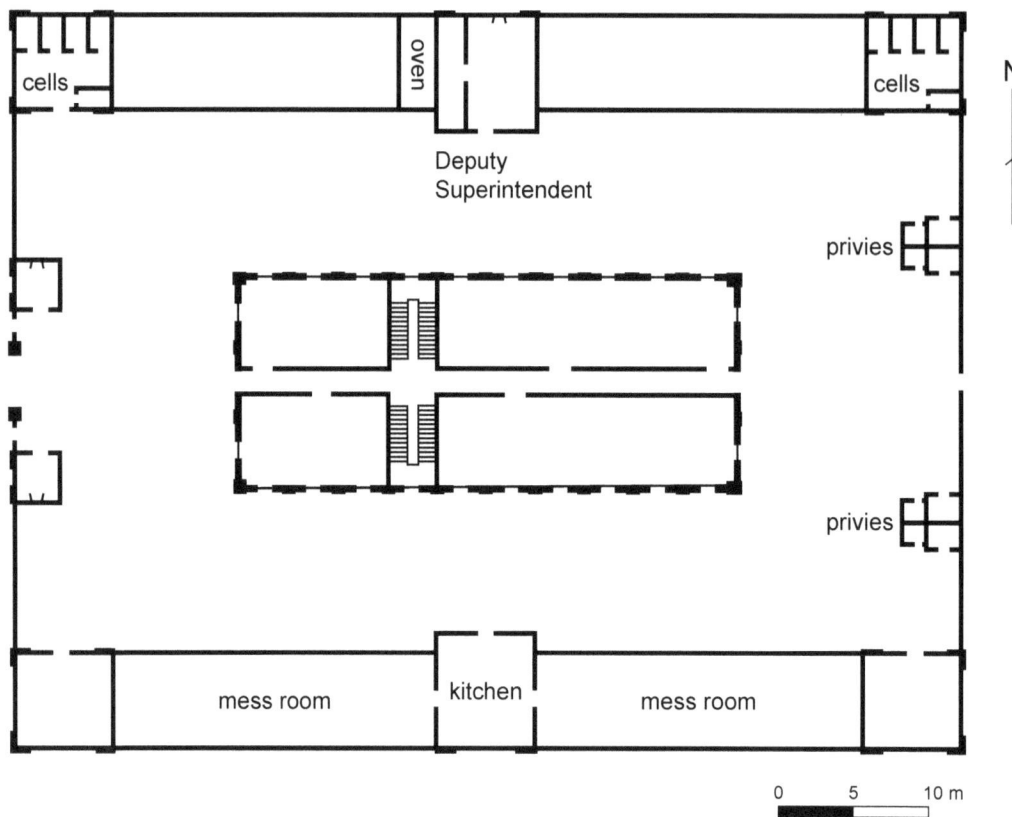

Figure 1.1: Plan of Hyde Park Barracks, adapted from Freycinet's 1819 plan (Historic Houses Trust 2003:5), Commissioner Bigge's 1822 plan (in Baker 1965:16), and S. L. Harris' 1824 plan (in Baker 1965:30).

believed that the convicts had too much free time, which they abused in robbery and drunkenness. He wanted convicts on government service subject to tighter discipline and easier mustering, so more work could be obtained from them. His response was to create a large barracks where the men would be confined every night during the week, but allowed to work on their own account on weekends (Hirst 1983:41–44).

The Barracks complex was constructed by skilled convict labour to a design specified by the convict architect, Francis Greenway (**Figure 1.1**). In Greenway's original Georgian design, the compound comprised a central dormitory building, enclosed by perimeter walls with corner pavilions that contained both cells and guard houses. Two ranges of additional buildings flanked the northern and southern perimeter walls, comprising a kitchen, bakery and mess, in addition to residential quarters for the Deputy Superintendent and his family. Open sheds were later built against the eastern and western compound walls to provide additional shelter. As a reward for services, Francis Greenway's conditional pardon was made absolute.

The Barracks was intended to house 600 convicts, but up to 1400 may have been accommodated there in later years (Cozens 1848). With more than 9000 male convicts in the colony by 1819, however, only a fraction were held at Hyde Park (Shaw 1966:96).

In the wards they slept in hammocks slung from wooden rails and beams. The work day extended more or less from dawn to dusk, with an hour's break for lunch. Supervision within the wards was minimal, and thieving, gambling and nocturnal escapes were reported as chronic problems (Ritchie 1971:17; Select Committee 1844).

The Hyde Park Barracks was built to provide accommodation for convicts, not as a prison. In Britain, during the later 18th and early 19th centuries, there was significant debate about crime, laws, punishment and gaols. Penal reformers such as John Howard and Jeremy Bentham promoted a new regime of punishment, directed not at the physical chastisement of the criminal, but at reforming 'the heart, the thoughts, the will, the inclinations' of the prisoner (Foucault 1977:16). The new way to discourage criminal behaviour was through punishment by confinement in prison, rather than by the infliction of bodily pain. The British government responded by building two new prisons, one at Millbank, which opened in 1816, and Pentonville, which opened in 1842, while continuing with the use of hulks as floating prisons, and transportation (Brodie et al. 2002:60, 94; Ignatieff 1978:93–95).

While convict transportation to Australia continued throughout this period of shifting ideas about the punishment and reform of criminals, the

Hyde Park Barracks, however, was constructed with little apparent awareness of these changing penal philosophies. There were no facilities to separate or isolate convicts, for example, and internal surveillance and control were also limited. Architectural historian James Semple Kerr argues that Greenway's barracks adapted a form used in the 18th century for a variety of domestic, agricultural and urban buildings and institutions (Kerr 1988:24). He also suggests that the composition and style of the Barracks was meant to embellish the urban environment, and that its function as a place of confinement was incidental (Kerr 1988:40). J. M. Freeland (1968:40) writes that the Hyde Park Barracks was 'just a barn — but a very handsome barn'.

Although the Hyde Park Barracks did not, and could not, function effectively as a prison, increasingly, in the 1830s and 1840s, it was used as a place of secondary punishment for refractory prisoners. Governor George Gipps observed in 1844 that the convicts in the Barracks 'are for the most part those, who in consequence of their misbehaviour have failed to receive indulgences ...

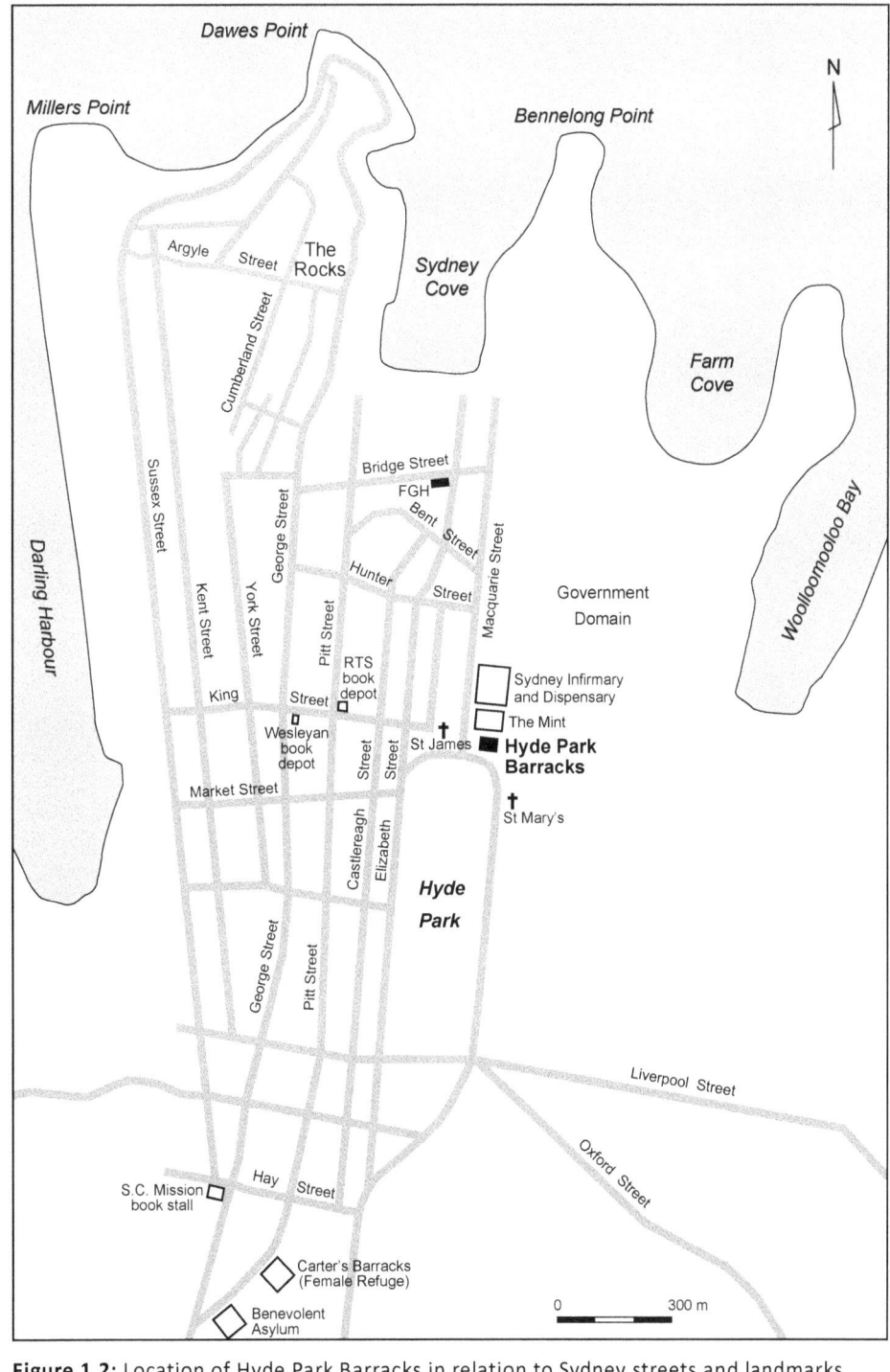

Figure 1.2: Location of Hyde Park Barracks in relation to Sydney streets and landmarks.

1. Introduction

they are in fact the refuse of the Convict system in New South Wales' (Gipps 1925[1844]:84). Well-behaved convicts continued to be rewarded with permission to live outside the Barracks, on their path to a ticket-of-leave (or conditional pardon), leaving the complex increasingly as an option for the punishment of secondary offenders.

The Court of General Sessions was established in the northern range of the Barracks complex in 1830, beginning a long occupation of the complex by the colonial courts. Magistrates dealt mostly with offences against the labour code (which mostly applied to convicts), including drunkenness, disobedience, neglect of work, absconding and insolence. Physical punishment for convict misdemeanours increased in severity during this period. The range of penalties magistrates could impose comprised flogging, or work in irons on road gangs, to fines, extensions of sentence, or being sent to Norfolk Island (Molesworth 1967 [1838]:24–25). A convict was appointed as an official scourger at the Barracks in 1822. The flogging triangle 'squatted obscenely' in the south-east corner of the Barracks yard, with flogging carried out in the presence of all the convicts, with 25–50 lashes being the norm.

Following the end of convict transportation to New South Wales in 1840, the continued presence of convicts in the Hyde Park Barracks became an embarrassing anomaly in the heart of Sydney (**Figure 1.2**). Surrounded by public buildings and churches, offices and businesses, the hundreds of convicts marching in and out were a daily reminder of the colony's convict origins. There were around 800 convicts occupying the Barracks at this time, many transported to the colony from Great Britain, and others, expiree convicts from Norfolk Island completing the residue of their sentence. Much of the public antagonism towards convicts was due to the fact that while transportation to New South Wales had ceased, the NSW government was still required to spend large sums accommodating the convicts, and to pay for a substantial police and court system to prosecute the crimes they committed. There was public resentment at the ongoing cost of paying for the 'criminal outcasts' of Great Britain, when colonial society was trying to leave the dark stain of convictism behind.

In 1848 the remaining 19 convicts still living at the Hyde Park Barracks were moved to Cockatoo Island in Sydney Harbour, and the main Barracks building was refitted to accommodate orphans and a new kind of mobile workforce: the single, female migrant:

> The building known as Hyde Park Barracks having survived the system of supplying this colony with Labour, to which it so long ministered, has been appropriated as a place in which the [Irish] Orphan Immigrants will be lodged until provided their places. Situated at the corner of Hyde Park [it] is an open place, which, though in immediate proximity to the business thoroughfares of Sydney, is not one itself, with the Government Domain behind it stretching to the Waters of Harbour, and an uninterrupted view to the Heads of Port Jackson, surrounded by a spacious yard enclosed by high walls, and close to the principal Church of England and Roman Catholic churches, and to the residences of the clergymen who officiate there, this building appears to possess every advantage that could be desired, with reference to the health, the seclusion and the moral and religious instruction of the inmates, and the convenience of persons coming to hire them. It consists of three stories, divided into large airy wards, and affords convenient accommodation for about 300 persons. The females are under the immediate superintendence of an experienced resident matron, who was appointed by the Colonial Land and Emigration Commissioners to the charge of the children who arrived last year in the *"Sir Edward Parry"*, and where efficiency in that situation caused her appointment to the office which she now fills. (*Annual Report of Immigration in NSW* 1848, page 5, SRNSW 4/4708 in HPB Research Folder: 'AONSW Immigration and Government Asylum Records')

The offices of the Agent for Immigration and the hiring rooms of the Female Immigration Depot were located on the ground floor, with temporary accommodation for new arrivals transferred from the Quarantine Station at North Head in Sydney Harbour provided on Levels 2 and 3. From 1849 to 1855 the Immigration Depot also accommodated the wives and children of convicts brought out to the colony at government expense to be reunited with their husbands and fathers (McIntyre 2011:25). Convicts had petitioned authorities to have their families sent out from Britain since at least the 1830s (Hirst 1983:129). The poor families of Irish emancipists dominated the scheme, with around 85 per cent of the almost one thousand family members sent out coming from Ireland (Berry 2005a).

The arrival of young female immigrants was part of the much wider movement of people during the 19th century from Britain to far-flung parts of the Empire. Governments sought to attract the labour they needed through assisted fares and cheap passages. Single women were in high demand as domestic servants, with the expectation that in time they would also become the wives and mothers of colonial Australians (Chilton 2007; Gothard 2001; Hammerton 1979; Rushen 2003).

In addition to the Female Immigration Depot and Immigration Office, the Hyde Park Barracks briefly accommodated several thousand Irish female orphans between 1848 and 1852 (McClaughlin

Figure 1.3: View of the Royal Mint and Hyde Park Barracks taken from the steeple of St James' Church c.1871, with The Domain, Woolloomooloo and Potts Point in the distance (Mitchell Library, State Library of NSW, SPF/322).

1991). Other government agencies resident in the northern and southern parts of the complex included the Government Printing Office (1848–1856), the Vaccine Institute (1857–1886), the NSW Volunteer Rifle Corps (1861–1870), the City Coroner (1862–1907), the Sydney District Court (1858–1978) and the Court of Requests (1856–1859). Cases in the District Court mostly involved the recovery of small amounts of money, property disputes, defamation, and breaches of contract, providing much work for barristers and solicitors filing in and out of the Hyde Park Barracks compound (Holt 1976:59).

In 1862, the top floor of the main building was given over for the use of the Government Asylum for Infirm and Destitute Women, following the colonial government's assumption of responsibility for the care of the aged and infirm. Over 150 women were transferred from the overcrowded Benevolent Asylum at the south end of Pitt Street. Transported in horse-drawn omnibuses, 101 women arrived on 15 February, 36 women on 1 March and 14 more women on 13 March (Hughes 2004:58). Matron of the Immigration Depot and from February 1862, of the Asylum, Lucy Applewhaite (later Hicks) also lived at the Hyde Park Barracks along with her husband John Applewhaite, Master of the Asylum, and their family. The presence of the Asylum for the care of aged and infirm women placed many demands on the old convict barracks, and many modifications were required over the next two decades (**Figure 1.3**).

Overcrowding was an ongoing problem, with almost 300 inmates at the Asylum by the 1880s. In 1886 the women were moved to a new purpose-built facility at Newington on the Parramatta River, and the Immigration Depot was relocated.

Thus began the third major phase of the Hyde Park Barracks' history: the judicial period. At this time, the area became known as Chancery Square, and buildings within the Hyde Park Barracks complex were extensively remodelled for use by the Department of Attorney General and Justice. Level 1 of the main building was occupied by the Land Evaluation Office, a small court, and judges', jury and witness rooms. The Clerk of the Peace and rooms of the Industrial Court took up much of Level 2, while the Master in Lunacy took over Level 3 with his clerks, reporters and records (Lucas 1990:25; Street *et al.* 1993). Two large courtrooms (Equity and Bankruptcy) were attached to the eastern end of the main building after the 1860s verandah was removed. Internal partitions were installed in the main building to divide up the large rooms into smaller spaces, while a number of doors were cut through the central corridor to provide access to

1. Introduction

these new offices (Davies 1990:8; Varman 1981:37). Around this time there was a proposal to replace the Barracks with a new building to house a public library. The Colonial Architect, James Barnet, sketched designs based on the style of the British Museum, but nothing further came of it (Chanin 2011:14).

By the turn of the century the entire complex was renamed Queen's Square, and comprised the main building and a jumble of makeshift structures that filled the courtyard. Government offices located at the complex at that time included the Metropolitan District Court, Coroners Court and Equity Court, the Master in Lunacy, the Clerk of Peace Office, the Registrar of Probates and the Estates Office. In the following decades numerous additions and alterations were made to the buildings, and there was a suggestion in 1935 to convert the central building into a museum (Thorp 1980:9:1). In 1946 a report recommended that the building be demolished (Baker 1965:42). The complex continued, however, to be used primarily for judicial purposes until 1979.

In 1975, under the auspices of the Public Works Department, restoration of the Hyde Park Barracks buildings began while still being occupied by the Department of Attorney General and Justice, and ancillary police departments. The Barracks was placed on the Register of the National Estate in 1978, and three years later was granted one of Australia's first Permanent Conservation Orders (PCO) under the New South Wales *Heritage Act* 1977.

In 1980 the NSW government announced that the Hyde Park Barracks would be converted to a museum of Sydney's history and that the physical fabric of the building complex would be restored to its original convict phase. When restoration work began, artefacts were revealed in the underfloor spaces of the central dormitory building as well as in service trenches within the grounds of the compound. Following test trenching, the Public Works Department embarked on Sydney's first large-scale public excavation, which attracted media attention and was assisted by the work of many volunteers.

The Museum of Applied Arts and Sciences (MAAS) opened the Hyde Park Barracks to the public in 1984, as the first museum of its kind to focus on the history of Sydney. In 1990, the Barracks was transferred to the Historic Houses Trust (HHT), and after refurbishment, was reopened as a 'museum of itself' with permanent displays on the second and third floors and temporary exhibitions in the Greenway Gallery on the first floor. By 2001 the Parole Courts, which had occupied the north-eastern perimeter structures of the Barracks, became the final portion of the complex to come under the management of the HHT.

In 2008, the Commonwealth Government included the Hyde Park Barracks as part of a serial listing of eleven convict places for World Heritage nomination (Australian Government 2008). The UNESCO World Heritage Committee accepted the listing in July 2010. The Trust's Hyde Park Barracks Museum continues to operate successfully today as a museum depicting its own history, especially its convict phase.

ARCHITECTURE OF THE HYDE PARK BARRACKS

Governor Macquarie formally reserved the area of Hyde Park in 1810, an area known as the Cricket Ground or the Racecourse, renaming the area in tribute to its far grander namesake in London. In 1816 he initiated construction of the Hyde Park Barracks without approval from the Home Office, later telling Lord Bathurst, Secretary of State for the Colonies, that it would be 'productive of many Good Consequences, as to the personal Comfort and Improvement of the Morals of the Male Convicts, in the immediate Service of Government at Sydney' (Macquarie 1925 [1817]:720). Ground was marked out for the building in November 1816, and work by skilled convict labour began in March 1817. On 20 May 1819 the first batch of 130 convicts moved in, a precursor to the official opening on 4 June 1819, when 589 convicts sat down to a special meal to mark the occasion. Macquarie enjoyed the spectacle of so many felons treated to an abundance of 'good beef and bread, plum pudding and punch', followed by official speeches (Broadbent and Hughes 1997:56; Ellis 1973:116).

Francis Greenway's simple, elegant design was a familiar 18th-century arrangement, with a dominant central building set in a rectangular walled compound and aligned on an east-west axis (Kerr 1984:39). Commissioner Bigge described the internal fittings of the Barracks in detail:

> ... the principal barrack ... is a handsome brick structure 130 ft in length and 50 ft in breadth, and contains 3 stories, that are divided by a lofty passage, separating one range of sleeping rooms from the other. There are 4 rooms on each floor, and of these 6 are 35 ft by 19 and 6 others are 65 ft by 19. In each room rows of hammocks are slung to strong wooden rails, supported by upright staunchions fixed to the floor and roofs. 20 inches or 2 ft in breadth and 7 ft in length are allowed for each hammock; and the 2 rows are separated from each other by a small passage of 3 ft. 70 men sleep in each of the long rooms and 35 in the small ones. Access to each floor is afforded by 2 staircases, placed in the centre of the building; and the ventilation even in the warmest seasons is well maintained. The doors of the sleeping rooms, and those communicating with the courtyard, are not locked during the night. One wardsman [a convict] is appointed to each room, who is responsible for the conduct of the others ... Another dormitory is provided

Figure 1.4: General view of Hyde Park Barracks main building (P. Davies 2008).

in one of the long buildings on the north side of the yard, 80 ft in length by 17, in which the convicts lately arrived, and those returned into barrack by order of the magistrate are lodged. They sleep on the matrasses [sic] that are brought from the convict ships, and spread them upon raised and sloping platforms of wood similar to those used in military guard rooms. The convicts employed in the kitchens and bakehouse are allowed to hang their hammocks there. (Quoted in Kerr 1984:40–41)

Greenway used soft red sandstock bricks set in lime mortar for the main building, and stone for the compound walls and gate piers (**Figure 1.4**). The base course and string courses were of sandstone. Pilasters in the main building served as load-bearing elements for the large floor beams and ceiling members, while the low hipped roof was covered in wooden shingles. A domed ventilator was placed in the centre of the roof, with a bell suspended from the centre. A clock was placed in the pediment over the main entrance, below which was inscribed:

L MACQUARIE ESQ
GOVERNOR 1817

Large glass windows were set in each of the three levels. These included rectangular windows set in semi-circular arched niches on the first level, rectangular windows in the second level, and square windows on the third level (**Figure 1.5**). Window glass was expensive in the early 19th century due to stiff British excise laws, and

Figure 1.5: Detail of Level 1 window (P. Davies 2008).

1. Introduction

technical limitations on the production of Crown glass meant that panes were generally less than 16 inches (400 mm) in size (Boow 1991:100–101). The generous use of glass in the Barracks provided a practical way of admitting natural light into the interior of the large building, and may also have been a subtle statement by Macquarie and Greenway about the kind of settlement and society they wanted to build.

The perimeter wall of the Barracks compound was only 10½ feet high and, over the years, proved little obstacle for convicts wanting to escape. Its elevation may have been determined in part by Greenway's reluctance to obscure views of his building.

The buildings ranged along the northern wall included a prominent central building, connected on either side to a long, low single storey wing, each terminating in a small square pavilion containing five small punishment cells, 7 ft by 4 ft, for the solitary confinement of refractory convicts. The buildings ranged along the southern wall included two long mess rooms, each 100 ft in length, with the large kitchen in between. Privies were built adjacent to the eastern wall of the compound, while wash houses and a drying shed were later constructed nearby. On the east side of the Barracks a brick wall enclosed a four acre garden, cleared and stumped by the convicts, with a gardener's lodge in the centre (Thorpe 1980:2.2). At the main western entrance there were two square lodges used by a clerk and a constable overseeing the movement of convicts.

Responses to the construction varied. A detailed and positive account, probably written by Greenway himself, appeared in the *Sydney Gazette and New South Wales Advertiser* for 17 July 1819. The building was described as 'a noble structure of admired architecture ... The aspect of the building is beautiful at a distance, but at a near approach conveys an idea of towering grandeur.' Others objected, however, that its function was subordinated to its form. Commissioner Bigge, for example, acknowledged that the style was 'simple and handsome', but complained that the external walls were too low. He was concerned that the need for security had been sacrificed to the building's ornamentation.

Joseph Fowles was the last person to describe the building as a convict barracks, in 1848. He referred to 'the pile of building called Hyde Park Barracks', and argued that 'none of these edifices have much architectural pretension, being constructed entirely of brick and devoid of ornament, yet, the proportions being good, the masses broad, and the lines bold and unbroken, they form an imposing and dignified whole' (Fowles 1962 [1848]:28). He also acknowledged that the Barracks was 'very well adapted for the purpose for which it was designed' (Fowles 1962 [1848]:81).

Modifications and Renovations

A range of modifications and repairs were made to the Hyde Park Barracks over the years. In 1821, for example, only two years after its opening, the entire roof of the main building was re-shingled, because the initial selection and laying of [Casuarina] shingles had been inadequate (Thorp 1980:2.2). 'Squint' or spy holes were made in the walls of the dormitories on the second and third levels, to permit the wardsmen to keep a closer watch on the inmates. In 1824 it was reported that the water closets were 'in a most offensive state, for want of Proper Sewers round the Building to carry off the Soil' (quoted in Baker 1965:30). The perimeter wall was also undergoing repair at this time. During the early 1840s, reticulation pipes were laid from Busby's Bore to various points in the city, and it is likely that the Barracks was connected for the first time to a permanent water supply (Spiers 1995:50; Thorp 1980:4.2; Varman 1993: phase V). In 1847 the roof was re-shingled again, and the walls were repainted.

The departure of the remaining convicts in 1848 and the arrival of immigrant women necessitated further changes to the fabric and appearance of the building. The hammock rails and supports were removed and replaced with iron-framed beds, which were held in place by 'bed battens' nailed to the floor (Varman 1981:13). The battens indicate that beds were arranged in two east-west rows in the dormitory rooms. Lime-washing of 'walls, ceiling and inside of roof' was also carried out as a hygienic measure (Thorp 1980:4.2). Four new external water closets were installed, along with a pump to convey water to the second floor. A 260-foot-long stonewall fence, 11 feet high, was also built to separate the Immigration Depot from the Government Printing Office in the north of the compound. Shutters were installed on the windows of the central dormitory building around 1856.

Around 1862 the southern stair was removed, leaving only the northern stair for access to the upper levels. This was done to create extra floor space on all three levels of the main building, with new landings built on Levels 2 and 3. The landings were removed during renovations in the 1980s, and reinterpreted with a 'ghost' hand railing.

In 1863 a section of yard at the rear of the main building was fenced off for the use of the recently arrived Asylum women (**Figure 1.6**). A new kitchen was also built at the south-east corner of the Barracks. By 1864 the dining room of the Depot, on the ground floor of the Barracks, had become so overcrowded that a shed was erected by the screening wall between the Depot and law courts (Spiers 1995:63). A balcony and staircase were also built at the eastern end of Level 3, to allow separate access for the aged and infirm women to their yard, privies and washhouse, without having to go through the Immigration Depot. A bell-cot was

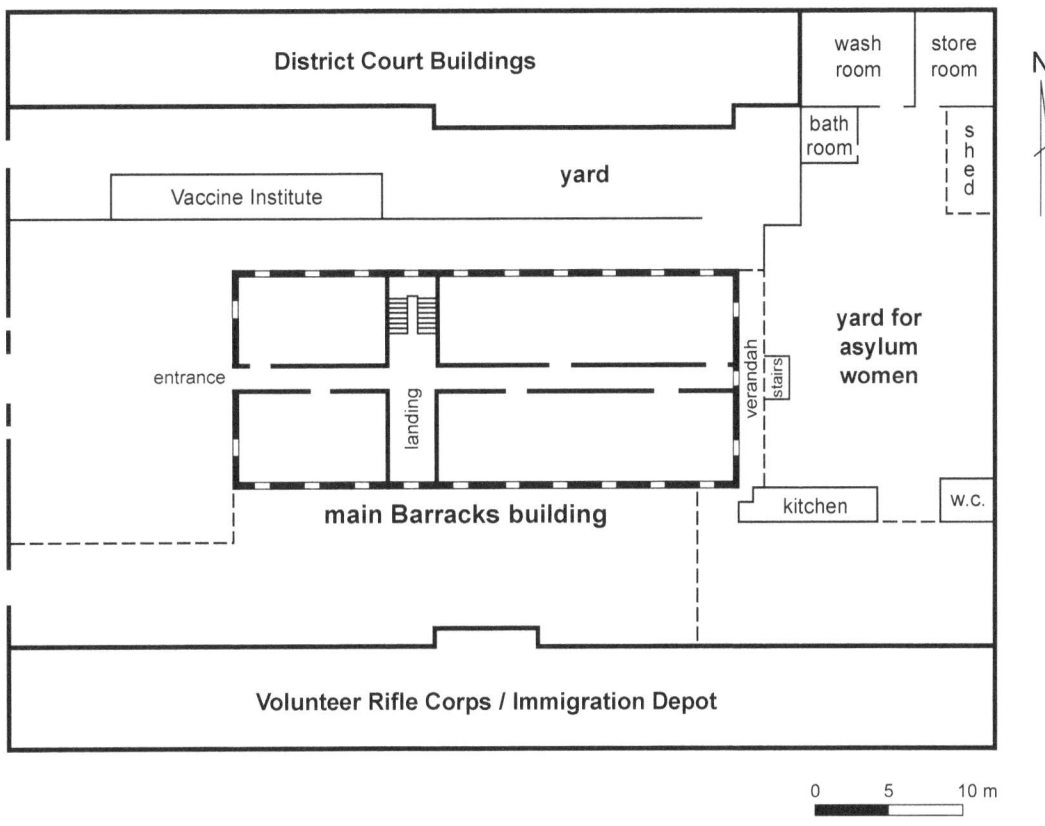

Figure 1.6: Simplified plan of Hyde Park Barracks, about 1870 (P. Davies 2011).

added to the roof of the Barracks in the late 1860s (Thorp 1980:6.2).

Modifications to the internal ceilings at this time were critical for the accumulation of underfloor archaeological deposits. Ceiling boards were introduced in most parts of the building with the arrival of the Immigration Depot in 1848. These were joined by tongue-and-groove fittings, which trapped many small artefacts that fell through the butted floorboards above. These were in turn replaced by lower lying ceiling boards which were installed during renovations at the beginning of the 1886 legal phase. In the few places where no ceiling boards had been installed in 1848 (e.g. the corridors on Levels 1 and 2) the ceiling boards of the legal phase provided the first opportunity for deposit to be accumulated below the floor boards. This change effectively sealed the cavities created by the introduction of ceiling boards in 1848 and the artefact assemblages which had accumulated within them for 38 years.

Writing about the Barracks

Although the Hyde Park Barracks is a well-known part of Australia's convict and colonial heritage, the historiography of the complex is very uneven. References to the building and its various occupants have appeared regularly over the years in books, articles and other publications, along with dozens of consultants' technical reports (Crook *et al.* 2003:15–17), however, there is no single comprehensive account of the Barracks and its occupant groups, and the associated archaeological material.

Convictism has been a popular theme in accounts of the Barracks, an emphasis reinforced by the inclusion of the site in 2010 on the World Heritage List as part of a serial nomination of convict places in Australia (Australian Government 2008; see Baker 1965; Bogle 1999; Emmett 1994; Irving and Cahill 2010:21–24; Moorhouse 1999:171–173; Robbins 2005). The museology of the Barracks, as a 'museum of itself', has also claimed critical attention (e.g. De Silvey 2006:334; Eggert 2009:31–40; Kelso 1995; Kirshenblatt-Gimblett 1998:168; Lydon 1996; Young 1992). The history and archaeology of the Immigration Depot[2] and the Destitute Asylum, however, and the century of civil and judicial administration that followed, are usually ignored in scholarly literature. Stephen Garton (1990), for example, described the government male destitute asylums at Parramatta and Liverpool, but not the

---

[2] Several historians have wrongly linked Caroline Chisholm with the Hyde Park Barracks, mistaking the short-lived Immigrants' Home she established in Bent Street (1841–1842) with the HPB Immigration Depot (e.g. Gothard 2001:167–168; Hamilton 2001:458). Chisholm was in fact in England from 1846–1854, when the Depot at the Barracks was established (Kiddle 1972:80, 182).

1. Introduction

Hyde Park Asylum for women. Historian Brian Dickey has written extensively about charity and welfare in colonial Australia, with a particular emphasis on New South Wales and South Australia, although much of his work on the former focused on the Benevolent Society of NSW and largely ignored the Hyde Park Asylum (Dickey 1966, 1973, 1976, 1987). Judith Godden's doctoral thesis on female philanthropy and charity in New South Wales from 1870 to 1900 mentions the Hyde Park Asylum only in passing (Godden 1983:66). The Asylum is also overlooked in many standard historical analyses of poverty in colonial NSW (e.g. Fitzgerald 1987; Kelly 1978; Mayne 1982; O'Brien 1988), while Kingston (1988:51) wrongly claims that only South Australia and Western Australia had state-subsidised benevolent asylums (Hughes 2004:3). A biography of Charles Cowper, the Colonial Secretary primarily responsible for establishing the Hyde Park Asylum, fails to mention this major achievement (Powell 1977). Joy Hughes (2004:1) describes the asylum as 'invisible'.

This silence may be due in part to the lack of readily accessible primary documents, with almost none of the Hyde Park Asylum's official records, including admission and discharge registers, ration returns, store books, letter books and other papers, having survived. Unlike its predecessor, the Benevolent Asylum, the Hyde Park institution was largely free of complaint and thus did not attract adverse newspaper attention — notwithstanding some public scrutiny in its later years (Hughes 2004:8). Primary historical material is available, however, scattered through archives from the Colonial Secretary, the Government Architect and the Public Works Department. Hughes' (2004) MA (Honours) thesis draws on this documentary archive to describe the Hyde Park Asylum in relation to the development of NSW colonial government policy on charity and welfare, placing the Asylum in a historical trajectory between the Sydney Benevolent Asylum and the Newington Asylum. Her work offers a valuable revision to the usual focus on convicts and immigrants, and illuminates in particular the life of Matron Lucy Hicks.[3]

In addition, two important sources of primary information about the Asylum emerged from official government inquiries. The 1874 Public Charities Commission reported on the workings and management of numerous charity institutions operating in the colony at the time. Matron Hicks gave evidence to the Commission on 24 September, which reveals her at the height of her control and influence. The Report of the Government Asylums Inquiry Board, which sat from August 1886 to March 1887, also casts important retrospective light on the operations at Hyde Park, and reveals a sharp decline in the standards of care. In total, Hicks gave evidence to the Board on nine separate occasions. Annual reports published by the Government Asylums Board, and the Inspector of Public Charities, also provide useful summary information about the costs and operations of the four institutions for the destitute under government control.

---

[3] For convenience, the Matron is referred to by her second and final name, Lucy Hicks, except when making reference to her life and work when she was known as Lucy Applewhaite, prior to 1870 when she married William Hicks.

2
THE UNDERFLOOR ASSEMBLAGE OF THE HYDE PARK BARRACKS

The most outstanding component of the Hyde Park Barracks Archaeology Collection is the underfloor assemblage, concealed for up to 160 years in the cavities below the floors on Levels 2 and 3. The assemblage is significant because its survival in the dry cavity spaces has preserved a wide range of fragile materials such as paper, textiles and other organic products that rarely survive in regular, subsurface archaeological contexts.

In this section we review the history of architectural changes to the Hyde Park Barracks as the context in which the formation and characteristics of its archaeological collection and associated processes of deposition took place (Schiffer 1987:64–69).[4]

Architectural Context: The Subfloor Cavities

When the Hyde Park Barracks was first constructed as a convict barracks, the floorboards were butted and fixed with machine-cut floor brads, which was typical for the time. Almost none of this original flooring has survived on the ground level, but the majority of boards on the first and second floors are original, although after decades of repairs and refits for various government departments, there were many areas of disturbance. The most affected areas were those around principal beams, near windows and under doorways (**Figure 2.1**). In other locations, boards were pulled up, buttressed with

Figure 2.1: Cavity spaces between the joists below the floor on Level 3, looking east. Note the stack of floor boards on the scaffold at left (V. Pavlovic 1982).

---

[4] Artefacts from the 'Underground' collection, recovered from excavations below the floor of Level 1 and elsewhere at the Barracks, are summarised in Appendix 3.

iron stirrups and then re-nailed (Varman 1981:11). Originally the boards ran across the width of the rooms but few had survived to their full length by the late 1970s (Varman 1981:7).

The original floorboards had been pit-sawn by convict workmen, with significant variations in width, thickness and evenness of cut caused by the different saws used, and the strength and skill of individual sawyers (Varman 1981:7). Later floorboards were cut by machine, and tongue-and-groove flooring became available by the 1840s. This means that as flooring was repaired and replaced over the years, a mix of boards was installed over the floor joists. As older timbers dried, shrank and split, gaps opened up between the boards and nails weakened their grip. By the Depot and Asylum years, it is probable that some sections of flooring were loose enough so that the floor boards could be lifted and items could be deposited in the subfloor spaces.

There is no clear evidence of the floor coverings used during the Asylum and Depot era, but it is likely that some areas of the building's floors were covered, although not for their full length of occupation, as indicated by the large quantities of material deposited beneath the floor. Linoleum was first developed in the 1860s although it did not become ubiquitous until the 1890s (Townrow 1990), so it seems unlikely that this would have been used during the Asylum period. Oral histories revealed that in the 20th century most floor areas were covered with linoleum or carpet, at least on Level 3, and it is likely that the floors were systematically covered with linoleum from 1886 when the law courts moved in.

The original ceilings of the Hyde Park Barracks were a mix of lath-and-plaster and exposed white-washed beams (Varman 1981:22). Ceiling boards were introduced in most parts of the building with the establishment of the Immigration Depot in 1848 (Potter 1981:48). The floor over the Matron's quarters on Level 2 was ceiled in 1865 'to prevent the inconvenience arising from the leakage which occasionally takes place from the upper rooms' (quoted in Thorp 1980:6.2). Ceiling boards either sealed the formerly exposed beams or, where lath-and-plaster ceilings had been installed, these were removed and replaced with the new boards. Lath-and-plaster boards survived at the western end of the ground floor hallway and the stair landing on Level 1, with traces recorded in the clock weight case on Level 3 (Varman 1981:22). Large quantities of artefacts were recovered from the subfloor spaces created above these lath-and-plaster remnants (JG59, JG60, JG61 and JG62).

The new ceiling boards were joined by tongue-and-groove fittings which trapped many tiny artefacts that had fallen through the butted floorboards above. These were in turn sealed by lower lying ceiling boards which were installed during the 1886 legal phase renovations and which were removed during the 1979–80 conservation works (Varman 1981:22). In the few places where no ceiling boards had been installed in 1848, such as the corridors on Levels 1 and 2, the ceiling boards of the legal phase provided the first opportunity for deposits to accumulate below the floor boards.

This sequence of floor and ceiling construction and modification has important consequences for the underfloor assemblage (**Figure 2.2**). Despite the great importance of the convict origins of the Barracks, the underfloor areas that are *potentially* of convict origin comprise only 3.6% of the floor space on Levels 2 and 3. Those dating to the women's phase, from 1848, comprise over 71% of the total area, and those dating from the legal phase, 16.2%. In four areas on the ground floor the ceiling boards collapsed during conservation

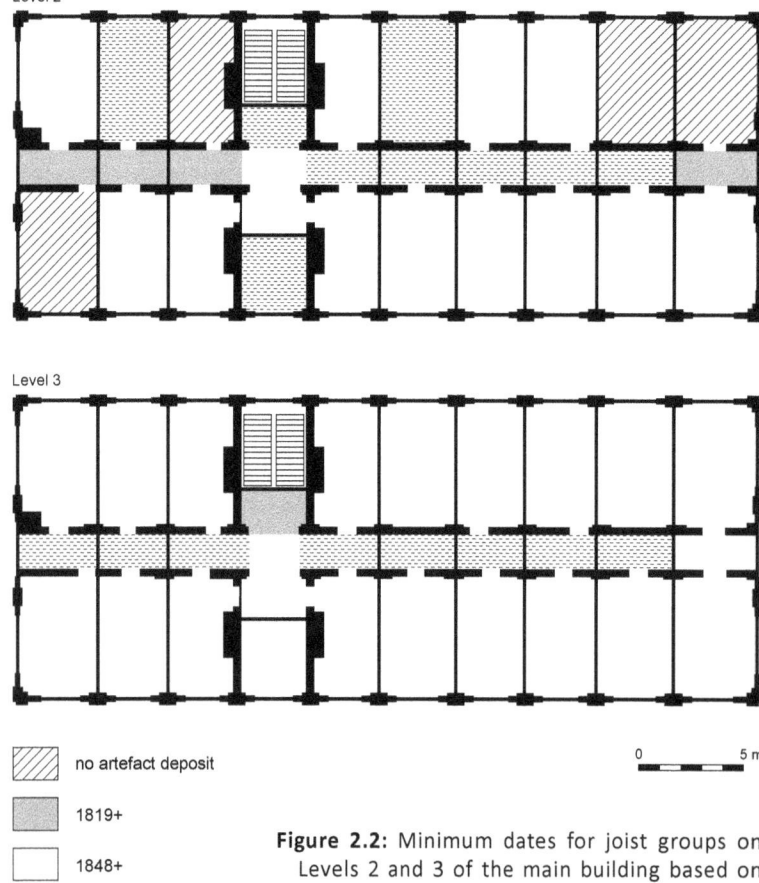

Figure 2.2: Minimum dates for joist groups on Levels 2 and 3 of the main building based on ceiling modifications (after Mider 1996 [1]:9–10; Varman 1981).

works and all the deposit that had accumulated from below the boards on Level 2 was lost. This represented 8.8% of the floor space.

Examined *in toto*, the Hyde Park Barracks assemblage is a palimpsest deposit, containing a range of materials dating from 1819 up to the mid-20th century, and includes material from the legal phase of office occupation.

Processes of Deposition: Accidental Loss, Rats and Concealment

The underfloor assemblage comprises a range of materials lost, swept or placed beneath the floorboards over a long period of time. The majority of underfloor deposits include an accumulation of small items such as buttons, beads, pins and paper clips that fell through the gaps of the boards when accidentally dropped, or incidentally swept between the cracks, along skirting boards, in fallen-through timber knots or other holes such as old nail shafts. Fragments of larger items, such as glass bottles or ceramic vessels, may also have been lost this way if a vessel shattered when dropped. Many of these items probably fell through the boards unnoticed.

The old and warped butted floorboards on Levels 2 and 3 would have provided ample opportunities to lose small items in this way. Sweeping and cleaning may also have resulted in the deliberate deposition of refuse under the floor. Large quantities of textile fragments and torn paper, for example, which accumulated on the floor under beds and in corners, may have been swept up and pushed below a conveniently loose floorboard.

It is likely that most items fell, or were placed, within a metre or so of where they were last used or accumulated. Once under the floor, they were concealed between joists that run perpendicular to the boards and were subject to further taphonomic processes. The first of these was due to disturbance or refuse deposition when boards were pulled up for maintenance work. Such human traffic in the underfloor spaces is likely to have caused damage to fragile items and other items in the deposit may have been moved or removed and discarded to make way for cables or other fixtures. It is also common that when a few boards have been pulled up, other 'above board' rubbish was probably discarded beneath them, prior to their reinstallation.

The second taphonomic process was disturbance from rats and other rodents. There is ample historical and archaeological evidence for rats at the Hyde Park Barracks. In 1864, Matron Hicks protested against Medical Officer Dr Walker's plan to lay rat poison in the building, owing to the smell and the 'injurious' effects it may have had on the expected immigrants (Daily Reports, 25 June 1864, SRNSW 9/6181b). Two years later Dr Walker was still struggling with the rats in his dispensary, which had become so infested with rodents that 'the destruction of Drugs and breakage of Glass is really very serious' (Memo, 5 Sept 1866, SRNSW 2/642A, see 'Medicine' for full quote). Ellen Jane Purnell, an inmate of the Asylum, claimed in 1886 that while Newington had some rats, it was nothing to the Hyde Park Barracks, which was 'a regular pig-stye' (Government Asylums Inquiry Board 1887:460).

At least six complete or near-complete rats' nests and a considerable number of rat carcasses have been recorded in the Barracks assemblage. Rats and mice form nests from any soft, portable material they find in their immediate environment, with each nest at the Barracks comprising paper, straw, grasses and large quantities of cotton scraps (Barnett 1976:148). Rats are highly adaptive creatures, readily exploiting the material culture of humans, as well as being very social animals, creating separate nest areas for sleeping, eating and disposing of wastes. The black rat (*Ratus ratus*) typically lives in the higher parts of a building, including walls and ceilings, whereas the brown rat (*Ratus norvegicus*) prefers ground burrows (Barnett 1976:4). Rats will range up to 50 metres from their nest to find food, often returning to the nest to eat in safety or to hoard the food (Hendrickson 1983:86; McDonald 2005). They can also climb vertical surfaces and squeeze into narrow spaces. Higginbotham considered that mice could easily have squeezed through mortise and tenon joins between the principal beams and joists on the upper floors, giving them 'free access throughout the underfloor spaces', but that rats, being larger rodents, may have been confined to joists along the window bays, where much gnawing was observed (Higginbotham 1981:32). Rats spend much of their waking time gnawing to keep their front incisors from growing too long, and can cut through wood, bone, concrete and even sheet metal (Hendrickson 1983:86). This behaviour is evident at the Barracks in the form of numerous gnawed books, buttons, textiles and wood offcuts.

Rodent activities have impact on the formation of the archaeological assemblage. Some items, especially lightweight and portable material such as fabric scraps, may have been 'stolen' by rats from above the floorboards during the night, and other items, lost below the boards, may have been relocated by rats within the underfloor space between rooms and even levels.

Mice skeletons were also recorded in the Barracks. Several were contained within a matchbox deposited below the floor at the eastern end of the corridor on Level 3 (UF17967). The skeletal material includes the remains of at least three individuals, represented by two well preserved skulls and segments of vertebral columns with articulated ribs. Further details of this item are provided in Davies and Garvey (2013).

In addition to accidental loss and rodent disturbance, another means of deposition below the floor was intentional discard or concealment. Notwithstanding the large gaps between the butted floorboards on Levels 2 and 3, many of the items recovered simply could not have been lost accidentally, or dragged by rats below the boards. Matchboxes and clay pipe bowls, for example, are too large to fall through the widest cracks or even large knots in floorboards, but may easily slip through or be placed in a small disused cut in a board. Larger objects, such as the complete pharmaceutical and schnapps bottles, can only have been deposited by lifting a board. Given that these large items were mostly found near windows and door frames where Varman (1981:7) notes that boards were shortened for repairs, the opportunities for lifting boards would have been greater. The possibility remains that the boards were lifted during renovation works (**Figure 2.3**), rather than by the inmates themselves.

In summary, the majority of the Hyde Park Barracks underfloor assemblage is likely to derive from accidental loss and incidental sweepings, most of which will survive in the general locale of where they were lost. A small but unquantifiable percentage of the assemblage probably derives from refuse following maintenance work, and a small number of items were probably deliberately concealed beneath the floorboards. Similarly, a small percentage of the assemblage was probably dragged beneath the floorboards by rats and mice, and a much greater proportion of the remaining deposit is likely to have been disturbed or relocated by rodents. It is also possible that some items were dragged from room to room, or even from floor to floor, for nest-building.

RECOVERY OF THE UNDERFLOOR ASSEMBLAGE

The archaeological collection at the Hyde Park Barracks is primarily the result of archaeological excavation and artefact recovery in the main building and grounds in 1980–1981. This process is described below in more detail in 'History of the Collection'. The underfloor assemblage was recovered from discrete spatial units on Levels 2 and 3. The spaces between each joist ('Joist Space' or JS) were grouped into areas partitioned by principal beams ('Joist Groups' or JG). All JGs were numbered from 1 to 62 (**Figure 2.4**). The JSs within each group were numbered from 1 to 14, running north to south in the main rooms and east to west in the corridor and stair-landing spaces (**Figure 2.4**).

Joist Spaces varied a little in size over the full extent of Levels 2 and 3. Generally, however, each subfloor JS measured about 400 mm in width, 200 mm in depth, and up to 3.70 m in length. The size of the underfloor area from which the artefacts were recovered included approximately 340 m^2 on Level 2 and 430 m^2 on Level 3, or about 770 m^2 as a whole.

This represents a considerable scale of archaeological 'excavation', and one that yielded a substantial collection of material refuse.

Floorboards were removed to allow the recovery of the underlying deposit, and were returned to their original location in the later stages of the restoration (Potter 1981:30). Larger items, including what appeared to be intact rats' nests, were removed manually while the remainder was recovered with industrial vacuum cleaners and bulk bagged for later analysis. Mider (1996 [1]:5) notes that the corridor areas were not vacuumed 'due to the high level of perceived disturbance from later building works (the installation of services)', which reduced the quantity of material recovered from these underfloor spaces.

Figure 2.3: Floor cavity on Level 3 (P. Davies 2009).

2. The Underfloor Assemblage of the Hyde Park Barracks

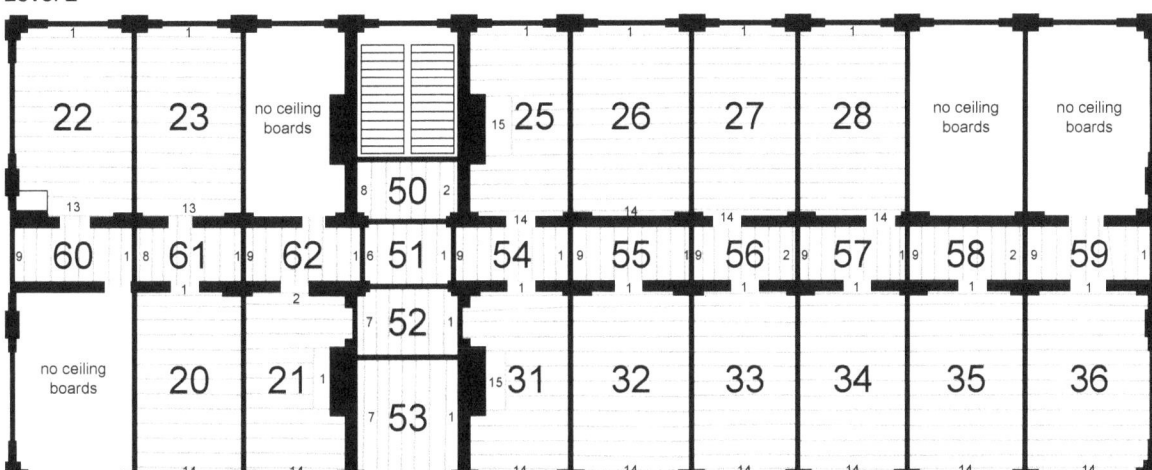

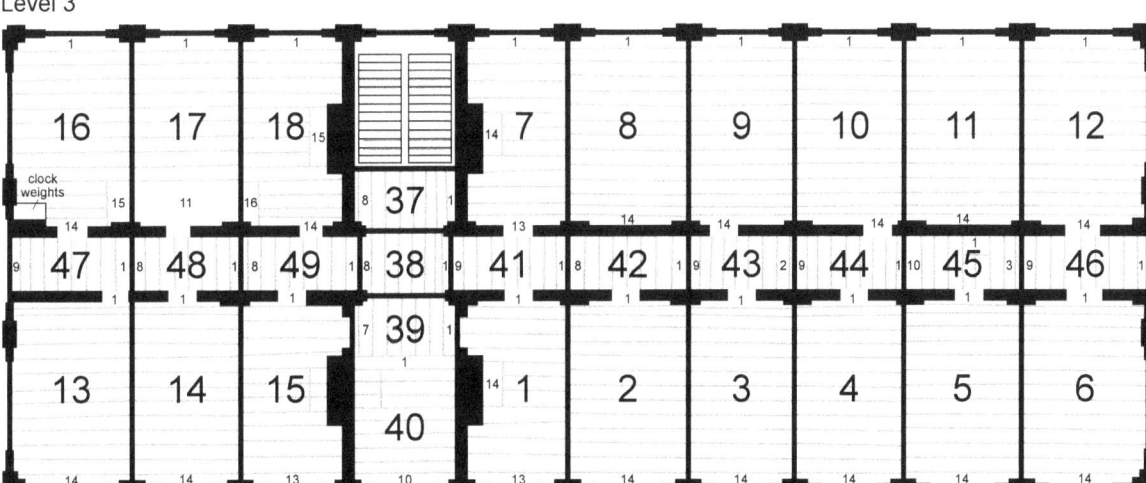

Figure 2.4: Plan of Level 2 and Level 3 showing joist groups (in large figures) and joist spaces.

Summary of the Underfloor Assemblage

The Hyde Park Barracks underfloor assemblage is characterised by both the diversity and the quantity of artefact forms represented, including large numbers of well preserved organic items (**Table 2.1** and **Table 2.3**). While most conventionally excavated assemblages are, typically, dominated by glass, ceramics and ferrous items, the Hyde Park Barracks material includes thousands of paper, textile, leather and other organic artefacts, along with large quantities of nails and other building debris. For some items, such as clay pipes, matches and matchboxes, pen nibs and textile offcuts, the underfloor collection includes some of the largest quantities of such material recorded from archaeological sites in Australia.

Assemblage component	Database records	Artefact count
Underfloor collection	18,286	80,037[5]
Underground collection	7,375	33,567[6]
Total	*25,661*	*113,606*

Table 2.1: Summary of Hyde Park Barracks artefact assemblage.

[5] Underfloor total includes 513 artefact fragments from unrecorded locations.
[6] Underground total includes artefacts from all excavations in courtyards and peripheral buildings of the HPB complex.

2. The Underfloor Assemblage of the Hyde Park Barracks

Level 2			Level 3		
Room	Joist group	Fragments	Room	Joist group	Fragments
L2-1	JG22	1,577	L3-1	JG16	1,033
	JG23	1,462		JG17	586
	Total	*3,039*		JG18	1,862
L2-2	JG50	81		*Total*	*3,481*
	JG51	481	L3-2	JG37	7,011
	Total	*562*		JG38	90
L2-3	JG25	578		*Total*	*7,101*
	JG26	509	L3-3	JG7	2,086
	JG27	1,794		JG8	844
	JG28	1,040		JG9	2,425
	Total	*3,921*		JG10	2,524
L2-5[7]	JG54	305		JG11	2,238
	JG55	196		JG12	2,684
	JG56	266		*Total*	*12,801*
	JG57	69	L3-4	JG41	218
	JG58	23		JG42	59
	JG59	2,722		JG43	118
	Total	*3,581*		JG44	97
L2-6	JG31	2,124		JG45	102
	JG32	2,583		JG46	1,363
	JG33	3,255		*Total*	*1,957*
	JG34	1,951	L3-5	JG1	1,765
	JG35	1,689		JG2	2,880
	JG36	1,810		JG3	955
	Total	*13,412*		JG4	487
L2-7	JG52	36		JG5	1,329
	JG53	0		JG6	1,981
	Total	*36*		*Total*	*9,397*
L2-8	JG20	1,371	L3-6	JG39	4,620
	JG21	1,034		JG40	1,353
	Total	*2,405*		*Total*	*5,973*
L2-9	JG60	912	L3-7	JG13	3,936
	JG61	368		JG14	2,467
	JG62	365		JG15	1,800
	Total	*1,645*		*Total*	*8,203*
			L3-8	JG47	305
				JG48	54
				JG49	179
				Total	*538*

Table 2.2: Summary count of artefact fragments by joist group and room number.

---

[7] Room 'L2-4' was not assigned in PWD plans.

2. The Underfloor Assemblage of the Hyde Park Barracks

Item	Level 1	Level 2	Level 3	Total
Ammunition	16	31	3	50
Bead	71	452	368	891
Bone	6,084	2,057	4,709	12,850
Bottle glass	1,284	831	3,002	5,117
Building materials	768	2,053	2,250	5,071
Button	355	193	396	944
Ceramic (table)	817	46	205	1,068
Cigar/ette	2	65	69	136
Clay tobacco pipe	2,090	302	1,006	3,398
Clerical fastener	134	150	694	978
Clothing accessory	28	45	51	124
Coal (fuel)	69	49	6	124
Coin/token	29	14	15	58
Comb	15	20	23	58
Cotton reel	4	20	72	96
Cutlery	135	15	75	225
Document		405	408	813
Electrical	95	506	250	851
Furnishing	103	86	39	228
Game piece	6	13	2	21
Garment		27	106	133
Hardware	144	694	308	1,146
Hook and eye	817	341	409	1,567
Hat (straw)		24	90	114
Jewellery	9	9	14	32
Jute rope		35	113	148
Leather	299	204	476	979
Lighting (lamp)	61	62	70	193
Match	17	2,070	3,320	5,407
Matchbox	1	25	417	443
Medicinal	48	37	379	464
Nail	2,431	7,357	7,042	16,830
Newspaper	22	422	321	765
Organic	1	262	646	909
Other	107	274	475	856
Packaging	193	63	102	358
Paper	23	2,349	8,214	10,586
Pen	71	99	302	472
Pencil (graphite)	3	37	20	60
Personal item	54	42	88	184
Pin	2,820	1,937	2,779	7,536
Printer's type		1		1
Religious item	1	16	229	246
Seed	468	1,206	2,730	4,404
Sewing tool	32	56	44	132
Shell	385	99	201	685
Slate pencil/board	22	44	9	75
Soap		13	14	27
Stoneware	87	5	80	172
String/cord		186	149	335
Table glass	8	12	21	41
Textile	352	2,882	7,120	10,354
Tool	13	27	47	87
Toy	28	36	16	80
Unidentified	638	611	613	1,862
Total	*21,260*	*28,917*	*50,607*	*100,784*

Table 2.3: Artefact fragment counts in the main building of the Hyde Park Barracks.

2. The Underfloor Assemblage of the Hyde Park Barracks

The deposition of artefact fragments across Levels 2 and 3 is relatively even, allowing for the loss of material from four joist groups (19, 24, 29 and 30) during conservation work. There is, however, a distinct concentration of material from the stair landing on Level 3 (discussed below) and in certain floor areas (Level 2: JG33, JG59; Level 3: JG13, 9–12; see **Table 2.2**). This may be the result of increased rodent activity, or the consequence of damaged floor boards allowing greater accumulation or lifting to dispose of refuse. The corridor areas generally have much less material because they were mostly ceiled later during the legal phase of occupation of the building.

The Hyde Park Barracks assemblage includes, in total, well over 100,000 artefact fragments (**Table 2.1**). The underground assemblage includes artefacts recovered from excavations in courtyards and peripheral buildings of the Hyde Park complex, as well as from Level 1. These represent approximately 29% of the total collection, with the remainder coming from the underfloor areas on Levels 2 and 3.

THE STAIRWELL LANDING ON LEVEL 3

One of the greatest concentrations of artefacts across the upper two floors of the main Barracks building comes from the stairway landing on Level 3, in Joist Groups 37, 38, 39 and 40. This includes an area of flooring in place of the original southern stairway (a mirror image of the one that survives today) that was probably installed in 1862 when the Asylum moved in, to create additional floor space on all three levels (**Figure 2.5**). We discuss the Level 3 landing here because of the large quantities of artefacts recovered from this area and their implications for the activities of the Asylum women.

A total of 13,074 artefact fragments were recorded in the landing spaces on each side of the corridor, including large quantities of clay pipes, textile offcuts, newsprint and religious texts. These represent 16.2% of the total underfloor assemblage in an area that comprises about 2.6% of the available floor space. In contrast, the floor spaces below the landing on Level 2 (JG 50, 51, 52 and 53) yielded only 598 artefact fragments, or 0.7% of the total underfloor assemblage. This relates in part to the removal of the staircase around 1862 and the removal of JG53. Nevertheless, the density of material below the Level 3 landing in comparison with the remainder of Levels 2 and 3 suggests that the deposits relate to specific activities on the landing itself.

The material from this small area is also interesting for the high integrity of the artefacts recovered from these deposits. There were 39 complete matchbox sets (with tray and cover), many with labels still attached and others with matches (mostly burnt) still inside. In addition to these there were 22 complete covers that found their way under

Figure 2.5: The surviving landing on Level 3 (P. Crook 2004).

the floor. There were also more than 40 complete or near-complete clay pipe bowls. While it might be easy to lose a fragment of a bowl or stem, dropping the whole bowl (usually 2 cm across and 3 cm high) through the floor cracks is far less likely. This is also the case for matchboxes, which measure roughly 6 x 4 x 2 cm, suggesting that they were deliberately stashed or trashed.

Most of the paper fragments date to the 1870s and 1880s, with 111 newspaper fragments dating from 1870 to 1886. There were also 39 datable matchboxes, most with tight date ranges within the 1870s and 1880s. These two independent means of dating — one being printed dates on newspapers or the mention of known, datable events, and matchboxes with known manufacturing dates — are rarely available to archaeologists and support the broad dating of this deposit to the 1870s and 1880s.

The stairwell landing deposit thus largely represents the last 10 or 15 years of the Asylum's life. The deposition of large quantities of material beneath the floorboards in this area may relate to a range of factors. Numbers of inmates increased relentlessly over the years, exacerbated by the closure of the Port Macquarie Asylum in 1869, and occasions when women were forced to sleep in the corridors, resulting in more women gathering in the few available communal spaces. The physical decay of the building may also be implicated, with areas of heavy traffic leading to loosening of old butted floorboards. Newspapers from the 1870s may well have come from William Hicks following his marriage to Lucy Applewhaite in 1870. It is also possible that the accumulating pressure of inmate numbers and other responsibilities weighed on the Matron such that it gradually undermined the workings of the institution, and undesirable behaviours developed beyond her watchful gaze.

History of the Collection

The record of the collection, the artefact catalogue, has been in the making from 1981 to the present day. Until 1998, the collection was divided into separate 'Underfloor' and 'Underground' collections, and each component had been organised, analysed, recorded and assessed by several project teams. Curators of the Hyde Park Barracks Museum developed a single database of the entire collection in 1998 by combining the 'Underground' and 'Underfloor' assemblages into a unified catalogue. In this section we briefly outline the history of excavation, assemblage formation and catalogue development at the Hyde Park Barracks over the last 30 years (**Table 2.4**).

Initial restorative work was carried out at the Hyde Park Barracks in the last years of the Attorney General's occupation during the late 1970s. The Public Works Department (PWD) then began more substantial construction work in 1979 to restore the Barracks to its convict phase in advance of its

Year/s	Project
1980	Excavation and analysis by Carol Powell
1980	Test-trenching by Wendy Thorp and team in the main building, north range and yard
1981	Excavation by Patricia Burritt and team of underfloor and underground deposits
1981–1983	Salvage excavation by Elizabeth Pinder
1981–1984	Salvage excavation by Graham Wilson at Bakehouse, Southern Gatehouse and Northern Gatehouse
1982	Artefact conservation by Glennda Marsh
1985–c.1994	Sydney University research design and preparation for catalogue of underfloor artefacts
1991	HPB Museum opened with display of artefacts
1994	Wendy Thorp Artefact Review and Management Recommendations: completed underground catalogue
1995	Finalisation and reporting of the catalogue of underfloor artefacts by Dana Mider
1996	Wendy Thorp unstratified artefacts report
1997	Peter Tonkin artefact 'stock-take' of underfloor and underground collections
1998–2001	The Hyde Park Barracks database
2001–2006	'Exploring the Archaeology of the Modern City' project by Tim Murray, Penny Crook, Laila Ellmoos and Sophie Pullar
2006–2011	'An Archaeology Institutional Refuge' project by Tim Murray, Penny Crook and Peter Davies

Table 2.4: Outline of projects affecting the Hyde Park Barracks collection and its catalogue.

2. The Underfloor Assemblage of the Hyde Park Barracks

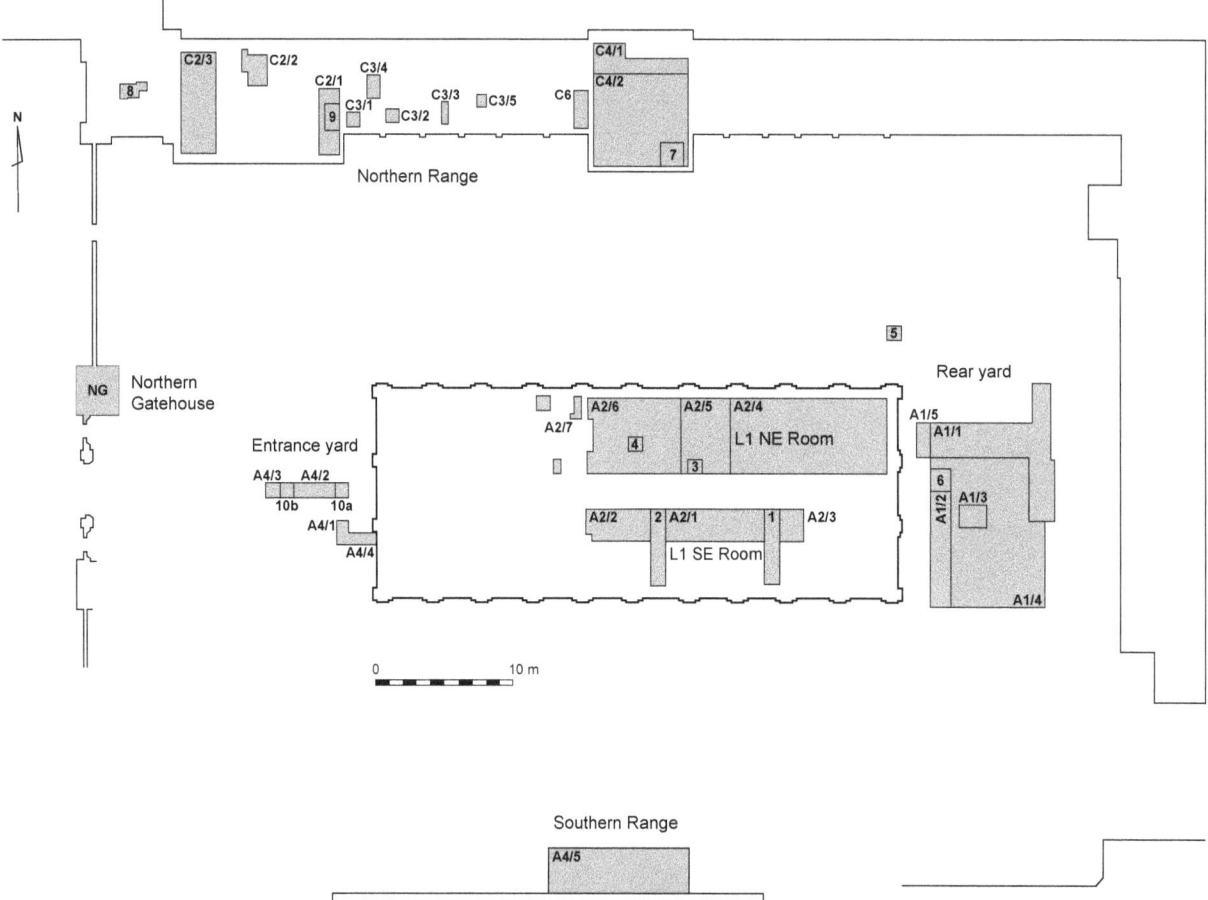

Figure 2.6: Location of excavation trenches; '4' = Stage 1 excavations (1980); 'A2/6' = Stage 2 excavations (1981).

conversion to a history museum. The warren of 'sub-standard accretions' that cluttered Greenway's original court was demolished and the many structures that had enclosed the main barrack building were removed (Proust 1996).

As restoration and construction work was underway, Carol Powell undertook archival research on the Hyde Park Barracks and the neighbouring buildings of the Sydney Mint, which were also being restored at the time. Powell also recorded important artefacts exposed during the conservation work (Potter 1981:1). It became apparent that the quantity of archaeological material at both complexes was extensive and archaeologist Wendy Thorp was commissioned in September 1980 to undertake a test-trenching program to better identify the nature and extent of the archaeological resource. These 'Stage 1' excavations took place beneath the floor of Level 1 and at several locations around the courtyard and within the buildings of the northern range (**Figure 2.6**).

At Thorp's recommendation, an additional and larger-scale excavation program was proposed, and Patricia Burritt was commissioned to undertake the work while the PWD's restoration project continued. This phase of the work came to be known as the 'Stage II' excavations and was conducted in 14 working weeks over an 11-month period from 23 December 1980, with 11 archaeologists, a conservator, a photographer and 250 volunteers (Burritt 1981:12, 31; Potter 1981:12, 31).

Both programs revealed archaeological material in trenches dug across the buildings and courtyards of the Hyde Park Barracks complex, and in the underfloor cavities of the main dormitory building. Many smaller excavations were undertaken as work continued in preparation for the opening of the museum in 1984. These were the result of the installation of pipes or the building of the Australian Monument to the Great Irish Famine (e.g. Wilson 1983). All disturbances to the ground surface since then have been supervised by an archaeologist.

The underground collection thus comprises artefacts retrieved from soil-based contexts in the grounds of the Hyde Park Barracks, distinct from the material retrieved from the underfloor spaces of the main building. The latter survives in superior condition to the former, and with a greater range of materials, hence the original division of the catalogue. The underground material comprises artefacts recovered during test-trenching by Wendy Thorp, excavation by Patricia Burritt in the main building and elsewhere, and salvage work undertaken by Graham Wilson at the Northern and Southern Gatehouses (Wilson 1983) and within the courtyard (Wilson 1986). Artefacts retrieved from other monitoring work (e.g. Pinder 1983; Graves 1994 and 1995; Tonkin 1997) do not appear in the database, while material from Tonkin's (1997) monitoring work is waiting for cataloguing and database entry.

On completion of the main excavations in 1981, the artefact assemblage was cleaned, sorted, inventoried and rebagged. The Museum of Applied Arts and Sciences (MAAS), which became manager of the Hyde Park Barracks Museum and its collection at the same time, undertook conservation work on several items. The collection was stored on site for some time and then moved to the MAAS store at Redfern. At the MAAS store, the material was physically affected by flood waters and its archaeological integrity diminished. Some objects, including items selected for display, were separated from their context numbers. Parts of the Mint and the Hyde Park Barracks collections were also mixed together (Wilson 1985:20).

In 1985, with funding from a National Estate Grant, Andrew Wilson (then of the MAAS) began a major review, re-catalogue and reassessment of the underfloor collection, which was moved to the University of Sydney for that purpose. The project involved the preparation of a 'research design' for the analysis, specifying elements of the catalogue and fields required, and tested the use of the proposed database system, Minark, on a bibliographic inventory of reports and references (Wilson 1985, 1989). Artefact recording was undertaken at the Centre for Historical Archaeology at the University of Sydney by Dana Mider, Andrew Wilson, Julie Dinsmoor and Tony English between 1990 and 1996 (Mider 1996). No analytical or interpretive work was undertaken in the scope of this project and no final report was produced.

Management of the Hyde Park Barracks and its collection was transferred to the Historic Houses Trust (HHT) of New South Wales in 1990. In the following year the majority of the collection was moved to its new home in the Archaeology Store and Study Room on Level 2 of the central dormitory building. This room was the first such dedicated archaeological research facility of its kind in Australia and its system for accessing artefacts in the boxes was established by consultant curator Margot Riley.

In the late 1980s the Department of Planning commissioned Wendy Thorp and Campbell Conservation Pty Ltd to review the Hyde Park Barracks, Royal Mint and First Government House archaeological collections and provide recommendations for their management (Thorp & Campbell Conservation 1990, 1994). The project, completed in 1994, required the 'sorting and consolidation' of the Hyde Park Barracks assemblage and was the first project to provide a comprehensive catalogue of the material, albeit only of the underground component. Artefacts were re-examined and re-bagged, with artefact recording information written directly on stamped paper bags in which the artefacts were kept.

In 1996 Dana Mider completed the catalogue of the underfloor collection for the Historic Houses Trust (Mider 1996). Her report, commissioned by the HHT in 1995, was the culmination of the work originally proposed under the National Estate Grant in 1985 and 1989. Mider, assisted by Claire Everett, also undertook an audit of the artefacts and their records, rematching several objects dissociated from their provenance with their original identification number. Although they remained in separate and somewhat incompatible databases, a detailed record of both parts of the Hyde Park Barracks collection was now complete.

In 1997 the HHT commissioned Peter Tonkin to undertake a 'stock take' of the collection held on site and at the HHT's Ultimo store. Tonkin identified several groups of provenanced artefacts that previously had not been gathered for cataloguing. These were catalogued by a small team of specialists and entered into the database.

In 1998 the Hyde Park Barracks began developing a database for public viewing of the archaeological collection. The two databases of underfloor and underground material were exported from Minark into Access, and reorganised into a new database structure that facilitated simple search mechanisms for broad categories of artefacts. Brian Robson undertook this work in consultation with assistant curators Gary Crockett and Samantha Fabry. By April 2001 the database was largely complete.

In 2001 the EAMC team, with funding from the Australian Research Council, began to utilise the data in this new Hyde Park Barracks database, which was customised with fields compatible with the EAMC Archaeology Database and designed to meet the project's analytical requirements (Crook et al. 2006). This project included a systematic reassessment of the artefact catalogue, site records and the collection itself to examine the surviving archaeological resources and determine the potential for future work (Crook et al. 2003). The assessment identified a wide range of problems, from data errors and incomplete records to missing labels and lost items, and a general lack of reliable information. This established the need for substantial further work on the collection, which involved upgrading the catalogue of artefacts recovered from the underfloor spaces, with a particular emphasis on splitting 'mixed bags' containing bulk accumulations of paper, textiles and 'mixed media'. Sophie Pullar carried out this work between October 2002 and January 2003, with additional research conducted between December 2003 and March 2004.

The result of this work included publication of a substantial volume (Crook and Murray 2006) presenting the results of the EAMC team's re-examination of the historical and archaeological resources from the Hyde Park Barracks. With support from the Australian Research Council, Peter Davies and Tim Murray, from La Trobe University in Melbourne, conducted a further stage of analysis between April 2008 and February 2011. This project continued the re-cataloguing of bulk bags, especially of 'mixed media' and textiles. It resulted in the correction of 4885 database records and the addition of 1225 new records. At the conclusion of the project, 85 per cent of records relating to the Underfloor collection had been revised. The remaining uncatalogued material is predominantly bone, seed and shell.

3
CHARITY AND IMMIGRATION IN 19TH-CENTURY NSW

Poverty and suffering were harsh realities for many people in colonial New South Wales. While there was generally a high demand for labour throughout the 19th century, accident and illness could bring destitution even in times of prosperity. Despite awareness of such problems, Australian authorities generally resisted poor laws and workhouses based on the English and Irish models, fearing that they could entrench a pauper class and undermine the moral fabric of society (Dickey 1992; Twomey 2002:56). Colonial authorities also believed that the high demand for labour in Australia meant that workhouses were not needed, and that their presence would undermine the reputation of the colonies as a place of opportunity and prosperity.

The result was a charity system that combined private philanthropy with public funding. Most charitable organisations depended on government subsidies to survive, and this gave colonial authorities considerable say in who received assistance and in what form it took. By the 1860s, governments were becoming increasingly involved in the provision of welfare services. While private charities mostly preferred to help (and reform) the 'deserving poor' such as 'fallen' women and orphan children, there was a growing need to help the sick, destitute, elderly and insane. Fear of and concern for 'fallen women' was at the heart of much charity and welfare in colonial society. The term applied not just to prostitutes but also to women who had conceived out of marriage, women guilty of 'disorderly conduct', as well as to female thieves, alcoholics and the 'feeble minded' (Kovesi 2006:50). The unemployed posed a particular problem as the able-bodied were traditionally denied assistance on the grounds that they were capable of supporting themselves. Such demands resulted in the creation of various government asylums for the aged and infirm, orphanages and industrial schools for children, and labour exchanges for the unemployed.

In the early years of settlement in Sydney various institutions were established to support the destitute. As early as 1796, Philip Gidley King, Commandant of the Norfolk Island penal station, founded two day schools, one for boys and one for girls, as well as a home for female orphans on the island, while a Female Orphan School was opened in Sydney in 1801 (Ramsland 1986:1–3). Relief was also provided by the New South Wales Society for Promoting Christian Knowledge and Benevolence, formed in May 1813 by journalist Edward Smith Hall. Another organisation, the Colonial Auxiliary Bible Society, was formed in 1817. Both these groups relied on private patronage to support their religious and welfare efforts. The two societies merged in June 1818 to form the Benevolent Society of New South Wales. The objectives of the society were to:

> relieve the poor, the distressed, the aged, and the infirm, and thereby to discountenance as much as possible mendacity and vagrancy, and to encourage industrious habits among the indigent poor, as well as to afford them religious instruction and consolation in their distresses. (*Benevolent Society of New South Wales* 1820:8 quoted in Cummins 1971:3)

Initially the society confined itself to outdoor relief, distributing cash, provisions or clothing on a weekly basis to the 'deserving poor'. However, the need to provide some kind of lodging became apparent, and Governor Macquarie agreed to the construction of a building, at public expense, for accommodating the pensioners. It was located at the corner of Pitt and Devonshire Streets, where the Central Railway Station now stands. The two-storey brick building, which opened to receive inmates on 12 October 1821, was 97 feet long and 25 feet wide, with detached kitchen and outhouses. The simple internal design featured men's and women's quarters on different floors, each separated from dining areas by a central corridor containing the staircase. The inscription on the foundation stone read:

> This Asylum for the Poor, Blind, Aged and Infirm, was erected in 1820, L. Macquarie Esq., being Governor

The asylum provided food and shelter to paupers, and able-bodied ones were expected to work. Inmates picked oakum, made clothes and shoes, baked bread and grew vegetables. The proportion of disabled, elderly and infirm inmates, however, made it necessary to provide medical assistance as well. By 1825 the building was already overcrowded, with 64 men and 29 women. This increased to 112 men and 32 women by 1830, with an average age of 65 years (Cummins 1971:5–6). By this stage a number of female paupers and pregnant women had also been admitted to the small hospital at the Female Factory in Parramatta (Salt 1984:111). Historian Anne O'Brien (2008:154) suggests that this early period of the society's work saw a shift from paternalism and compassion for the victims of poverty to a desire to correct and reform them, a reflection of the influence of the new poor law movement at this time (Himmelfarb 1984:147–155).

The need for extensions and medical facilities resulted in the construction of a North Wing to the asylum in 1831 and a South Wing in 1839. The institution by now served increasingly as a hospital as well, supporting those with chronic diseases, while the Sydney Dispensary (formerly the Rum Hospital) handled acute cases. Sick and infirm patients at the asylum had separate accommodation from those in the workhouse. Chronic conditions included diarrhoea, dysentery and diseases of the lungs and eyes. Dr William Bland was the first of a number of visiting and resident surgeons and doctors, while nursing care was provided by the inmates in return for gratuities.

Limited outdoor relief continued to be available in this period via several ladies' organisations, whose members visited pauper women in their homes. These included the Sydney Dorcas Society for Protestants (founded in 1830), the Strangers' Friend Society for Catholics (1835), and the Ladies' Dorcas Society for Distressed Jewish Mothers (from 1844), (Hughes 2004:20). A Female School of Industry opened in 1826 to accommodate girls who would be fed, clothed and trained as servants (Peyser 1939:119–120). Historian Christina Twomey suggests that despite colonial resistance to the English workhouse model of poor relief, the opening of benevolent asylums was often associated with civic pride, and regarded as a marker of a Christian community (Twomey 2002:56).

The end of convict transportation to New South Wales in 1840 and the increase in free immigration meant growing demand for poor relief. A number of institutions were established in this period to accommodate vulnerable paupers. These included the Roman Catholic Orphan School (1836), the Sydney Female Refuge (1848), the House of the Good Shepherd (1848) and the Destitute Children's Asylum, which opened in Paddington in 1852 and transferred to Randwick in 1858 (Austral/Godden Mackay 1997; Ramsland 1986:52–54). In 1867 an industrial training school for destitute children was established on the ship *Vernon*, moored in Sydney Harbour, which by 1891 had trained more than 2300 boys (Parkes 1892[1]:246).

The Sydney Female Refuge Society was established in 1848 with the explicit purpose of reclaiming 'unfortunate and abandoned Females', that is, ex-prostitutes (Godden 1987:292). About 300 females passed through the society's refuge between 1849 and 1855, with numbers fluctuating between about 20 and 50 women. The society aimed to improve the prospects of the 'fallen' by training them in habits of good industry and set them back on the path of 'rectitude and virtue' (Sydney Female Refuge Society 1856:5). There was a heavy emphasis on Protestant religious instruction, moral training and industrial pursuits, which involved washing and needlework carried out on a commercial scale. The House of the Good Shepherd, a similar institution, was established by three Sisters of Charity in 1848, to provide refuge for former Catholic prostitutes (Godden 1987:292). Both institutions appear to have been granted accommodation in the former convict Carters'

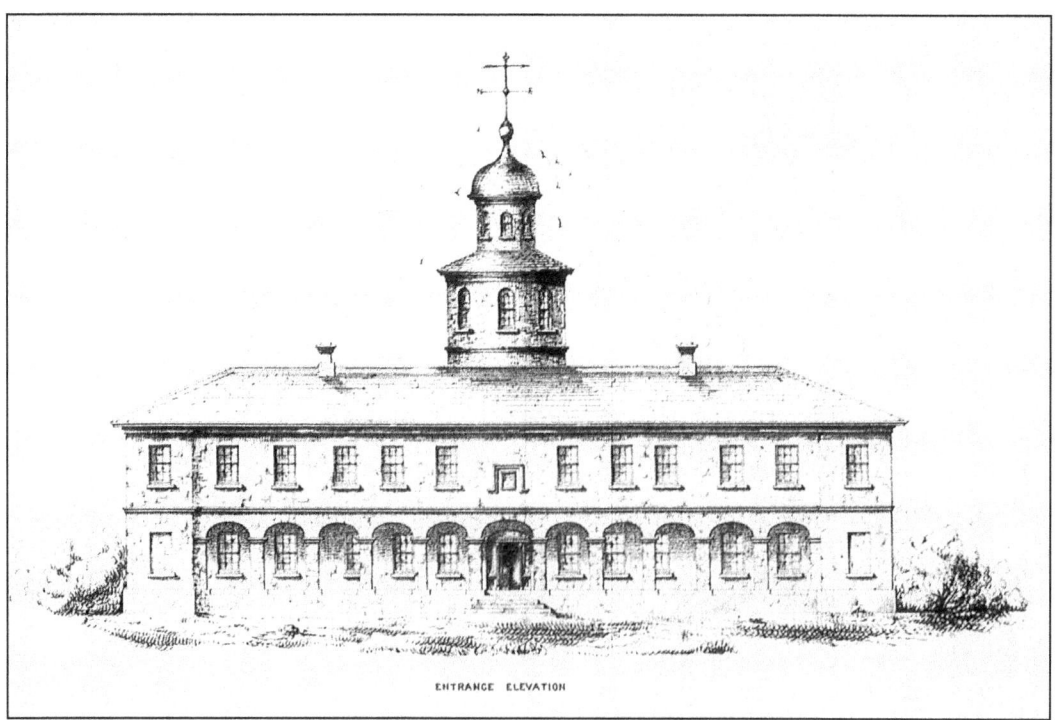

Figure 3.1: Sydney Benevolent Asylum, 1861 (source: Select Committee 1862: Appendix B).

Barracks, adjacent to the Benevolent Asylum at the south end of Pitt Street (**Figure 3.1**).

By 1849 there were almost 500 inmates in the Benevolent Asylum, half of whom were sick or infirm and in need of special accommodation. This included those who were blind, lame, 'paralytic' and 'idiotic'[8] (Cummins 1971:7). As a result of overcrowding, beds were laid on floors and dormitories reeked of body stench and excreta. The Asylum was described at this time as 'little better than a huge charnel house' (Rathbone 1994:33), but the Benevolent Society was also recognised as the 'Government Almoner', providing relief in place of an official poor law (Horsburgh 1977:77).

Relief from overcrowding came in 1851, when the male inmates were transferred to the Liverpool Hospital, which had been vacant for some years after it ceased to function as a convict hospital. At the time scrutiny of community-run charitable institutions such as the Benevolent Society increased (Hughes 2004:26–51; Select Committee 1862). As governments were forced to provide more support for such places, the concept of the relief of poverty as a moral option for the individual changed to that of collective responsibility for the welfare of the community as a whole. The ongoing debates culminated in the creation of the Board of Government Asylums for the Infirm and Destitute in 1862, with Frederic King appointed as Secretary. In addition to the acquisition of Liverpool Hospital, another asylum was established in 1862 in Macquarie Street, Parramatta, for blind and senile males. The mentally deranged were cared for by government lunatic asylums at Tarban Creek and Parramatta (Cummins 2003:33–41). In 1862, 150 women were also transferred to the newly established Hyde Park Barracks Asylum for the Infirm and Destitute, and the government became fully responsible for the management and operation of three colonial destitute asylums (Cummins 2003:53).

GOVERNMENT WELFARE

With the establishment of the Board of Government Asylums, the colonial government assumed substantial responsibility for the funding and care of destitute paupers. In addition to managing the Hyde Park Asylum for women, and Liverpool and George Street, Parramatta, for men, the Board opened an asylum in 1866 at Port Macquarie, in the former convict quarters, for both men and women. Lucy Applewhaite was opposed to the move, claiming 'There was never a more cruel thing than moving the institution to Port Macquarie', and that for the inmates 'It would be a great misery to them ... they would rather starve in the streets of Sydney' (Q2379, 2391, Public Charities Commission 1874:77). By May of the following year, however, there were 47 women in residence, but the asylum was abandoned in 1869 owing to the cost of maintenance and difficulties in supervising its management (Government Asylums Board 1870:1; Hughes 2004:77). The closure led to the return of 55 of its inmates to the Hyde Park Asylum, pushing numbers there to over 200 women. Another asylum was established in Macquarie Street, Parramatta in 1875 as an erysipelas hospital for male and female paupers, and later it accommodated indigent inmates. At the same time, private charities flourished, with many devoted to assisting unemployed domestic servants and unmarried pregnant women, while government remained the main provider of support to aged and infirm women.

The Board met twice weekly in a boardroom set up in the Hyde Park Barracks. Members decided on applications for admission based on genuine physical infirmity and true destitution, for people without relatives or friends who could take them in and support them. Although the Board was responsible for deciding the merits of each applicant, it was frequently over-ruled by the Colonial Secretary, the courts, and other government agencies. The asylums, including Hyde Park Barracks, became dumping grounds for society's outcasts, including the blind, epileptics, the physically and intellectually disabled, and the chronically and terminally ill — there was nowhere else for them to go (Hughes 2004:96). The inevitable result was over-crowding and constant pressure to find room for the growing numbers of impoverished invalids. At the 1873 Inquiry it was claimed that some inmates at Hyde Park Asylum were sleeping in its corridors (Q1272, Public Charities Commission 1874).

Accommodation at the Hyde Park Asylum was much cheaper for the government, however, than providing room for the sick poor in hospitals, thanks largely to Lucy Hicks' economical management and her constant striving 'to make the institution as self-supporting as possible' (Public Charities Commission 1874, Special Appendix 4). The average cost per head at Hyde Park in 1862 was £15 8s 4d (Hughes 2004:217). Twenty-three years later this figure had *decreased* to £15 3s 2d, while hospital accommodation could cost three times as much (Government Asylums Inquiry Board 1885:2).

During this time the government introduced legislation to help manage the growing problem of poverty and infirmity. A *Workhouse Act*, for example, was introduced in 1866 to control social deviants and paupers. Its aim was to get vagrants and 'irreclaimable' drunks off the streets and into a nominated workhouse. Charles Cowper objected to the bill on the basis that it allowed for the indefinite imprisonment of paupers by the government (Dickey 1966:16). The legislation was repealed in 1869,

---

[8] 'Idiocy' was a 19th-century scientific term indicating extreme mental retardation, with a mental age of two or less. 'Imbecility' was the term for intellectual disability less severe than idiocy, while 'lunacy' referred to mental illness or legal insanity.

without ever being brought into use. The *Public Institutions Inspection Act* of 1866 provided for the appointment of an Inspector of Public Charities to inspect all hospitals, orphan schools and asylums funded wholly or partially from public revenue. From 1869 Frederic King took up the new role of Inspector, while continuing to serve as Secretary to the Government Asylums Board (Hughes 2004:107).

The need for welfare services expanded as the population grew. The City Night Refuge and Soup Kitchen, for example, was established in Kent Street in June 1868 to provide a meal or a bed for the night to the destitute. It was the initiative of Police Magistrate D. C. F. Scott, and combined with a pre-existing soup kitchen in Dixon Street in the Haymarket neighbourhood. The Refuge provided temporary support for individuals until they could gain admission to one of the government asylums (Dickey 1966:15; Peyser 1939:196–198). In 1870 there was a proposal to convert the Victoria Barracks in Paddington into a hospital for the treatment of 'chronic and incurable cases of disease' (Victoria Barracks 1870–71, p.150). This was intended to relieve pressure on the Sydney Infirmary and the destitute asylums, but the proposal was not acted on.

The Government Asylums Board was abolished in 1876, and replaced with a new Department of Government Asylums for the Infirm and Destitute, with Frederic King appointed as Manager. In response to suggestions that inmates should be forced to do useful work, King stressed, in his annual report, that 'the Asylums are not poorhouses', and that if inmates recovered their health and strength sufficiently to earn a living they left the asylum or were put out (Government Asylums Board 1876:930).

As the government expanded its management of institutional welfare during this period, philanthropy and charity continued to provide significant support to the poor and infirm. In 1878 the Sydney branch of the Charity Organisation Society (COS) was established, based on the British organisation founded in 1869. The society functioned as a charity referral service, aiming to co-ordinate assistance provided by different agencies and improve the efficiency of delivering aid to the 'deserving poor' by centralised record keeping and investigation of individual cases. The main philosophy of the COS was that indiscriminate charity was debasing to all concerned (Cage 1992:93).

By 1880 the government's asylums were increasingly functioning as convalescent hospitals, as patients discharged from the Sydney Infirmary often lacked the health and strength to earn a living and ended up in one of the destitute asylums. The expansion of railway lines also brought the metropolitan asylums within reach of paupers from country areas. The death toll also increased at Hyde Park Barracks, as patients unable gain entry to a hospital were admitted to the Asylum in the last stage of illness. As inmate numbers at Hyde Park approached 300, work began on new facilities at Newington in 1884 (Government Asylums Board 1883:631). Construction had not been completed when the first inmates arrived in February 1886.

Female Immigrants

When the last convicts had been removed from the Hyde Park Barracks in 1848, the main building was largely given over to the use of an Immigration Depot. The protection of single women migrating to Australia was a matter of significant concern for the authorities, arguably more so than the need to provide for the aged, infirm and destitute. The colony's future was dependent on its reputation as a place of security and opportunity. Young Irish, English, Scottish and Welsh women were to be the domestic servants and future wives of the colony, and their safe, healthy and uncorrupted arrival was considered a vital element in the economic and social development of New South Wales. Concern for their welfare was motivated by the colonial authority's determination to ensure that the female immigrants did not join the colony's destitute.

British campaigns to assist women emigrants to travel to the Australian colonies began in the 1830s (Chilton 2005; Gothard 2001:10; Rushen 2003). In the 1840s, the end of convict transportation to New South Wales sparked renewed interest in securing migrant labour, and hundreds of thousands of refugees were fleeing from the consequences of the Great Famine in Ireland. Under a new scheme, orphans from Irish poorhouses and industrious single women were brought to Australia under free passage, and from 1848 they were received at the Hyde Park Barracks where they remained — protected from unscrupulous employers and vagabonds — until suitable work could be found. While making a new home in Australia was a goal for most of the arrivals, others clung to the possibility of further migration and a return 'home' as an important assertion of belonging and identity (Fitzpatrick 1995:534).

Single women migrants were supposed to be between the ages of 18 and 35, but at times older women and girls as young as 15 could apply. Immigration assistance was restricted to the healthy and those of good moral character. In the 1870s and 1880s, single women migrating to New South Wales arrived under selection (advertised) or nomination schemes, and involved the payment of £2 by the young women themselves, or by nominating friends or relatives (Berry 2005a; Gothard 2001:182).

Regulations specified that unmarried women arriving in New South Wales were to be received into an immigrants' home and provided with accommodation for up to eight days, under the authority of the Agent for Immigration. This was often extended to include young female children, who were brought to the Barracks while their parents remained on ship, with the aim of freeing the girls from the cramped conditions on board (*SMH* 24 May 1878, p.5). In the period from 1860 to 1886, more than 7000 government-assisted single female immigrants were hired from the Hyde Park Depot (Gothard 2001:220–221). While they waited for employment or reunion with family, the young women spent their time writing letters, reading, sewing and receiving religious instruction.

On hiring days, the immigrant women were usually quickly assigned to eager employers. Journalist John Stanley James (writing as 'The Vagabond') reported on the scene in 1878:

> In ten minutes every servant was engaged. There was little preliminary bargaining, the hirers knew too well that they must not let a chance slip of obtaining a "help", and as a rule the first girl on whom a lady fastened was engaged. The wages were from eight to fifteen shillings a week ... (*SMH* 24 May 1878, p.5)[9]

James also thought, however, that the semi-public hiring rooms at the Barracks were totally unsuited to their purpose. He described the Depot as:

> ... one of those ugly public buildings ranging along Macquarie-street, remnants of the bad old times, and which would be better if burnt down ... the accommodation [for immigrants] is most inadequate, although everything possible appears to be done by Mrs. Hicks to make the girls comfortable and happy ... There is not half enough accommodation, nor anything like a sufficient staff to work this properly ... (*SMH* 24 May 1878, p.5)

The Hyde Park Barracks was not, however, the first or only depot established to receive single immigrant females arriving in the Australian colonies during the 19th century. Caroline Chisholm, for example, who had arrived in Australia in 1838, established the 'Female Immigrants' Home' in 1841 to help distressed single females who lacked employment due to the drought and economic depression of the period. The Home was located in part of the old wooden Immigration Barracks in Bent Street,[10] behind the First Government House, and soon provided shelter for more than 90 women (Hughes 1994:145; Kiddle 1972:39). Chisholm also established depots in numerous country towns, where immigrant women were supported until they found work with local employers. When the Sydney Immigrants' Home closed in 1842, Chisholm had helped more than 2000 people, including finding employment for more than 1400 single women, many of whom would otherwise have become paupers (Hoban 1973:94).

Figure 3.2: White cotton fragment with ink hand-writing, possibly part of a name-tag (UF5479; P. Davies 2010).

Immigration facilities were also set up in other colonies, cities and towns to protect (and control) young women, who needed food, shelter and time to adjust from shipboard life, prior to taking employment (Pescod 2003). Single men were regarded as competent to arrange their own employment, but single women were thought to be vulnerable to 'immorality', as well as needing instruction in local conditions, and in some cases, domestic work skills. Facilities for those accommodated varied considerably, and were often designed as temporary shelters of minimal comfort, so as to discourage the women from lingering.

Irish Female Orphans

Between 1848 and 1852 the Hyde Park Barracks was also used to accommodate Irish female orphans. The traumatic consequences of the Irish famine coincided with the growing demand for labour in the Australian colonies in the late 1840s. Earl Grey, Secretary of State for the Colonies, tried to alleviate the labour shortage and imbalance in the sexes in

> Alice Peacock, aged 14, arrived with 104 single women on the *Samuel Plimsoll* from Plymouth in June 1879. As she was over 12, Alice travelled in the single women's compartment rather than with her parents. Her father David, a labourer from Cornwall, was a constable for the single women on the voyage. Her mother Elizabeth, like Alice, came from London.
>
> After three weeks at the Quarantine Station (there was typhoid & typhus fever on the ship), Alice came with the single women to the Hyde Park Barracks. Her parents remained on the ship until her father found work. They then collected Alice from the Barracks for the long journey to Adelong near Tumut, in southern New South Wales, where they were to live.

---

[9] Eight shillings per week converted to £20 16s per annum; fifteen shillings equalled £39 0s per annum. Wages for female domestic servants included board and lodging (Gothard 2001:212).

[10] The building was erected by Governor Bourke in the early 1830s to accommodate celebrations for the Royal Birthday (Hughes 1994:145). By 1837 it was being used as temporary housing for immigrants.

Australia, by introducing assisted immigration for Irish orphans, especially females. Between October 1848 and August 1850, over 4000 female orphans were brought to Australia from the workhouses of famine Ireland, most of them between 14 and 17 years of age. Numbers included 2253 sent to NSW, 1255 to Victoria and 606 to Adelaide. There were also 61 sent to the Cape of Good Hope (O'Connor 1995:257–258; O'Farrell 1987:74). The first group arrived at the Barracks from the ship *Earl Grey* in October 1848. The girls were indentured for 12 months, with committees of 'Gentlemen' responsible for their distribution. Many girls took positions as domestic servants in rural areas, although some resented being sent into the countryside (Hamilton 2001:458).

The Orphan Committees dictated the terms on which the young women could be hired out. Fourteen-year-olds, for example, were to earn seven pounds per annum, 15-year-olds eight pounds and so on (Hoban 1973:223). These wages were below market rates, partly to defend the class system in place, and partly to compensate for the low skill levels of the orphan girls. In return they were to receive instruction in the craft of service, and suitable food, lodging and medical assistance. They were also to be free to attend the divine service of their choice on Sundays (McClaughlin 1991:15–16). The Irish Poor Law Unions had already provided each young woman with clothing, which included six shifts, two flannel petticoats, six pairs of stockings, two pairs of shoes, two gowns, and a shawl and bonnet, perhaps the first such outfit most had ever owned. Each was also provided with a bible and prayer book, soap, needles and thread, all to be stored in a stout, locked wooden box (McClaughlin 1991:89).

Irish newspapers condemned the practice of transporting helpless and pure Irish orphans to the distant cesspool of the Australian colonies, but the girls themselves were eager to go, and the first arrivals were quickly employed on good wages (O'Farrell 1987:74). Some young women deliberately entered workhouses to secure assisted passage to Australia (Hammerton 2004:162).

Irish orphans sent to Sydney were accommodated in the Hyde Park Barracks, where wards on the upper floors were fitted up as quarters for the 'comfort and protection' of these young women (Pescod 2003:19; *SMH* 30 September 1848). The Immigration Agent, Francis Merewether, emphasised that the Barracks possessed 'every advantage which could be desired, with reference to the health, the seclusion, and the moral and religious instruction of the inmates, and the convenience of persons coming to hire them' (quoted in McClaughlin 1991:15).

Another 4000 'orphan' girls were brought to New South Wales between 1850 and 1852. Although not all of them were orphans, or children, or Irish, they came to be known as such, and single Irish women came to be regarded as a 'servant' class, with all the faults of an uneducated, semi-savage people (Higman 2002:75–76). Improving economic conditions in Ireland by the mid-1850s, however, meant good positions were becoming available for increasing numbers of domestic servants there, and the rate of emigration by young females to Australia began to slow (Gothard 2001:42). In subsequent years, child migration from the United Kingdom increased again, and many thousands were sent to Canada, South Africa, Australia and New Zealand (Kershaw and Sacks 2008).

The Irish orphan scheme was a mixed success. In 1858 it was found that hundreds of girls had been returned to the Barracks as incompetent. There was considerable debate as to whether the girls themselves, mostly young and with little or no training in domestic service, were to blame, or if their employers had been 'very hard upon them', objecting to the 'dirty Irish, and ignorant Irish papists' (Select Committee 1858:403). In 1849 alone, more than 200 of the orphans had their Indentures cancelled by the Court of Petty Sessions. Reasons included bad conduct, being absent without permission, disobedience, insolence, idleness, neglect of duties, and several charges of assault (Select Committee 1858: Appendix J). Another cause for complaint was the desire of the Irish girls to attend Mass on Sunday mornings, when their employers much preferred to allow them out on Sunday evenings as being less disruptive to households.

Some of the girls returned to the Barracks were punished as virtual prisoners. Up to 50 at a time were confined in a separate building in the complex, under the supervision of a sergeant of police, and made to pick oakum 'to keep them employed' (Select Committee 1858:403). The room was known as The Penitentiary, and the girls worked, ate and slept here, allowed only a little exercise in an adjoining yard. When the Sisters of Charity visited and complained at the 'unwholesome' nature of the room, the orphan girls were sent to work in country areas and prevented from being hired in town again.

These cases, however, were in the minority, and most Irish orphan girls achieved modest success in their new lives in Australia. Mrs Capps, Matron of the Hyde Park Barracks from 1848 to 1853, admitted that for the most part she had very little trouble with them, even when there were 600 in the building and she had no assistant to help. Based on her own experience, Mrs Capps believed that the Irish girls were the best behaved, followed by 'the Scotch' and lastly the English. She was also impressed at the hard work and industriousness shown by the Irish orphan girls, and their willingness to send home money saved from the 'pittance' of their salaries (Select Committee 1858:402).

4
THE WORKINGS OF AN INSTITUTION

The Destitute Asylum and Immigration Depot were two separate institutions, serving quite different purposes: one, the long-term care of aged, disabled and at times terminally ill women who could no longer support themselves; and the other, the short-term care of single women making a new life in the colony. Despite these different purposes, the aims of both institutions were very similar: providing shelter, food and medical care to women who, for the time they spent at the Hyde Park Barracks, were without support from the usual family and social networks.

It was perhaps these common needs that prompted the colonial government to manage both facilities from the same building, and under the same Superintendent: Matron Lucy Hicks. While each facility was financed from separate budgets, and the complex itself was compartmentalised with separate entrances, the line between Depot and Asylum was much harder to identify in the daily management of the institutions.

When the 150 or so inmates were transferred from the overcrowded Benevolent Asylum in 1862, they were allocated the third floor of the Hyde Park Barracks and a dedicated entrance was constructed at the eastern end of the building. Matron Hicks moved Asylum inmates into Immigration Depot wards when immigrant numbers were low (Q2306, Public Charities Commission 1874:74). During both the 1873 and 1886 parliamentary inquiries, Matron Hicks was adamant that immigrant and aged women were segregated, but in practice an absolute separation may not have been possible. In the 1886 Inquiry conducted after the Asylum had moved to Newington, it was reported that:

> At Hyde Park, Mrs. Hicks states she superintended the Immigration Barracks, as well as the Infirm and Destitute Asylum. The institutions were practically merged as regards furniture and utensils — that is, if the Infirm and Destitute Asylum required anything the Immigration Barracks could spare it was taken, and vice versa. No inventory existed at Hyde Park. (Government Asylums Inquiry Board 1887, Appendix C, p.52)

It is likely also that the immigrant women relied on the Asylum dispensary from time to time. While partitions may have separated wards and parts of the building, the noises, chatter and moaning of aged women could not have been excluded from the floors below. In the 1860s, liquid matter could not be excluded from the floors below either. In 1865 there was a request to fit ceilings above the matron's and sub-matron's apartments, in the front rooms on Level 2, to prevent 'the inconvenience arising from the leakage[11] which occasionally takes place from the upper rooms' (Immigration Agent to Undersecretary for Lands, 2 March 1865, quoted in Thorp 1980:VI.2).

The inmates nevertheless enjoyed a much healthier physical environment in the Barracks than in the old Benevolent Asylum. From the top floor windows they took in views to the east over the Domain to Woolloomooloo, while the sandstone spires of St Mary's Cathedral rose to the south. Nearby was the expanse of Hyde Park, while directly across the road to the west were St James' Church of England, the Supreme Court and the top of King Street which led down to Sydney's busy retail district (Hughes 2004:57). By the mid-19th century, Macquarie Street had become one of Sydney's most desirable residential locations (Mackaness and Butler-Bowdon 2005:53).

There are no internal floor plans of the Asylum when it was in the Barracks; and while the physical evidence of partitions and other room markings have been destroyed or superseded by later occupation, the struggle for, and negotiation of, space within the main and auxiliary buildings are apparent in the various government reports, special inquiries and general correspondence from 1862 to 1887.

The tug-of-war between the two main institutions, the Immigrant Depot and Offices and the Asylum, was often interrupted by other annoyances, such as the census calculations, the Master in Lunacy and other government departments which vied for corners of the ageing building (for evidence of their occupation, see 'Official and Administrative Records'). The complex was subjected to shifting arrangements of wards, offices, hiring rooms, yards and hospital rooms at various times. The Colonial Architect was called in on many occasions to build a kitchen, a washhouse, a new entrance and water closets, and to make repairs such as removing lead pipes, cementing the yard and sheathing the shingled roof with corrugated iron (in 1880).

---

[11] It is uncertain if this 'leakage' refers to the general problems of the leaking roof during wet weather or spills and other accidents occurring during the daily routine of the Asylum.

4. The Workings of an Institution

The negotiation of space eventually favoured the Destitute Asylum and the pressing needs of ageing women over the fluctuating numbers of single immigrant women. By 1873, the Asylum had taken over about half of the main building and acquired the ancillary buildings of the NSW Volunteer Rifle Corp, although these were inadequate for use at the time.

Owing to its physical dominance within the Barracks building, the following discussion of the operational concerns and daily activities at the Hyde Park Barracks during the period from 1848 to 1886 is focused more strongly upon the operation of the Asylum than on the Immigrants' Depot. We work on the assumption that Level 3 was under the exclusive use of the Asylum from 1862 to 1886, and that the majority of the assemblage recovered from that level can be confidently attributed to the Asylum inmates. While inmates did occupy Level 2 from time to time, the assemblage on this level is more likely to be the result of use by the Immigration Depot, and the Matron's family. We generalise an association of Level 3 with the Asylum and Level 2 (excluding the southern section) with the Depot.

Room Use

For the entire occupation of the Hyde Park Barracks as an Immigrants' Depot and Destitute Asylum, we have no maps or diagrams of the internal layout of the main building. From evidence given at the 1873 Inquiry, however, along with various requests sent to the Colonial Architect for repairs, we can speculate on how the rooms may have been used. For example, Lucy Hicks reported:

> The Government did speak of turning my apartments into two wards, and that would give accommodation within the building for forty more women; and they would build me a cottage at the gate. (Q2298, Public Charities Commission 1874:74)

This suggests that the matron's apartments were in the main building and that they were equivalent to the size of a 40-woman ward, and probably in an area with two distinct parts. The likely place for such accommodation would have been the two smaller, western rooms on Level 2 at the front of the Barracks overlooking Queens Square (**Figure 4.1**). Being close to the stair, the matron had easy access to other parts of the building, and it is possible that the corridor was enclosed with a door and partition to give the family more privacy — although there is no physical evidence to suggest this either way.

The female immigrants, when in residence at the Barracks, mainly occupied the large northern room on Level 1 as a dining room and living area, and the large room above on Level 2, 'plainly furnished but everything clean withal' (*SMH* 24 May 1878, p.5). This is confirmed by Mrs. Hicks' 1873 testimony.

When asked how much of the main building was set apart for the immigrants, she replied:

> Two large rooms, a large ward, and a dining hall. I had formerly three other rooms and an office, but Mr. Wise, at the time the Census was in preparation, applied and got these rooms, and his having them has put me to very great inconvenience. I have now no office or any other accommodation. (Q2302, Public Charities Commission 1874:74)

The office and very probably the 'three other rooms' would have been on the ground floor, a level always occupied by offices and semi-public functions such as the Hiring Room of the Immigrants' Depot. This is reinforced by Matron Hicks' later comments on cutting out calico in preparation for making the women's clothing:

> ... I have felt greatly the loss of that office I used to have at the bottom of the stairs where I used to cut out ... Many times I had an hour to cut out, and I could lock the room up and leave it; but now I am obliged to keep at it, and say I am not at home, for I cannot leave the material when once I begin to cut it out. (Q2368–2369, Public Charities Commission 1874:76)

Level 1

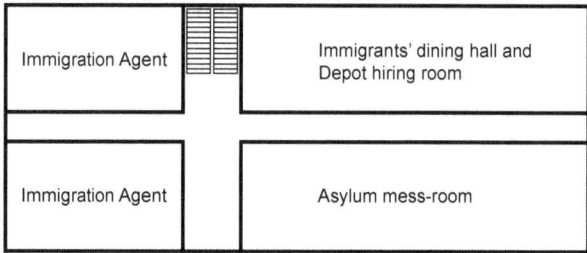

Level 2

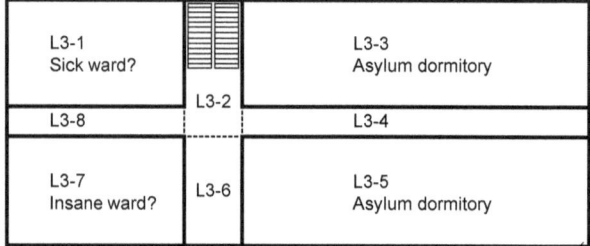

Level 3

Figure 4.1: Schematic plan of room functions and numbers.

She went on to explain that the rooms had ceased to be used for preparing the census, but that she still did not have access to them. In another line of enquiry regarding the accommodation of disabled inmates:

> Q2316 The room in which they [the 'idiots'] were seemed very damp and dark? The room is dull, but I see them cheerful. I always make it my business to say, "Well, girls, are you comfortable here?" and I never have any complaints.
> Q2317 How many are there there? I have eight in that room; one has St. Vitus's dance[12] very badly — cannot sit up from it. I cannot say that they are all idiots. There are eight very bad cases in that room.
>
> (Public Charities Commission 1874:75)

It is likely that the ward to accommodate these eight cases was on Level 3, and was probably one of the smaller rooms at the western end of the building. The Asylum inmates used two large rooms at the eastern end of Level 3 as dormitories. The small room opposite the idiots' ward may have accommodated women with acute or infectious diseases. In the absence of a dead house, this is probably also where bodies were washed and prepared for burial. Inmate nurse Ann Jeffreys (or Coffrey) advised Matron Hicks 'not to come up' following Priscilla Pritchard's death by mortification (gangrene) because 'it was a bad case' (*SMH* 30 August 1866, p.5). Coffins were left in the lobby (which John Applewhaite noted was on the same floor as the hospital wards (ibid) which was probably on Level 2 (see 'Death and Burial' section below).

The dispensary was a small timber building attached to the rear, eastern side of the building, completed in April 1862 (Hughes 2004:74). The visiting doctor George Walker complained about the saturation of the building from water running off the roof, and later from the flow of excrement coming from the water closets above him (Hughes 2004:80).

In 1882 Matron Hicks and her family moved out of their quarters in the Barracks and took accommodation in Phillip Street. The Asylums Board used the rooms on Level 2 to accommodate 40 extra inmates, bringing the daily average to almost 300 (Government Asylums Board 1882:626).

The Matron

Editions of *Cassell's Household Guide* in the 1880s outline the duties of matrons in English workhouses in a section entitled 'Occupations Accessible to Women':

> The last occupation suitable to women under Local Government and other official Boards is that of matrons of workhouses. There seems no good reason why women from the middle and educated classes should not hold this situation. The one usually urged is that the positions of master and matron are generally held by a man and his wife, and that a superior woman could not hold a subordinate post under a master of the stamp at present employed. A recent authority writing on this subject says that, 'as gentlemen of small means, military and naval officers on half-pay, and many others, have accepted the governorship of prisons, there can be no reason why they should not take charge of workhouses.' The entire charge of a workhouse, containing from 500 to 700 souls, would seem as worthy of any man's powers as any sphere of work that could be pointed out ... In all workhouses the position of both master and matron is most important. Their authority is very great, and the post affords immense facilities for doing good ...
>
> Board, lodging, washing, and attendance, are all found; and the combined salaries of master and matron generally amount, in the larger workhouses, to over £200 per annum. Here, also, the work mainly consists in superintending their subordinates.
>
> The general duties of the matron are to superintend the female inmates, to look after the cutting-out of clothes, &c., to visit the sick in the infirmaries once a day, to see that the kitchen and laundry-work are properly attended to, and the whole house scrupulously clean and tidy. She has also to give out the stores of linen and of provisions, and to see that the children are well, and to superintend the schoolmistress. Many, if not all, of these duties are such as every lady habitually undertakes in her own home; and when, in addition to this, we understand that the work of a matron is a real work of Christian charity, it is not too much to say that the post is a suitable one for any educated woman, with some force of character, and sound health. The classes of people who come under her charge are the old, and the sick, and orphans, and deserted children, who will look to the matron for all they will ever know of a mother's loving care. In addition to this, to a good religious woman, there would be the opportunity of sometimes being able to hold out a hand of mercy to a lost and miserable sister; who, under her kindly ministrations, might yet aspire to a better life. (*Cassell's Household Guide* c.1880:173)

While the Hyde Park Asylum had no young children in its care, this is a fairly accurate description of the duties that the Matron of the Immigration

---

[12] St. Vitus's Dance or Sydenham's Chorea is a motor control disorder which usually affects children. It is associated with rheumatic fever and characterised by jerky, uncontrollable movements, either of the face or of the arms and legs.

4. The Workings of an Institution

Depot, and later, the Matron of the Asylum, was expected to undertake, and the kind of woman she ought to be. She was responsible for maintaining discipline, enforcing personal hygiene, supervising the preparation of meals, ensuring the cleanliness of cooking and eating utensils, and airing the building and bedding (Hughes 2004:153).

When the Immigration Depot was established at the Hyde Park Barracks in 1848, quarters for a live-in matron were provided. The first matron was a Mrs Capps (see section 'Irish Female Orphans') who served from 1848 to 1853, while Grace Tinckham was matron of the Depot in 1860 (*Statistics of NSW* 1860:21). Tinckham was followed by Hicks (then known as Lucy Applewhaite) who came to have the most enduring impact on the shape of the Immigration Depot and Destitute Asylum. She retained the position of matron until and shortly after the move to Newington in 1886.

Lucy was appointed matron on 13 May 1861 with an annual salary of £70, while her husband John commenced duties on 20 July 1861 as a clerk in the Hyde Park Immigration Office at a salary of 10 shillings per day (Hughes 2004:150–152). When the Government Benevolent Asylum was established at the Hyde Park Barracks in 1862, Lucy became matron of both the Immigration Depot and the Asylum, while John seems to have relinquished his position as clerk in the Immigration Office and become Master of the Asylum alone. His annual salary for the first year of setting up the Asylum was £200 and then it was reduced to £100 the following year. Lucy's salary as matron of the Asylum was £100 and in 1863 her salary as the Immigration Depot matron increased from £70 to £100 (Hughes 2004:153).

When asked at the 1873 Inquiry about the wages she received in the early years of the Asylum, she replied:

> Well, I held a double appointment in the Government Service previously. When Mr. Cowper — Sir Charles Cowper — placed me there, I was matron of the Immigrants' Depôt, and Mr. Applewhaite was a clerk in the Immigration Department, with a salary of £285 per annum. We had a very good appointment then; and when the old people were brought there, Mr. Cowper wished us to undertake the duties connected with the Asylum, and promised us a salary of £300 per annum. When the other institution was formed our salaries for the Asylum duties were reduced to £200 per annum, and to make good the promise of the Government £100 each was given from immigration. (Q2273, Public Charities Commission 1874:74)

When her husband died in 1869, she took over his duties and eventually her income was reduced to '£200 a year from the Asylum, and ... a nominal salary of £20 a year from the immigration' (Q2274). In the 1870s, as the number of female immigrants fluctuated from year to year, her salary as Depot matron rose to £35 in 1872 and to £50 in 1877, so she was still earning £250 in her own right. For much of her time at the Barracks, Lucy was among the most highly paid matrons in New South Wales (Hughes 2004:158, 169). By way of comparison, Dr Robert Ward, the Surgeon and Dispenser at the Hyde Park Barracks, was paid £225 per year, although this was likely to be one of several salaries or income streams.

Initially Lucy was supported by a sub-matron, originally Alice Gorman[13], and then by Mrs Kennedy, who resigned in August 1864. It is unknown whether there was some conflict between the two because it appears Mrs Kennedy gave notice on 30 March 1864, but then withdrew it. The Daily Reports written by Matron Hicks give little away. The entry for 1 August 1864 simply reads: 'Mrs Kennedy Sub-matron has left the Institution today' (Daily Reports SRNSW 9/6181b).

It is unclear who held this post thereafter but in the 1873 Inquiry, Matron Hicks indicated that her daughter, although 'not an officer of the institution', maintained the stock book (Q2281, p.73). Lucy's 24-year-old daughter, Mary E. Applewhaite, was officially appointed sub-matron on 1 January 1875 with an annual salary of £50 (Hughes 2004:168). She held the post until her death in 1885, when Mrs. Cecilia J. Hyrons was appointed sub-matron (Government Asylums Inquiry Board 1887:526). Another daughter, Miss Clara Applewhaite, also assisted Mrs Hicks as an unpaid officer in 1886 (Government Asylums Inquiry Board 1887:446). This pattern of daughters helping their mothers to superintend welfare institutions was repeated elsewhere in the colony, and includes Mary Burnside and her daughter Jane at the Liverpool Asylum, and Catherine Dennis and one of her daughters at Parramatta (Hughes 2004:172).

THE INMATES

While the matron was responsible for the care of the inmates, she was not responsible for deciding who could be admitted to the Asylum. This was decided by the Board of Government Asylums for the Infirm and Destitute, a situation for which Matron Hicks was glad (Q2387, Public Charities Commission 1874:77). The sick and indigent must have waited anxiously during the Board's sitting days to learn whether a bed could be found for them. Distinguishing between the urgency of needs within

---

[13] Mrs Gorman was working at the Asylum again in 1886 after the move to Newington. At the Inquiry, Mrs Gorman indicated that she 'was employed at the Immigration Depôt years ago'. According to Lucy Hicks, this was in 1863 (Government Asylums Inquiry Board 1887:448, 455).

a population suffering the after-effects of half a century of convict transportation, mass migration, illness and economic downturns was a difficult task. Many deserving cases were turned away at the gate.

The prerequisites for admission to the Asylum were infirmity and inability to support oneself. Destitution alone was not enough, as Board members shared the prevailing view that the poor were to blame for their own misfortune. Cases for possible admission to the Asylum were brought to the attention of the Board by the Benevolent Society, other charities, clergy, well-meaning employers, the police, and the Sydney Infirmary, nearby on Macquarie Street. The cases referred by the Infirmary often caused the greatest disruption to the Asylum. These were patients deemed to have chronic conditions and long-term diseases, such as cancer and mental illness, which could not be cured by the medical resources of the dispensary.

Some of the mentally ill women were abusive or inclined to using obscenities, undressed and destroyed their clothing, or wandered around the wards at night and removed the bedclothes of other inmates. Some were also violent and attacked other inmates or inflicted injuries on themselves. Many suffered paranoid grievances such as fearing the matron or doctor sought to poison them or had stolen their children. Those with senile dementia were unaware of their surroundings and could not recall their names or other personal details (Hughes 2004:71). Mrs Hicks complained of receiving insane persons:

> We have to keep them for ten days or a fortnight sometimes, and I have only a small room to put them in, and that one woman will perhaps keep 100 poor old souls awake night after night. (Q2373, Public Charities Commission 1874:76)

Such cases were the exception. These inmates should have been referred to the lunatic asylums at Tarban Creek or Newcastle. The more common chronic medical conditions affecting the inmates at Hyde Park were blindness, idiocy and crippled limbs. At least one case of St. Vitus's Dance was recorded in the 1873 Inquiry.[14] These inmates were lodged in the same small ward, and one of the able-bodied inmates was responsible for their care. The majority of inmates suffered from the effects of ageing and had no family networks to fall back on. The oldest recorded inmate at the Hyde Park Asylum was 106 in 1873 (Q2291, Public Charities Commission 1874:74). While her name is unknown, she was probably an ex-convict:

> One who has attained the age 106 'goes,' says Mrs. Hicks, 'into a tub every Saturday morning like my own baby.' This old woman, whom we saw in her bed, is doubtless an ex-convict. She told us that she had come out in Governor —'s time (we could not catch the name), a genteel way of concealing the manner of her arrival (Hill and Hill 1875:336).

For many of these bed-ridden, chronically ill or elderly inmates, their admission to the Asylum was their final life transition, even though many survived for several years. Agnes Barr was the 'oldest inmate'. She was transferred from the Benevolent Asylum on 15 February 1862, spent every day of the next 24 years at Hyde Park Barracks, before ending up at Newington in 1886 (Q4441, Government Asylums Inquiry Board 1887:540). For the able-bodied inmates, however, the Asylum was more like a depot, where they stayed for short periods while their illnesses were at their worst, and were discharged as soon as they were well enough to work outside, or a new situation arose.[15] This strategic, temporary use of the Asylum by many inmates suggests that the institution functioned not only as a place of *refuge* but also of *respite*, which the women used to help survive and endure life's crises (see De Cunzo 1995:110–113).

Some of the women were acutely conscious of their fall in life. Hugh Robinson, the Inspector of Public Charities, reported in 1879 that many of the inmates at the Hyde Park Asylum were 'of the most irreproachable character who once occupied highly respectable positions, and who are now destitute through no fault of their own'. These women felt uncomfortable at being forced into close and constant contact with other inmates of coarse habits and speech (Inspector of Public Charities 1879:856).

Some destitute women, however, refused to accept institutionalisation of any kind. In February 1876, for example, Sergeant Attwell of the Sydney Police took officers of the Sewage and Health Board to visit Sarah O'Neill. Sarah lived in a one-room brick house in Wattle Street near Blackwattle Swamp, where waste from the Colonial Sugar Refinery drained by. One window was boarded over with scraps of iron, while the other was used as a doorway for Sarah and her fowls, although according to a local shopkeeper she would often not leave the house for months on end. The room contained only a few mats and rags, and had no water. She lived there rent-free, kept alive by the produce of her chickens and scraps of food left by neighbours. When Attwell called out, in jest, that he had come to take her to the [Hyde Park] Asylum, 'the wild looking uncombed elderly woman' retorted that none of the O'Neills ever saw the inside of an asylum, and offered him some eggs. She had been born in Ireland and lived in the colony for 20 years, the last nine of them 'in this hole'

---

[14] See footnote 12.
[15] Most of the inmates interviewed during the parliamentary inquiries were able-bodied and held in-house positions. When asked how long they had been in the Asylum, many replied 'five or six years, on and off' (e.g. Eliza Allen, Ann Ballard, Mary Burns, Margaret Gannon, Kate Gilmore).

(Suburban Sewage and Health Board 11 Progress Report 1875–76, quoted in Fitzgerald 1987:169).

Minnie Perks (or Perkins) is an example of the young women who could fall between the cracks of the charity system. She was a young Aboriginal girl, 'apparently intelligent and of sound intellect', but 'quite blind' (Hughes 2004:117). She was rejected by the Sydney Infirmary because she was not sick, from the Newcastle Asylum for Imbeciles because she was mentally competent, and from the Deaf, Dumb and Blind Institution because she was too old. Aged about 15 years, she was reluctantly admitted to the Hyde Park Asylum in 1874, as no one else would take her (Hughes 2004:118). She died there in 1877, aged 19, of chronic cerebritis (NSW Death Certificate 1878/80).

The vast majority of inmates at the Hyde Park Asylum remain anonymous, reduced to statistics in the Board's annual reports. Joy Hughes (2004:58, n.29) has calculated that around 6000 women passed through the doors of the Hyde Park Asylum over its 24 years of operation, but we know the names of only a fraction, gleaned mostly from witness statements provided to parliamentary inquiries. The initial intake of around 150 women transferred from the Benevolent Society in 1862 included only 9 who were born in the colony. Of the remainder, half arrived as immigrants or the wives of soldiers, and the rest were convicts. A few had been in the Benevolent Asylum for more than 20 years (*Empire* 17 February 1862). Half were widows, while 20 were deserted and 4 had husbands in gaol. Fifteen of the women had some degree of blindness, 8 were physically handicapped and 5 were of unsound mind. Young mothers who were drunk or infirm were separated from their children, who were sent to orphanages (Hughes 2004:59–60). The following brief biographical notations for some of the inmates provide some insight into the misery confronting infirm and destitute women.

Alice Clifton
Admitted March 1862, aged 24
Worked as prostitute to survive; bore five children by at least four different fathers; died in 1879, aged about 41.

Hannah Dodds
Admitted 15 February 1862
Transported from Ireland on the *Hooghly* in 1831, she spent most of her adult life in and out of the Benevolent Asylum, Hyde Park, Tarban Creek and Gladesville Asylums.

Amelia Howe
Admitted 15 February 1862, aged 21, Jewish
Travelled from England to Melbourne on the *Ballarat* in 1854 under Caroline Chisholm's Family Colonisation Loan Society. Her husband was in Cockatoo Gaol. Destitute, her 'bad hands' forced her to leave domestic service.

Bridget Cullen
Admitted 18 October 1884, aged 70, Roman Catholic
Born Longford, Ireland. Came out as passenger with her father, a soldier. Mostly living about Sydney. Transferred from Hyde Park to Newington Asylum. Memory failing, blind, and almost totally deaf.

Ellen Howard
Admitted 27 May 1886, aged 36
Emigrant per *Marlinsay* 1864. Married. Has not seen her husband for 10 years. Used to do needlework in Sydney but has been paralysed for 3 years.

Joanna Hunt (née Brown)
Admitted 15 February 1862, aged 50, Roman Catholic
Arrived as convict in 1829 on *Princess Royal*; married Jonathon Hunt in 1840. Jailed more than 20 times for drunkenness; suffered alcoholic poisoning; died Darlinghurst Gaol in 1869.

Mary Ann Kennedy
Admitted 1862
Arrived from Ireland in 1849; spent 24 years in the Hyde Park Asylum, the last four bedridden as an invalid, before transfer to Newington in 1886. She died in 1887, aged 67.

Bridget Keys
Admitted 11 September 1868, aged 17, Roman Catholic
Born Yass NSW; partially blind and unable to work; no family to support her. Jailed repeatedly for vagrancy and her own protection.

Louisa King
Admitted 1 March 1862, aged 24
Arrived December 1858 aged 20 at Hyde Park Immigration Depot from the *Forest Monarch*. Epileptic; no friends or relatives in the colony. In and out of Sydney Infirmary and Benevolent Asylum suffering fits. Gave birth to son Samuel (out of wedlock) on 12 October 1861; infant died several weeks later; admitted to Benevolent Asylum 'very ill' and transferred to Hyde Park Asylum in March 1862.

Margaret McDonald (née Hogan)
Admitted 15 February 1862
Irish convict transported on *Elizabeth* in 1828; married emancipist Matthew McDonald (*Earl St Vincent* 1818) in 1831; After 30 years of marriage both were admitted, ill and destitute, to the Benevolent Society in January 1862. Matthew was sent to the Liverpool Asylum and Margaret to Hyde Park. It is not known but likely that they did not see each other again.

Mary Ann Murray
Admitted 18 November 1880, aged 70, Roman Catholic
Born Hull, Yorkshire. Came to colony as convict aboard *Buffalo* for theft. Husband deserted her 10

years ago. Blind. Old inmate of Hyde Park Asylum. No relatives.

Ann Sheldrick
Admitted 13 March 1862, aged 18
Born in Hackney, London, arrived in NSW in 1858 with her parents and two brothers on the *Stebonheath*. Described as 'idiotic and subject to fits', she was probably the Ann Sheldrake who died in 1866 at Parramatta, aged 23.

(Source: SRNSW 7/3801, vol. C–D, p.283; vol. H–J, p.784; and vol. K–M, p.1203; Hughes 2004:60–85, 102–110; Smith 1988:111–115)

These sad stories were corroborated by City Missionary, Stephen Robins, who testified at the 1873 Inquiry. When questioned about whether the inmates were fit for work outside the Asylum (and thus undeserving of their place there), he responded:

> ... I could not see any women there who were able to do anything more than the work of the house. They are very old women there. There is one woman of the name Elizabeth Mills, who asked me to get her a situation. She is one of the nurses up-stairs, and she says that she does not like stopping there, and she does not know where to go to outside. She has no home, and would go for small wages if she could get them. It requires some one with strength to nurse these old women. That is the only woman whom I saw that could do anything. There was another woman of the name of Dawes. I do not think that any one could take her for a servant, because she is very deaf. They are all very old women, except the blind ones and a few that are paralyzed. It does not seem to be scarcely enough to do the work of the house. (Q2514, Public Charities Commission 1874:83)

Other women were rejected by their family members who were well able to care for them. Clara Morris was transferred from the Sydney Infirmary to the Parramatta Lunatic Asylum in 1865, and transferred to Hyde Park in 1872, around the age of 55. Although partially paralysed she was never considered insane, and attributed her long institutionalisation to the neglect of her family. She was briefly reunited with her son Frank in Queensland in 1874, but he sent her back to the Asylum in Sydney because 'she is nothing but a drag on me ... she should never have left your Institution which was & is quite good enough a home for her' (quoted in Hughes 2004:88). The Asylums Board had no option but to exercise compassion and readmit her.

ASYLUM WORK

The Hyde Park Asylum was a place of work as well as a place of refuge. It was largely self-supporting and able-bodied inmates were responsible for '... all the work of the institution, including cooking, laundry, hospitals, wards, cleaning, making and repairing all clothes and house linen, &c.' (Public Charities Commission 1874:109). According to the official reports, the only paid officers of the Asylum were the matron, the visiting medical officer, a head laundress and, in the early 1860s and (as mentioned) after 1875, a sub-matron. In 1866, Julia Williams was also on the payroll as a nurse at 12s. per week (*SMH* 30 August 1866, p.5).

All the remaining chores relating to feeding, cleaning, clothing and caring for up to 310 women. were undertaken by the inmates themselves, for small wages. In 1873, 21 inmates earned between tuppence and one shilling for a day's work, as set out in the following schedule of workers at the Hyde Park Asylum:

Officers employed at the Hyde Park Asylum —
Surgeon, Dr Ward   £122 per annum
Matron, L. H. Hicks   £190 per annum

Servants —
Head laundress, Nancy Bell   12s. per week

Servants selected from inmates —
Head cook, Ann Bertha   1s. per diem
2nd cook   6d.
3rd cook   4d.
Assistant laundress   6d.
4 assistant laundresses at   4d.
Head wardswoman, M. Haggerty 1s.
Assistant wardswoman, 1 at   6d.
Assistant wardswoman, 3 at   4d.
Assistant wardswoman, 2 at   3d.
Head hospital nurses, 2 at   6d.
Assistant hospital nurses, 2 at 4d.
Care-taker of needlework   2d.
Messenger, M. Jackson   4d.

(Source: Public Charities Commission 1874, Special Appendix 4, p.109)

The Hyde Park Asylum was thus comparatively cheap to run, a fact the Government Asylums Board was always keen to point out in its annual reports. In 1873, for example, the average cost per inmate was £11 16s (Government Asylums Board 1873:222). This compared very favourably to the Magdalen Asylum in Melbourne, where inmates 'cost' almost £25 each per annum, although they experienced similar living and work conditions (James 1969:242).

By the time of the 1886 Inquiry, and after the move to Newington, many more inmates were paid gratuities for their labour as bathwomen, dairymaids and wardswomen in the new wards. At Newington there were four bathwomen to assist inmates who could not bathe themselves, and to change the water between baths (two women shared a tub of fresh water). They worked from 9 am until 2 pm each Saturday to bathe all the women, 20 at a time in ten

4. The Workings of an Institution

tubs (Q1246–1257, Government Asylums Inquiry Board 1887:471).

With the possible exception of hat-making, the women were not engaged in the production or manufacture of goods for sale outside of the Asylum, unlike their male counterparts at the Liverpool Asylum. The women did not operate a commercial laundry, nor were they permitted to undertake 'out-door needlework', even on an individual basis (Public Charities Commission 1874:109). All their efforts were funnelled into the operation of the institution.

Control

In 1862, when the colonial government assumed responsibility for providing indoor relief to the infirm and destitute, Chairman Chris Rolleston published eight pages of 'Regulations for the Internal Management of the Government Asylums for the Infirm and Destitute' to be hung up in each dormitory, and to be read aloud to assembled inmates once a month. These rules provided guidelines for the daily routine, meal times, procedures for handling misconduct and so on, and were similar to those found in hundreds of other almshouses and poorhouses in major towns and cities across the western world.

Such explicit rules, however, appear to have been of little use at the Hyde Park Asylum, and by 1886 there were no printed rules. This was a cause of

Regulations for the Internal Management of the Government Asylums for the Infirm and Destitute[16]

Provisions
1. The daily ration of each inmate shall be in accordance with a scale to be fixed from time to time by the Board.
2. Snuff and tobacco in small quantities may, on recommendation of the Surgeon or Matron, be allowed to such of the inmates as use tobacco, or withheld from such as misconduct themselves.

Clothing
3. Each inmate shall be provided with a complete change of suitable clothing, upon entrance, if required.

Bedding
4. Each inmate shall, upon entrance, be supplied with a stretcher, a bed, and suitable bedding.

Stores
5. Each mess shall be provided with suitable mess utensils, including a table, forms, soup vessel, dishes, plates, pannikins, knives, forks, spoons, and salts.
6. No person discharged for misconduct shall take away anything belonging to the Institution, except clothing in wear at the time; and any person absconding may be prosecuted as for a theft of anything belonging to the Institution which such person may have absconded with.

Presents
7. No present is to be made to any inmate, except through the Master or Matron.

Drink
8. No present shall consist of or include drink of any kind; and the Master and Matron are strictly charged by every means in their power to prevent the inmates from being supplied with drink, otherwise than as may be ordered by the surgeon, and are authorised, in their discretion, to search for and seize any that may have been smuggled, or may be attempted to be smuggled into the buildings, taking care to report the same at the next Meeting of the Board.

Classification
9. The sick shall be separated from the healthy, and treated in all respects as the Surgeon may direct, irrespective of these Regulations.
10. The healthy shall be divided into messes, of from eight to ten in each, and the persons appointed by the Matron to be heads of Messes shall aid at all times in keeping those associated with them to a due observance of the Regulations of the Asylum.

---

[16] These regulations were drawn up in 1862 by Christopher Rolleston, chairman of the Board of Government Asylums. He also issued *By-Laws of the Board for Managing the Government Asylums for the Infirm and Destitute* (1862), which defined the role of the board, the criteria for admissions and the duties of the secretary and asylum staff.

Gratuity to Heads of Messes
11. The heads of messes shall be allowed a gratuity in tea, sugar, butter, tobacco, snuff, or some article of dress, as they may individually prefer, not exceeding one shilling in value weekly.

Rising
12. The hour of rising shall be in Spring and Summer six, and in Autumn and Winter seven a.m.

Washing, Dressing, &c.
13. Half an hour shall be allowed for washing and dressing.

Airing
14. After being dressed, if the weather permit, the inmates shall, in the order of their messes, take three quarters of an hour's airing in the Outer Domain, under care of the Master, assisted by the heads of messes.

Meals
15. Breakfast shall be on the table in Spring and Summer at half-past seven, and in Autumn and Winter at half-past eight o'clock a.m.; and Dinner at one, and Tea at half-past five o'clock p.m., throughout the year.

16. The heads of messes shall be responsible to the Matron for the becoming conduct of those associated with them at the respective Tables throughout the hour allowed for each meal.

Occupation
17. The inmates shall do all the needlework, washing, tidying, and cleansing required in the Institution; and the Matron shall apportion these several employments, as well as any other she may think conducive to health and comfort, according to the ability and aptitude of the several inmates for the work to be done; and the head of each mess shall be responsible to the Matron for the faithful performance of the labour allotted to those associated with her.

Recreation
18. The times for recreation shall be — half an hour after breakfast, three quarters of an hour after dinner, and half an hour after tea, which may be taken within the building, or in the yard, as the Matron shall direct.

Smoking
19. Smoking shall be allowed only in the place appointed by the Matron to be used for that purpose.

Bath
20. The inmates shall take the bath in messes, once in every week, and oftener if needful, generally, or in particular cases; and such bath may be hot or cold, as the Matron may think fit; and the heads of messes shall assist the Matron in seeing that this regulation is properly carried out.

Rest
21. The hour for retiring to rest shall be — in Spring and Summer, half-past Seven; and in Autumn and Winter, half-past Six p.m.

Sundays and Other Public Holidays
22. The inmates of the several denominations may attend Divine Service on Sundays and other holidays, under the care of persons appointed by the Clergymen of their respective Churches, who shall be responsible for their return to the Institution immediately after the close of the Service, and that they bring with them nothing contrary to the regulations of the Institution.

23. No work that can, in the opinion of the Matron, be dispensed with, shall be required of inmates on Sunday or any other public holiday; and ministers of religion, or members of any religious order, shall have every facility for the religious instruction of those of their own faith, within the Institution, care being taken by the Master or Matron that, in case of any visit for such purpose at the same time from persons of different persuasions, separate accommodation be provided for each.

Misconduct
24. The Master shall report to the Board any infraction of these Regulations, or any other misconduct on the part of any of the inmates, that ought to be made known to the Board.

4. The Workings of an Institution

> Regulations to be Read Monthly
> 25. The Master shall keep a copy of these Regulations hung up in each dormitory, and shall read them to the assembled inmates once in each month.
>
> Application of Regulations
> 26. These Regulations shall apply, so far as applicable, as well to the Asylums at Liverpool and Parramatta as to the Asylum at Hyde Park.

great concern to the Government Asylums Inquiry Board investigating the operation of the Newington Asylum six months after the move from Hyde Park, but Mrs Hicks insisted that rules were unnecessary in the aged-care facility that she managed. When asked whether rules had been issued to her, she replied:

> Not for years. We had some, but they were absurd for these old people. You have to give way to them a little, and sometimes you have to punish. I was called up last night to the cancer ward [at Newington], and found two old women fighting like tigers. One said she would see the other weltering in her gore. I had to take one and put her in the Roman Catholic hospital. (Q38, Government Asylums Inquiry Board 1887:448)

Hicks argued that routines of the Asylum were well enough understood, particularly by the wardswomen. Her position of authority was also clear: 'I say, "Come, girls, do so and so," and they do it, and do it well' (Q47, Government Asylums Inquiry Board 1887:418).

While mostly confined within the Asylum walls, inmates were permitted excursions, but as only three women were permitted leave on any given day, they had to 'wait for their turn' (Q2290, Public Charities Commission 1874:74). Leave was also granted under special circumstances, such as the death of a family member or friend. During the smallpox outbreak of 1881, the Hyde Park Asylum was quarantined to protect the inmates and these excursions were suspended.

The daily routine of the Asylum was flexible. Assuming it changed little following the transfer to Newington, the inmates rose at 6.30 a.m. in summer and 7 a.m. in winter — 'It is the greatest difficulty to keep these old people in bed' — the water was boiled for tea and sugar, dinner was served at 1 p.m. or later if the butcher was untimely, tea at 5 p.m. and then to bed shortly after. The doors to the wards were not locked; musters were taken when the matron thought it 'necessary', certainly not on a weekly basis — 'you see it is a long job' (Q88, Government Asylums Inquiry Board 1887:448–449).

Even if the regulations were followed loosely, it is apparent that many of the women were required to work less than seven hours per day during the week, with only essential work required on Sundays.

Matron Hicks' resistance to formal strictures was clearly out of step with some of the contemporary approaches to institutional control, as indicated by the following exchange:

> 92. *Chairman.*] Do you make any classification of the inmates? No; decidedly not.
> 93. *Dr. Ashburton Thompson.*] You mean ordinary social classification? No.
> 94. *Chairman.*] But you do classify the blind and ill? Of course; there is a classification of them and of gouty cases.
> 95. *Mr. Robison.*] What about the blind people? I find some of these the worst class we have here.
> 96. But you mix them among the others? Always. I find the old people very good to each other; always ready to help a blind person.
> 97. *Chairman.*] You have already said that you discharge inmates. Have you any means of keeping them in? No; they are not prisoners. A lawyer told me years ago I had not power to keep a woman in if she wished to leave.
>
> (Evidence of Mrs. Hicks, 19 August 1886, Government Asylums Inquiry Board 1887:449)

Ultimately this liberal view of institutional management contributed to her downfall. She was condemned by the Board as negligent in her duties to detect and prevent abuses within the Asylum and responsible for the untimely death of several inmates on their transfer to Newington in 1886. After 25 years of managing the provision of indoor relief, the government demanded a more controlled and restrictive regime. While this did not bode well for the Matron in the end, her approach that left the Institution 'free from control or inspection' (Government Asylums Inquiry Board 1887:419) may have been to the liking of the inmates. While it is difficult to generalise the experience of the thousands of women admitted to the Asylum from the testimony of the few dozen who gave evidence at the 1873 and 1886 inquiries, the *majority* had no complaint with the matron's management of the institution. Their criticisms were primarily directed at the state of the facilities at both Hyde Park and Newington.

Sanitation

Since the days of the convict occupation, ablution facilities were provided in outbuildings along the eastern wall of the Hyde Park Barracks complex, but the main building had no water or drainage facilities. At the time of its construction in 1817, indoor plumbing was a luxury for the wealthy, and certainly not a necessity for the convict inmates. While chamber pots would have been used in the main building in the evenings, outside privies would have worked sufficiently well for the 600-plus able-bodied men who lived in the Barracks.

When the last convicts were removed in 1848 the building was made ready for the reception of female immigrants and Irish female orphans. General repairs to the main building included lime-washing of much of the interior (Thorp 1980:IV:2). Several additional measures were undertaken in 1862 to improve sanitary conditions for the Asylum women. Grated apertures were installed in the walls under the windows, with openings near the ceilings in the opposite walls to ensure cross-ventilation. The walls were 'roughly whitewashed', and folding iron beds from the Immigration Depot were brought upstairs for the Destitute Asylum. In addition, a pump was supplied to provide fresh water for washing on Level 3 (*Sydney Mail* 15 March 1862, p.2).

The sanitary facilities of the Barracks, however, became a source of bitter complaint within just two years of the establishment of the Asylum on the third floor. In February 1864, the Asylum's Medical Officer, George Walker, raised concerns about 'the means adopted for getting rid of night soil — refuse water and other impurities from the Establishment ... [and the] non Existence of proper Water Closets to the sick Wards' (SRNSW 2/642A quoted in Berry 2001:14). He suggested that only an 'intervention of special mercy' had spared the inmates from 'severe and fatal epidemics' and noted also that visitors to the Hiring Room of the Immigration Depot complained 'loudly of the stench and nausea' that he described as an 'Atmospheric Poison'. He also urged the Board to punish those inmates who were not incapacitated but who 'from actual laziness or the baser motive of giving trouble — are in the habit of soiling their beds '(SRNSW 2/642A quoted in Hughes 2004:74).

A report on the drainage of the Hyde Park Asylum in April 1864 described the problem in more detail:

> Another complaint is the heavy and unwholsome [sic] air in the building this must arise in a great measure from the necessity of carrying down all the night tubs in through the stair case which is in the very centre of the Building the effect of which will take some hours to allow the fetid air to be carried off.
>
> It is proposed to erect a verandah on the end facing the east with four water closets one convenient to each dormitory, a door in [the] end of each dormitory to lead to the closet and as it is probable night tubs would still have to be used [in] a stair erected from those balconys [sic] to the ground as shown by the Plan accompanying the stair in the centre of the Building would not be required for those purposes and the Patients would have all the benefit of the fresh air on those Balconys when they would not be able to descend the stair ... (SRNSW 2/642A quoted in Berry 2001:14).

In following the miasmatic theory of disease, Walker blamed the stench and foul air for causing the death of Mary Tracy in February 1864, who died from diarrhoea while afflicted with *purpurea* (SRNSW 2/642A, quoted in Hughes 2004:75). In 1865, George Walker again complained that:

> No drainage exists in the Institution ... the means of carrying off refuse Water ... [from] the building seems to be very limited and imperfect. This is manifest from the Accumulation of stagnant liquid to be found in every place in the Yards ...
>
> [There is] A Cart load of Bones and a full Ash-pit within a few yards of the Cooking Aparatus ... I have to suggest that these Accumulations should be cleared Away Every Week.
>
> I am informed by the Emigration Agent that in upwards of four thousand Emigrants may be Expected this Year as on a former occasion — more than three hundred were housed on the premises in Addition to the inmates of your Institution, it is desirable to improve the means for Conducting to their health and safety before warmer weather sets in. (SRNSW 2/642A, letter dated 6 August 1865 from George Walker MD Hyde Park Asylum Medical Officer to the Chairman of the Board of the Hyde Park Asylum, quoted in Berry 2001:15).

Walker was also concerned about other aspects of the Barracks environment. He complained about the excessive noise generated by the band rehearsals of the Volunteers' Brigade. He urged the Asylums Board to deal with the disturbance, so that the sick outcasts 'should have some fair play and not be drummed into their coffins' (Walker to Government Asylums Board 24 Nov 1862, quoted in Hughes 2004:69). Two weeks later the Brigade Adjutant advised that the nightly drumming would cease.

Ashpits had previously been cleared on request from the Matron in her daily book, along with other routine maintenance tasks such as chimney sweeping. In 1864 it was agreed to construct a three-storey verandah with four 'patent valve' water closets on the eastern face of the main Barracks building at a cost of £326 (Berry 2001:15).

4. The Workings of an Institution

In 1865 there were further modifications, when the Colonial Architect installed ceilings in the matron's quarters to prevent 'leakage' from the hospital wards above, although it is uncertain if this came from incontinent inmates or a leaking roof. The modifications were regarded as 'very necessary' and were estimated to cost around £60 (Thorp 1980:VI:2). In addition, a block of water closets was finally installed in 1867 behind the kitchen in the south-eastern corner of the yard, along with a separate privy for the Matron (Hughes 2004:80).

Historian Joy Hughes describes the likely scene in the Barracks compound that would have greeted a visitor at this time:

> There was the cacophony of the Volunteer Rifles and band parading in their yard, the excited chatter of young female immigrants, infirm pauper applicants at the asylum door on board days or the crowds of prospective employers on hiring day, the general public awaiting hearings at the district court, smoke belching from the asylum's kitchen and laundry, cooking smells emanating from the kitchen and the cartload of bones outside, rats amok, stagnant surface water, fetid privies, the pervasive odour of night pails indoors, washing flapping on clotheslines, the incessant clucking of the matron's thirty-five chooks and the pathetic garden plot devoured by her goats (Hughes 2004:81).

It is evident from the historical and archaeological evidence that Matron Hicks regarded hygiene very seriously. When a new inmate was admitted, the matron insisted she take a bath, even a sponge bath if arriving late at night. Her clothing was soaked and washed, and replaced with a complete change of Asylum clothes. If the new arrival had the 'itch' (scabies) or some infectious skin condition, her old clothing was burnt (Q2373–2376, Public Charities Commission 1874:76). There is no evidence, however, that the women's hair was cut short, either as a hygienic measure or as part of institutional austerity (Ignatieff 1978:144).

When the *Abyssinian* arrived in Sydney in 1862, Matron Applewhaite reported:

> I found this Morning upon inspecting the Blankets in the Dormitories that they were much covered with vermin the [shipboard] Matron informs me that for at least six weeks the girls have not been able to wash any of there [sic] clothes consequently have scarcely a clean article to put on. (Hyde Park Daily Reports, 1 June 1862, 9/6181, SRNSW, quoted in Gothard 2001:116).

During the 19th century, taking a bath became more common and was associated with improved sanitation, good health and personal cleanliness (Eveleigh 2002:64). As late as 1880 in Sydney, most homes had little or no fixtures for indoor bathing, and piped hot water remained a rarity (Cannon 1988:238). The Asylum inmates, however, enjoyed the benefit of 'hot and cold taps' for their Saturday morning bath (Q2367: Public Charities Commission 1874:76). In 1865 the bathroom was fitted with three six-foot baths served with hot water supplied by a copper from the adjoining laundry (Hughes 2004:78).

Along with the inmates themselves, the inmates' clothing was washed every week in the Asylum laundry. Nancy Bell was the Head laundress and, as noted, worked at the Asylum for more than 20 years. She was in charge of washing (and drying) not only the inmates' clothing, but also all of the bed sheets, towels and other items as well. She used 'soap and soda, blue and starch' for the washing, and went through 20–30 pounds each week (Q1209–1212, Government Asylums Inquiry Board 1887:470). In the 1870s she earned 12 shillings per week (about £31 per year), well above the wages of many female domestic servants of the era (Gothard 2001:221). She had up to 10 women helping her each day, and her status as an employee, rather than an inmate, reinforced the value placed on sanitation and hygiene within the institution.

Various items used for personal cleaning were identified in the underfloor assemblage material. These included 14 worn pieces of soap from the Asylum on Level 3, and 13 pieces from the Immigration Depot on Level 2. Hard soap was made by boiling oil or fat with a lye of caustic soda. All of the pieces preserved are small and worn, and may have been discarded as too small for further convenient use. It is probable that these fragments are the result of the bed-side sponge bathing of women unable to make it to the bath house.

The remains of eight lice-combs were found on Level 3 and two from Level 2 (**Figure 4.2**). Two toothbrushes were found on Level 2 (UF27, UF8534) but none on Level 3, which is a small number and may suggest that dental hygiene was less important than bodily and hair cleanliness among the inmates, or toothbrushes were in shorter supply.[17] One of the toothbrushes (UF27) was marked 'S. Maw & Son, London, for W T Pinhey, Chemist, Sydney'. The Maw firm was the largest drug wholesaler in Britain in the 19th century, and this mark dates the brush to the 1860s (Mattick 2010:70). Pinhey was a major figure in NSW pharmacy from the 1860s to the 1880s, building up a substantial business in George Street, Sydney, from the early 1850s (Haines 1976:35, 55–57). The Applewhaites purchased medicines for

---

[17] Toothbrushes did not become common in the UK and US until the 1870s and 1880s (Mattick 2010:15–18) so it is not surprising that so few are found in an Asylum during this period. Given the standards of dental care at the time, and the age and circumstances of the women who occupied the Asylum it is possible that many of the inmates had chronic dental problems and some may have had no teeth at all.

4. The Workings of an Institution

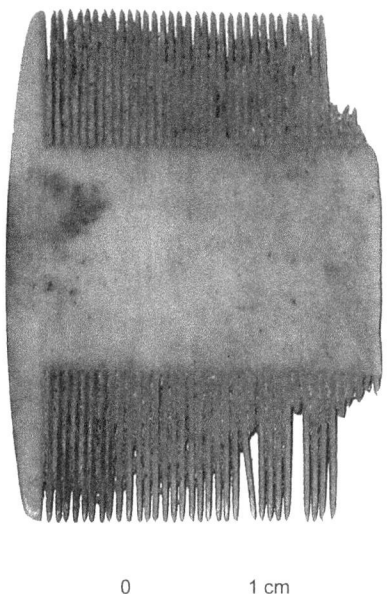

Figure 4.2: Bone lice-comb from the Hyde Park Asylum (UF7560; P. Davies 2009).

their family from Pinhey between the years 1861 and 1864 (NSW Supreme Court, Insolvency Papers, SRNSW 2/9226, no. 8090). He may have supplied the Hyde Park Asylum and other institutions on a regular basis. A bottle of 'Floriline' (UF7006) for the teeth and breath came from the northern ward on Level 2.

Inmates were also active in keeping the premises clean. In 1865 the Asylums Board asked the Colonial Architect to pave the shed in which the women sat during the day as their continuous sweeping of the gravel floor had created dangerous potholes. In the same year the Colonial Architect was also requested to supply a load of 'soft sand stone' for scrubbing the floors — the women took great pride in their 'snowy boards' (Hughes 2004:78–79). A wooden scrubbing brush with intact bristles (UF34) from the southern dormitory on Level 3 may be a remnant of this activity.

MEDICINE

At the Hyde Park Barracks all pharmaceutical items and medical comforts were administered by the visiting doctor. A dispensary attached to the rear of the building was completed in April 1862, but the small timber building was to be a source of frequent complaint. In 1866, the serving Medical Officer, Dr George Walker, complained bitterly about its position and condition, barely four years after its construction:

> I am compelled to request attention to the present state of the Dispensary attached to this institution. It is so much infested by rats that the destruction of Drugs and breakage of Glass is really very serious. The Animals eat the corks and upset the Bottles and the place is continually covered with their Dung. To this source of annoyance must be added that of damp which is so great that during rainy weather the walls are teaming with moisture, they are also so saturated with fluid excrement from the water closet above as to be perfectly pestilential. A Gentleman from the Colonial Architect's Office recently inspected the place and [told] me he would recommend its being lined with Galvanized iron. But it is already sufficiently and frequently unbearably hot and means must be taken to render it water tight. The Drug Bill of this Institution need never be a very serious item if care is taken to preserve the Stock from deterioration by Moisture or Vermin. At present the destruction is considerable. Many drugs are moulded and unserviceable and not a day passes without my finding something thrown down and broken by the Rats which even eat the Ointments and Pill Mass.
>
> George Walker MD
> Medical Officer

(SRNSW 2/642A — memo dated 5 September 1866 from Dr George Walker, Hyde Park Asylum, Medical Officer, to the Colonial Architect)

Several pharmaceutical bottles issued from the dispensary were recovered from Levels 2 and 3 of the main dormitory building, and because of the unique preservation conditions of the underfloor deposits, several have survived with their labels intact. The names of patients can still be read: Alice Fry (UF26), [Margaret?] Jackson (UF25) and F. [probably Francis] Cunningham (UF6624). Two of the bottles (UF6624 and UF3059) have two layers of labels. In the context of the institution, this is an unsurprising indication of the reuse of bottles, but one that raises questions about the hygiene standards of recycling medicinal vessels in this period. If the bottle had been sterilised by boiling, for example, the underlying label ought to have peeled off or boiled away (**Figures 4.3** and **4.4**).

There are several other examples of bottles with non-Asylum paper labels marked 'Raspberry Vinegar' (a cordial used for sore throats and coughs; UF4574), 'Tinct[ure of] Digitalis' (for regulating the heartbeat, treating dropsy and as a topical treatment for wounds; UF395), 'Aconit' (pain relief for various conditions including neuralgia, rheumatism and arthritis; UF11600) and 'Chloroform' (anaesthetic; UF377, UF413 and UF8351).

Most of the fragments of dispensary-issued labels were found on light-blue, oval-sectioned bottles made for pharmaceutical use that were common in colonial Australia at this time. Others, such as the Alice Fry label, were found on dark olive green, square-sectioned bottles typically associated by historical

41

4. The Workings of an Institution

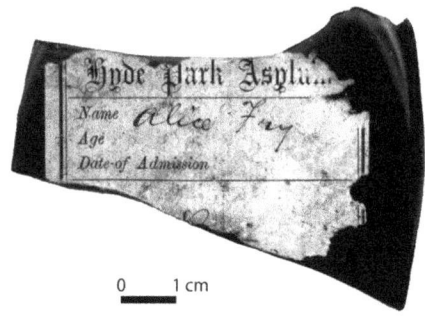

Figure 4.3: Hyde Park Asylum Dispensary Label for Alice Fry on a dark olive-green gin or schnapps bottle. Alice Fry died on 5 February 1868, aged 56 years, of a uterine tumour (UF26; P. Davies 2009).

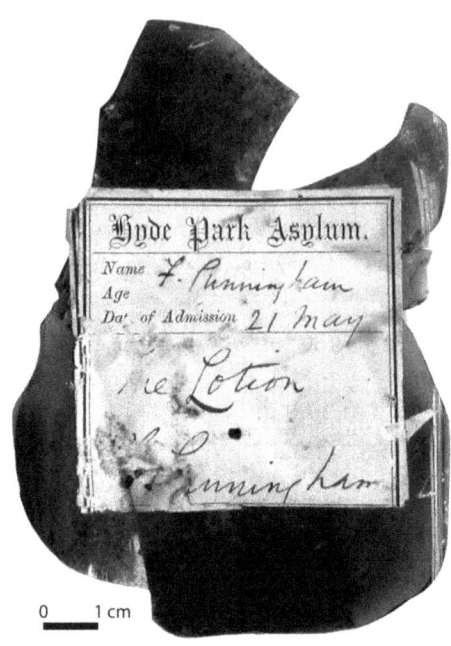

Figure 4.4: Hyde Park Asylum Dispensary Label for 'F Cunningham' on a gin or schnapps bottle. Francis Cunningham was part of the first intake of inmates in 1862 (UF6624; P. Davies 2009).

archaeologists with gin or schnapps. Square case bottles were a standard part of the 'kit' of military surgeons in the early 19th century (Starr 2001:43–44), and the Barracks examples may be a holdover from this practice. Whether Fry's prescription happened to be spirits or, when short of bottles the Medical Officer used whatever vessels were available at short notice, or 'Gin/Schnapps' bottles were commonly used for pharmaceutical concoctions, is uncertain. It is known, however, that some brands of schnapps including Udolpho Wolfe's popular 'Aromatic Schnapps' (4 examples of which were found on Level 3), were promoted at this time for its medicinal properties (Vader and Murray 1975:39–40).

There is, however, other more concrete evidence for 'making-do' when it comes to dispensing medicines. A small wooden disk, 40 mm across, is marked 'The Ointment / Mrs Harris' in brown ink (UF17601; **Figure 4.5**). It was probably from a circular matchbox or some other small, light, disposable box, and seems to have been used as a label in the absence of a paper one, possibly tied or glued to the bottle.

In addition to the medicines issued by the Dispensary, there was evidence of prepared, commercial remedies including a laxative tonic, 'Dinneford's Solution of Magnesia' (UF4520) and, among the paper fragments, two packets of 'Cockle's Antibilious Pills' for settling the stomach (UF4233, UF17281). A bottle of 'Barry's Tricopherous' skin and hair ointment came from the large southern dormitory on Level 3.

It is known from the parliamentary inquiries and the Daily Reports that sick inmates were prescribed alcohol and nourishing meals in addition to medicinal treatments. 'Grog', for example, was an alcoholic mixture of rum and water. Women and children in the Immigration Depot were given arrowroot, milk and rice. Traditional treatments were arranged by Matron Hicks. The Day Book entry for 8 July 1864 reported that a mustard poultice had been applied to immigrant Margaret Dailby who complained of a sore throat.

The parliamentary inquiry of 1886 revealed that inmates too were responsible for dispensing medicines in the sick wards, and to the great dismay of the Board of Inquiry, some of these women were illiterate or had limited reading skills. In the cancer ward, for example, Annie Mack could read 'printing' but not the hand-written dosage instructions, while Ann Simpson could not read or write at all (Q2014, Q1616, Government Asylums Inquiry Board 1887:484, 477). Both relied on the recall of instructions given to them on the doctor's weekly visits, or the assistance of literate staff such as Miss Applewhaite.

The medicines were stored on the mantelpiece in each ward and some patients were able to take their own dosage when required, sometimes with serious consequences. Ellen Purnell, who could read but not write, mistakenly took a poisonous lotion instead of medicine, apparently by accident rather

Figure 4.5: Wooden disc with hand-written identification: 'The Ointment / Mrs Harris' (UF17601; P. Crook 2003).

4. The Workings of an Institution

	Level 2	Level 3	Total
Bottle fragment	116	335	451
Bottle label	7	38	45
Medicinal packet	2	2	4
Vial	5	12	17
Total fragments	*130*	*387*	*517*

Table 4.1: Fragments of pharmaceutical items in the main building.

than inability to read the label (Q2403, Government Asylums Inquiry Board 1887:493).

The distribution of pharmaceutical items across Levels 2 and 3 suggests that sick wards probably operated on both floors at one time, with a greater use of Level 3 for remedial purposes (**Table 4.1**).

DEATH AND BURIAL

As expected in an institution of its kind, many women died while they were inmates at Hyde Park Asylum (**Figure 4.6**). Annual Reports of the Government Asylums Board from 1873 included summary information on the number of deaths, while from 1875 the causes of death were also reported. Conditions such as 'Brain disease', 'Senile decay', 'Diarrhoea' and Phthisis (tuberculosis) claimed the most lives, revealing the limits of medical diagnosis in this period, and the suffering that many of the women endured.

Mrs Hicks found the inmates 'very good to the dying and the dead'. Every corpse was bathed and dressed in a clean chemise and nightcap, for which the oldest clothes were specially put aside. There was no dead house, and the deceased were placed in coffins in the hospital ward and carried out by an undertaker. They were buried quickly, sometimes on the same day as their death — particularly in the case of infectious diseases. Some remained at the Asylum in their coffins or laid out behind screens for several hours or sometimes overnight (*SMH* 30 August 1866, p.5; Hughes 2004:197). If unclaimed by relatives, the women were buried in pauper graves at government cost.

In 1866, Richard Switson, the undertaker paid to provide coffins to the Asylum and carry them to their respective places of burial, was found guilty of fraudulently burying two Roman Catholic inmates in one coffin (with the corpse of an unknown infant) and 'charging for two'. He was also accused of failing to bury three Protestant inmates having claimed they were buried at Camperdown, although no record of their burial was known. The evidence presented at trial (*SMH* 29–31 August 1866, pp.5) provides yet another sad tale of the ill-treatment and mismanagement of pauper women, even in death. It also provides some interesting detail about the operations of the Hyde Park Asylum:

> Lucy Ann [sic] Applewhaite, being sworn, deposed: I am matron in the Hyde Park Asylum, the following paupers were inmates — Ann Miller, Ann Terry, Priscilla Pritchard, Mary Coffee, and Margaret Williams, persons of that name died in the asylum; I saw their dead bodies there; the nurses, as usual, placed them in coffins, and the defendant, to the best of my belief, brought the coffins; ... when the body of Pritchard was put into the coffin, she

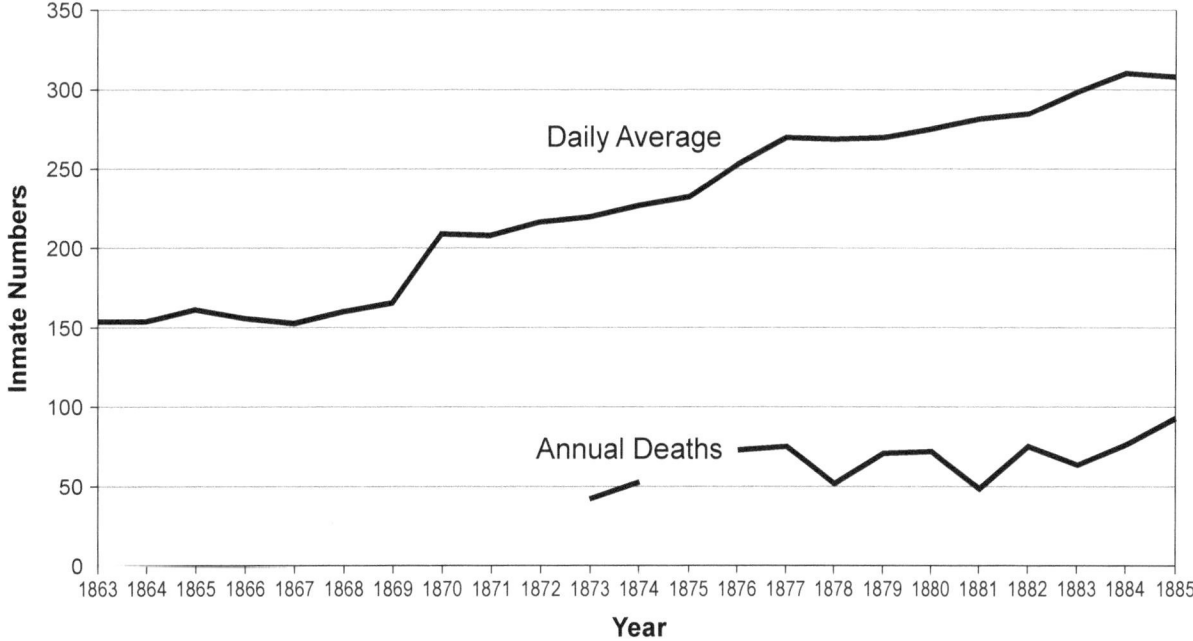

Figure 4.6: Daily average of inmate numbers at the Hyde Park Asylum, and annual death-rate (source: Hughes 2004:218).

---

[18] Gangrene.

having died of mortification[18], I stood at the bottom of the stairs whilst the coffin was being nailed down; ... there were two women lying dead at the same time — Rose Kelly and Priscilla Pritchard; Kelly was in her coffin, and defendant promised to come back with another coffin for Pritchard; ... going up-stairs I told defendant to be very particular about them, one being a Roman Catholic and the other a Protestant, and said, "Mind you mark the coffins", he said, "all right"; we put a cross in black lead pencil on the coffin of the Roman Catholic, some short time after he returned and brought a coffin for Pritchard; I made the mark on the coffin of Kelly with a little pencil mark, and the defendant said there would be no fear of burying them together ...

Somewhat gruesomely, the testimony of inmate and nurse Ann Jeffreys regarding the exhumation of Mary Coffee and Margaret Williams from the Roman Catholic Burial ground, Devonshire Street, on 12 August 1866 (one month after their burial) provides rare evidence of the medical afflictions and personal appearance of these inmates:

> I was present at the exhumation of a coffin at the Roman Catholic Cemetery a fortnight last Sunday; I saw the coffin taken from the ground, and when the lid was raised I saw the bodies of two women and there was a bundle at the foot of the coffin ... I recognised the two women, the top body was that of Mary Coffee, and the lower one that of Margaret Williams; one body was laid above the other; I recognised Coffee, because she had quite a moustache and beard; and Williams because she was buried with her arm across her stomach, and she had one knee bent up; I saw their faces distinctly; I should not know it was Coffee except for the beard and moustache; I recognised the clothes she had on; I put her in the coffin myself in the same clothes; I had known Coffee for about three years in the Asylum, or it might be more; she was a very old woman, I do not think she was quite 100, but upwards of 90; I cannot say exactly; she was a shortish woman, and stout, but not very heavy, I have not the slightest doubt this was the body of Mary Coffee; I saw the face of the body I recognised as Williams; I have no doubt it was Williams' body; I have known her six years, I believe Coffee died of old age, she did not die of dropsy; she was two years under my charge and care. (*SMH* 31 August 1866, p.5)

Mary Coffee is registered as 101 years on her birth certificate. She was a short, stout woman with 'quite a moustache and beard'. Williams had suffered as a cripple for many years and in death, her coffin had to be 'made large' to accommodate her bent knee, which is probably why the undertaker, Switson (or his 'man' as Switson argued), saw fit to bury three paupers in it.

Switson was sentenced to eighteen months hard labour in Sydney Gaol. After 1867, deceased inmates from the Asylum were interred in the Rookwood Necropolis in consecrated grounds of the various denominations (Hughes 2004:90).

VISITORS AND SPECIAL OCCASIONS

Women in the Asylum and Immigration Depot were generally confined within its walls, unless they were granted permission to leave or were sent on errands. They were not, however, entirely cut off from the outside world. The Hyde Park Asylum was accessible for visits by friends and relatives of the inmates, and there were many visits by well-meaning individuals and organisations, including the Ladies Evangelical Association, the Sisters of Mercy and the Flower Mission Ladies (*SMH* 1 February 1882). While the motivations for these visits were largely religious, and arguably political advocacy, they also provided an important distraction from the daily routine for the Asylum inmates.

At the 1886 Inquiry, one of the visitors on the Ladies' Board, Miss Eleanor Bedford reported that many inmates disliked the isolation of the new Newington Asylum:

> They said they had never been so wretched at Hyde Park; that Hyde Park was a paradise to this; there the old women had friends who could visit them easily. (Q2322, Government Asylum Inquiry Board 1887:490)

Eliza Pottie was also a member of the Ladies' Board, and from the 1870s onwards she undertook charity work for destitute women and children in Sydney. By the 1880s she was one of Sydney's leading evangelicals, distributing religious tracts to children and working for the welfare of women, girls and animals (Dickey 1994:312–313). She often visited the Hyde Park Barracks Asylum, and her testimony to the Newington Inquiry was highly critical of conditions at the institution (Q2354, Government Asylum Inquiry Board 1887:491–492).

Distinguished travellers also visited the institution. The sisters Rosamond and Florence Hill, for example, published an account of their visit in their book *What We Saw in Australia*, published in London in 1875. They described the Hyde Park Asylum as:

> ... standing on high ground in a beautiful situation, and in one of the fashionable quarters of the town ... It contains more than two hundred inmates, the greater proportion of whom are old or sick. The few young women are either blind, cripple, or idiots, for whom there is no other refuge. As the asylum is in the metropolis, it does not require a resident medical officer, but is managed by the matron, Mrs. Hicks, whose qualifications

are as remarkable as those of Mrs. Burnside [Matron of the Parramatta Asylum]. She and one laundress are the only [paid] officers in the institution, the whole of the work, nursing included, being performed by the inmates, who also make all their own clothing, with the exception of boots and shoes.

The house affords good bathing accommodation, and the old women have their warm baths regularly ... At meals the old women are divided into messes of eight, the strongest being chosen captain of the mess. She fetches the dinner, and, we conclude, carves for her mess-mates; but every woman pours her own tea. Small gratuities are given for the work performed, as at Liverpool, and the women looked as cheerful and happy as the old men there. Their annual cost per head is only 10*l.* 16*s.* 11½*d.* (Hill and Hill 1875:336–337)

It is also possible that Marie Rye, who promoted female emigration from England, visited the Hyde Park Barracks in 1865 during her trip to Australia and New Zealand. Rye wrote to Florence Nightingale about conditions in Sydney's institutions, including the Infirmary and Gladesville Lunatic Asylum, and she is unlikely to have missed an opportunity to inspect the Immigration Depot as well (Godden 2004:52).

Another well known visitor to the Hyde Park Asylum was the prominent local merchant and philanthropist Quong Tart. In later years his wife recalled:

On one occasion, in the year 1885, he was asked, along with others, to speak at a treat given to the inmates of the Asylum for Women at the head of King Street. Speaking of that address a daily paper of that day said, "Mr. Tart's speech differed from that of others in that while they spoke high-sounding words, he determined to make the treat an annual affair," and this he afterwards attempted to do, not only for the unfortunates of that asylum alone, but for the indigent poor in the benevolent asylums of the State. How far he succeeded in this attempt may be seen by casually scanning the large list of institutions where every year such festivals were held. (Tart 1911:25)

Tart maintained his relationship with the Asylum after its move to Newington:

"When nearing the wharf on the day of the feast of the inmates of the Newington Asylum," says "The Echo" of 16th October, 1888, "Mr. Tart seemed suddenly seized with a fit; he waved his arms and rushed about the deck, shouting out to the old women how glad he was to see them. The moment they recognised who it was, the look of joyous gratitude that came over those wrinkled faces was worth going over from Sydney to see. The moment

4. The Workings of an Institution

he reached the enclosure he was surrounded by the poor old creatures, who danced round and clapped their hands like children in a pantomime. 'Ah! God bless you for a good 'un Mr. Tart!' 'The Lord preserve you and yours, dear Mr. Tart!' 'Have you brought Mrs. Tart?' and dozens of similar ejaculations, and when he told them Mrs. Tart would be there directly with the little 'Tart,' which they mustn't eat, their enthusiasm knew no bounds."

"Long time since I saw you!" "Now, you have a good bit of fun to-day, but don't flirt with the gentlemen from Sydney!" "How are you, Mary? I must have a dance with you when Mrs. Tart goes away," and similar expressions, with a kindly word for all, as he wended his way amongst them, raising his hat each time he shook hands with one of them, with as much grace as he would have done to his own wife.

It was no unusual sight on feast day at the asylums for his name to be blazoned forth with mottoes expressing welcome and thankfulness — "A Glorious Welcome to Quong Tart and His Friends!" "Vive Quong Tart le Grand!" "Will ye nae come back again?" were among the decorative mottoes at the Parramatta Asylum in 1886. (Tart 1911:26)

On such occasions the women were issued with 'new dresses and aprons and the like' (Q3213, Governments Asylums Inquiry Board 1887:508). Religious and public holidays were also honoured in the Asylum with special feasts:

QUEEN'S BIRTHDAY was celebrated at the Hyde Park Asylum on Wednesday with the usual tokens of re-joicing. The old ladies were regaled with a bountiful dinner of roast beef and plum pudding, washed down with a glass of ale. A harper and violinist were afterwards introduced, to whose music some of the old girls danced jigs as merrily as they would have done some 50 or 60 years ago. The whole party seemed to enjoy themselves greatly, and were loud in their praises to the matron (Mrs. Hicks) and the Government, to whom they were indebted for the treat. (*SMH* 29 May 1882, p.5)

These banquets were important events for the inmates of the overcrowded Hyde Park Asylum which Frederic King described, in 1886, as unsuitable for the care of the old women, there being:

Little room for recreation, and the wards are badly adapted for the healthy accommodation of large numbers of aged, and in many cases bed-ridden paupers. (Government Asylums Board 1876:928)

The overcrowding of the inmates was also observed by Lady Carrington, wife of the Governor of New South Wales, who visited the Asylum in 1886, a few weeks before the move to Newington. The vice-regal couple displayed an interest in helping the poor during their five-year term in Sydney, banqueting a thousand poor boys and establishing the Jubilee Fund in 1887 to help to provide relief for distressed women (Hughes 2004:177; Martin 1969). Lady Carrington:

> ... [visited] some of the old women; with some of these she shook hands, and said a few kindly words. Amongst the poor creatures seen were a few who were so enfeebled that they were unable to leave their beds, and in these Lady Carrington seemed to be particularly interested. The inmates of the asylum, who were ranged in the yard, manifested their pleasure at seeing the lady of the Governor by giving hearty cheers. (*SMH* 21 January 1886, p.9)

OFFICIAL AND ADMINISTRATIVE RECORDS

Documentary evidence of government administration was found among the artefact assemblage, and included items from other institutions that shared the Hyde Park Barracks with the Asylum and Immigration Depot, or occupied the main building after its conversion to government and legal offices. The latter category includes documents from the NSW Parliamentary Library (UF4279), fragments from the *Government Gazette*, and numerous fragments of blue forms from the 1871 Census. The Census Office is known to have occupied rooms in the main building (probably on the ground floor), much to the annoyance of Matron Hicks.[19]

Several documents derive from the Master in Lunacy's office, including scraps of notepaper and part of a file for 'Isabella Hughes, Lunatic', dated 1891, relating to monies owed to the government (UF135). Judicial stationery included an envelope from the District Court of NSW (UF8315) and miscellaneous papers from the Supreme Court, along with a typed document addressed to the Equity Court (UF4303). A pink paper fragment (UF17749) from the City Coroner related to 'children', while two legal documents dated 1890 concern an Eliza Skinner (UF208 and UF209).

There were also at least 4 documents associated with the office of the Agent for Immigration, which occupied the building in conjunction with the Depot. These included a notice to single female immigrants wishing to be hired (UF11585 and UF11612); regulations relating to the cost of immigration (UF17756) and a handwritten document relating to the numbers of immigrants present (UF3311). There were also several 'Ship Surgeon's Requisitions' for medical comforts to be given to female immigrants (see 'Names: Individuals and Institutions').

It is unknown how some of these documents found their way to the upper floors, but as in the case of the newspaper fragments, it is possible that scrap paper had meaningful uses in the self-sufficient asylum, and once its clerical purpose had been served, it was provided to the matron for her use. These documents are an important reminder of the fact that the Asylum was by no means the exclusive occupier of the Hyde Park Barracks, and consequently neither is the archaeological assemblage an exclusive representation of Asylum life.

General stationery items were found, including paper clips and file clips, numerous lengths of pink legal ribbon, blobs of red sealing wax, and scraps of pink blotting paper. There were also 390 metal pen nibs from a wide range of manufacturers, including Joseph Gillott (Birmingham), John Mitchell, William Mitchell (England), Hinks Wells & Co (Birmingham), MacNiven and Cameron (Edinburgh), Collins Bros & Co (England), M. Myers & Son (England) D. Leonardt & Co (Birmingham), R. Esterbrook (USA), C. Brandauer & Co (Birmingham) and J. Swain. Mass-production of metal pen nibs started in the 1820s.

The tail (or 'queue') of a barrister's horse hair wig was found beneath the hallway on Level 2 (UF5478). Wigs were first adopted by the legal profession in England in the 17th century, and worn by judges and barristers to emphasise the dignity of the court. Legal attire in early colonial Australia lacked the formality of the English courts, largely to avoid claims of false status by those with little legal training. By the 1850s, however, full English judicial regalia were increasingly worn in Australian colonial courts, to confer a degree of formality and anonymity on members of the judiciary.

---

[19] At least 34 fragments of the 1871 Census papers have been identified: UF17341, UF17371, UF17377, UF17452, UF17462, UF17467, UF17476, UF17488, UF17588, UF17597, UF17604, UF17616, UF17621, UF17672, UF17742, UF17762 and UF7468.

5
DAILY LIFE IN THE ASYLUM

COMMUNAL MEALS

The women of the Asylum sat down to three simple, monotonous meals every day. Breakfast and supper consisted of dry bread and black tea, while the main dinner meal was served around 1 pm. This generally included boiled meat and a watery vegetable soup. The daily allowance for each woman was half a loaf of bread, one pound of beef or mutton and one pint of tea. Inmates could help themselves to dripping from the kitchen to spread on the bread, but only women in the hospital wards were permitted milk in their tea. The tea ration could also be supplemented by gifts, rewards or gratuities for daily work, or by purchasing or exchanging supplies with other inmates.

The women were organised into messes comprising 8 inmates and the strongest woman among the group was appointed the 'captain'. These women carried in the loaves of bread, the boiled beef or mutton 'hot in the joint' and the pot of tea, for breaking, carving and pouring amongst the mess. According to Mrs Hicks, the women preferred boiled to roasted meat which was reserved for 'special days' when large legs of roast mutton were served[20] (Q2321–2347, Public Charities Commission 1874:75).

The Asylum may have had the use of the large southern room on Level 1 as a dining room (Hughes 2004:57). A kitchen was located at the south-east corner of the main building, and this was replaced with a larger complex by 1870 (Spiers 1995:125; Varman 1993). The kitchen was thus convenient to the dining room for the Asylum women.

Large quantities of cutlery were found in the subfloor cavities on Level 3, including forks, spoons, teaspoons, serving spoons and bone- and wood-handled knives (**Table 5.1**). There was also an unusual concentration of 19 well preserved cutlery items found under the floor below a window in the large southern dormitory in the Asylum, the explanation for which remains uncertain (JG3 JS14). The presence of cutlery in the dormitories may indicate that some bed-ridden women ate their meals in bed. Only 15 cutlery items, however, were recovered under the floor on Level 2, which probably reflects the fact that the women from the Immigrant Depot took their meals in the large northern room down on Level 1.

Cutlery	Level 2	Level 3	Total
Fork	2	6	8
Knife	6	24	30
Serving spoon	–	7	7
Spoon	1	13	14
Teaspoon	2	9	11
Unidentified	4	16	20
Total fragments	*15*	*75*	*90*

Table 5.1: Distribution of cutlery items on Level 2 and Level 3.

It is very unlikely that the Applewhaite-Hicks family shared meals or utensils with the Asylum women. A kitchen range, for example, had been installed in 1848 in the Matron's apartment on Level 2. The family shared this with the sub-matron and the immigrant ship's matron before her departure. Its constant use over the years caused it to fall to pieces and it was replaced in 1866 (Hughes 2004:79). Mrs Hicks probably had her own china service and the family most likely ate in their quarters, or perhaps used the Asylum or Immigrants' dining room off-schedule to the main meals. The Matron also kept her own animals, including three dozen chickens and several goats, which destroyed the small garden in front of the Hyde Park Barracks, while her cow was de-pastured in the Domain (Q3927, Government Asylums Inquiry Board 1887:527). These animals may have been used to supplement Asylum rations and keep costs down.

The diet of the Asylum women remained basically unchanged for 24 years, except for 'special days' and the occasional feast (see following section). In 1885 Frederic King, the Manager of Government Asylums, defended the Asylum's meals as:

> ... suitable food for old and worn out persons ... it would be difficult to find a more health giving dietary ... [I]t has not been attempted ... to supply luxuries to people who, even in the days of their health and independence, were never accustomed to them. Sound, wholesome, and plenty of food has been given, and there is no fair ground for complaint by the inmates.
> (Government Asylums Board 1885:720)

---

[20] Large quantities of animal bone from the underfloor spaces were recorded in the original artefact catalogue, but were not analysed as part of our project. These include 2057 fragments from Level 2 and 4709 fragments from Level 3. There are also 3936 seeds in the underfloor collection, including many examples of peach, apricot and cherry.

5. Daily Life in the Asylum

Surveys of dietary scales at other asylums in New South Wales and the other colonies, however, indicated that greater effort was made to provide more appetising food. At the Melbourne Benevolent Asylum, for example, inmates had porridge for breakfast along with bread and tea, with food such as pies and fish donated at times by local traders. Catholic meatless Fridays were also accommodated with rice pudding, while special diets were available to those under medical care, and included whisky and wine, milk, butter, eggs, and arrowroot (Government Asylums Inquiry Board 1887:708; Kehoe 1998:43–45). Queensland destitute asylums served gruel two mornings a week, along with a variety of dishes including Irish stew, corned beef, and boiled or roast meat (Hughes 2004:89). Meals at New South Wales lunatic asylums were also more varied, with roast mutton or beef or meat pie or Irish stew, and a wide variety of vegetables such as pumpkin, tomatoes, artichokes, onions, leeks, carrots and cauliflower (Hughes 2004:89–90). Meals at the Adelaide Destitute Asylum, however, were much the same as those at Hyde Park, with boiled mutton, soup and tea served every day (Government Asylums Inquiry Board 1887:710; Hill and Hill 1875:144).

Nevertheless the dining arrangements at the Hyde Park Barracks were far better than those at the Parramatta Asylum for men, where soup and boiled meat was intentionally served cold and the soup — reported to be made with rotten meat — was distributed from slop pails and served in cups that were reused for tea without washing (Q2332–2338, Public Charities Commission 1874:2, 75).

In her evidence to the 1873 Inquiry, Mrs Hicks reported that the women of the Asylum sat down to eat with tin plates (probably versatile soup plates) and cups, each with their own knives and forks, and soup was served from 'nice soup-tureens' — probably of the tin or enamel variety, although possibly from tureens of utilitarian whiteware china.

Asylums, orphanages and other institutions in the United Kingdom and the United States provided crockery for their inmates (Dawson 2000; Hughes 1992; De Cunzo 1995:50–74). In the 1870s, and in the cases of the Craiglockhart Poorhouse in Edinburgh, the Royal Edinburgh Asylum and the Wanstead Infant Orphan Asylum in London, crockery was made especially for, and marked with the names of, these institutions.

The Wanstead Asylum crockery was plain with matching copperplate script 'Infant Orphan Asylum Hall' on various plates, mugs and slop bowls that were dumped in Eagle Pond in north-east London in the 1940s — some 70 years after the vessels were first produced (Hughes 1992:386). The Craiglockhart Poorhouse and Royal Edinburgh Asylum crockery were designed in the typical form and decoration of later 19th-century 'hotel ware', having red and blue band-and-line borders at the rim and coats of arms. The Craiglockhart wares are also marked with a ribbon banner 'CITY OF EDINBURGH POOR HOUSE' and the mugs had reinforced handles typical of hard-wearing, cheap crockery of that period (Dawson 2000: section 3.3). The Royal Edinburgh Asylum vessels appear to be of slightly better quality — a key concern of the Asylum Board. In 1877, they approached W. T. Copeland & Sons to produce the Asylum's crockery, 'hitherto supplied with articles of a somewhat inferior kind', for the '90 to 100 high class patients and ... about 650 patients of a humbler rank' (quoted in Dawson 2000 and Crook and Murray 2006:62).

It was not simply the presence of 'high-class' patients that compelled all of these institutions to supply china rather than tin or enamelled ware — the infant orphans and poorhouses too had crockery, albeit of a more roughly finished kind. In London and in Edinburgh, these boards of management were much closer to the source of crockery production (in the Midlands of England and also in Scotland) and could arrange orders with greater ease than colonial boards of management might have done. Factor in the cost of shipping and the difficulty a feeble inmate might have lifting heavy crockery, and the use of enamelled tin serving ware at the Hyde Park Barracks was quite reasonable.

The ceramic assemblage from Levels 2 and 3 of the main building is scant, comprising just 0.3% of the assemblage by fragment count. Of the recorded ceramic sherds from Levels 2 and 3, 38% are estimated to be less than 10% complete. This leaves us with a very small assemblage, too fragmented to pursue a substantial analysis of functional categories, or identify the kinds of ceramic vessels we might expect in institutional or infirmary accommodation, such as pap boats, sick feeders or bouillon cups (for drinking broth or beef tea), vessels which may well have been supplied in enamel and tin wares.

The remains of numerous glass condiment bottles suggest that various food additives were available to the women as well, including Worcestershire sauce and malt vinegar. A bottle preserved with a paper label from Crosse & Blackwell of London (UF2367) once held pickled onions. A total of 177 fragments from Level 2 represent a minimum of five condiment bottles, while 371 fragments from Level 3 represent a MNV of 11.

SMOKING

Smoking was another small treat enjoyed by many of the Asylum women, an activity permitted within the Asylum under certain conditions. The 1862 Regulations specified that small quantities of snuff and tobacco could be made available to the inmates by the surgeon or matron. Lucy Hicks provided four figs of tobacco each month to those inmates who wanted it, while clay pipes may have been donated by visiting City Missionaries. Tobacco was also

5. Daily Life in the Asylum

	Level 1	Level 2	Level 3	Rear yard	Total
Clay pipes	2,090	302	1,006	516	3,914
Matches	17	2,070	3,320		5,407
Matchboxes	1	25	417		433
Total fragments	*2,108*	*2,397*	*4,743*	*516*	*9,754*

Table 5.2: Fragments of all smoking items from specific areas at the Hyde Park Barracks.

traded for goods and favours within the Asylum. Mary Wright, for example, was an elderly blind inmate who exchanged 'a box of matches or a bit of tobacco' for someone to lead her around (Q2279, Government Asylums Inquiry Board 1887:488).

Due to the substantial risk of fire the Asylum women were supposed to smoke in designated areas. Inmates and officials had a front-row view when St Mary's Cathedral, located only a short distance to the south of the barracks, burnt to the ground in 1865. Most of the internal architecture of the Barracks was timber and the roof was made of wooden shingles, while the clothing and bedding of several hundred women were also highly flammable, as were the cotton scraps they spent their days sewing. The underfloor spaces were a tinderbox of textiles, newsprint and other paper — it was fortunate that no major fire ever broke out.

The barracks' large windows admitted good natural light during the day but there were only a few fireplaces to provide feeble light after dark. Authorities installed gas lighting in 1866, with padlocks fitted to each lantern, to prevent the women from lighting up at night and smoking their pipes in bed 'after the hours of Midnight' (Government Asylums Board, quoted in Hughes 2004:79). The recovery of thousands of used matches from the underfloor spaces, however, suggests that smoking persisted in the dormitories. In the absence of historical or archaeological evidence for the use of candles, many of the matches may have been struck simply to provide a few moments of light in the dark.

Clay tobacco pipes from the Hyde Park Barracks represent one of the largest known archaeological collections from an institutional site in Australia. The assemblage of 4,111 clay pipe fragments includes 1,006 pieces from Level 3, 302 from Level 2, and 516 fragments from the rear (eastern) yard. More than 2,000 fragments came from excavated deposits on Level 1 of the main building and date from across the 19th century, including examples securely dated to the convict period. In addition there were more than 400 matchboxes and thousands of wooden matches, many of which may have been used for lighting lamps, candles or fires, as well as for smoking (**Table 5.2**). The distribution of this material provides important insights into the habits and recreation of the Asylum inmates, and their use of spaces within the institution.

Smoking was meant to be restricted to specific places within the complex to prevent fires. Although there is no formal record of where such places were located, the concentration of clay pipes on the Level 3 stair landing[21] suggests this was a designated area. The overall distribution of pipes across the complex and in parts of the dormitories themselves reveals the scale of smoking within the Barracks and suggests that tobacco consumption was a pervasive element of everyday life in the institution.

The five most commonly stamped pipes of this period bore the marks of pipemakers Duncan McDougall and Thomas Davidson of Glasgow, Charles Crop of London and tobacconist Thomas Saywell and warehousemen Myers & Solomon of Sydney (**Table 5.3**). With the exception of Myers & Solomon, these and many other common pipes were also present in the archaeological record of the Sydney Night Refuge in Kent Street (Carney c.1991). The Night Refuge, run by the Sydney City

Figure 5.1: Well preserved and heavily stained clay pipe from Level 3 with wad of tobacco stuck in bowl (UF3269; P. Davies 2008).

---

[21] The stair landing is one of the underfloor areas in the Barracks complex with pre-1848 ceiling boards. Some of the clay pipes, particularly those made during the convict era and discussed below, may pre-date the Asylum and Depot occupation.

5. Daily Life in the Asylum

Mission, relied entirely on subscription (Carney and Kelly 1991:25) and the donations of wealthy Sydney merchants. It is very likely that some of the pipes in that assemblage were donated in this way, and conceivable that similar donations were made to the female inmates of the Hyde Park Asylum, if not via Matron Hicks, then by regular visitors including City Missionaries.

Maker/Distributor	Location	Date range	Level 1	Level 2	Level 3	Rear yard
*William Aldis	Sydney	1839–1868	4			
[Desiree] Barth	London	1855–1890				1
William Christie	Glasgow	1857–1891	3			1
William Christie	Gallowgate, London	1860–1876	1		1	1
William Cluer	Sydney	1802–1846	11		4	
Charles Crop	London	1856–1924	4		1	4
Thomas Davidson	Glasgow	1862–1911	26	6	12	24
William Davis		1810–1840	1		1	
*Hugh Dixson	Sydney	1839–1904	4		2	1
Joseph Elliot	Sydney	1828–1840	52		17	1
Samuel Elliott	Sydney	1828–1840	25		8	
John Ford	Stepney	1810–1909			1	
B Jacobs	London				1	
J[onathon] Leak	Sydney	1822–1839	6		1	
*Thomas 'Dan' Lowrey	Dublin	1879–1897				1
MG		1820–1860	7	3	4	
MPP		1810–1840	28		14	
Duncan McDougall	Glasgow	1846–1891	95	13	42	38
P McLean	South Tay Street, Dundee	1861–1883			2	
David Miller	Liverpool	1870–1880	12		2	1
*Thomas Milo	Strand, London	1852–1870	1			
Anson Moreton	Sydney	1829–1840	1			
John Moreton	Sydney	1822–1847	1			
William Murray	Glasgow	1830–1861				1
H N[athan] & Co	London				1	
*Myers & Solomon	Sydney	1863–1927	1	1	5	1
*Edwin Penfold	Sydney	1855–1890	3	1	3	3
Thomas Reeve	Hampstead, London	1828	2			
Reynolds & Blake	England		1			
*Thomas Saywell	Sydney	1865–1905	3		5	4
Sippel Brothers	Sydney	1864–1901				1
William Southern & Co	Broseley, Shropshire	1850–1900	1			
F S Sparnaay & Son	Rotterdam					1
Franz Verzjyl	Gouda		1			
Thomas White	Edinburgh	1823–1876	15		1	7
William White	Glasgow	1806–1891	6		1	4
Unidentified maker	Netherlands		2			3
Total Fragments			*317*	*24*	*129*	*98*

*distributed by

Table 5.3: Clay pipe makers and distributors represented at the Hyde Park Barracks (dates from Davey 1987; Wilson 1999; Crook *et al.* 2005:65).

5. Daily Life in the Asylum

Level 2	Hicks quarters north	Hicks quarters south	Depot ward north	Depot ward south	Stair landing
Clay pipe fragments	9	21	67	168	8
Clay pipe MNV	3	8	7	38	1

Table 5.4: Level 2 clay tobacco pipe minimum object count, based on mouthpiece and bowl/shank representation (after Bradley 2000:126).[22]

Level 3	Sick ward north	Sick ward south	Asylum ward north	Asylum ward south	Stair landing
Clay pipe fragments	25	48	180	182	541
Clay pipe MNV	6	25	31	50	62

Table 5.5: Level 3 clay tobacco pipe minimum object count, based on mouthpiece and bowl/shank representation (after Bradley 2000:126).

The clay pipe assemblage from the Hyde Park Barracks is very similar to contemporary collections recorded elsewhere in Australia, including those from The Rocks in Sydney and from the Commonwealth Block in Melbourne, with a high degree of overlap in terms of makers and motifs with the Barracks material (Courtney 1998:98; Williamson 2004, 2006; Wilson 1999). By the 1860s and 1870s, the Australian market for pipes was increasingly dominated by a few large Scottish manufacturers, with smaller quantities deriving from English and European makers (Gojak and Stuart 1999:43). Consumer choice for pipe motifs decreased during the 19th century, as local pipe distribution was controlled by a small number of importers. In spite of the hundreds of motifs produced by pipe manufacturers (e.g. Gallagher 1987), only a limited range of these wares are found in Australian archaeological assemblages of the period. Motifs represented in the Hyde Park Barracks collection thus generally reflect what was available in local stores rather than the aspirations and values of the inmates and immigrants.

The collection includes very few examples of Irish-themed pipes, such as the navvy-style *Dudeen* pipes with a short stem, thick bowl wall and rouletted bowl rim (Gojak and Stuart 1999:45). Numerous examples of these were found, however, at Cadmans Cottage and at the Cumberland/Gloucester Streets site in The Rocks (Gojak 1995; Wilson 1999:318–319). Two examples of Irish pipes were recovered from the rear yard at the Barracks, one marked 'Cork' on either side of the stem (UF3150), and another marked 'Dan Lowreys / Music Hall' (UF3330). Thomas 'Dan' Lowrey operated music halls in Dublin during the

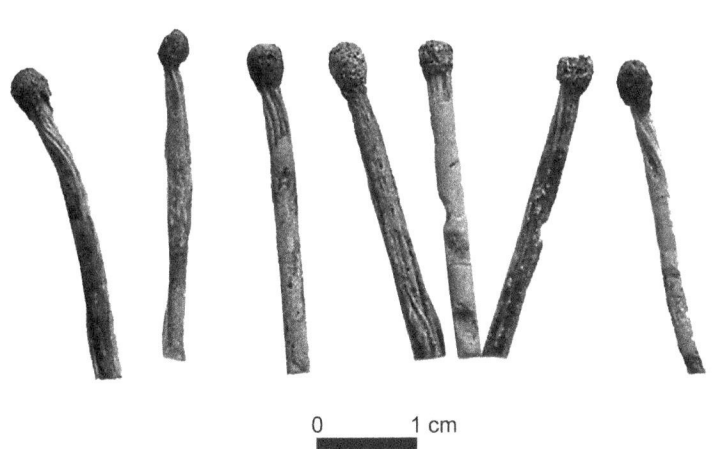

Figure 5.2: Hardened string matches from Level 3 (UF4404; P. Crook 2003).

Figure 5.3: Heavily used pipe bowl made by P. McLean of Dundee. The cross-hatched heart served as a match strike (UF3132, P. Davies 2008).

---

[22] MNV counts for clay tobacco pipes are based on the number of shank/bowl junctures and mouthpieces or bites, as each pipe had one each of these attributes. The highest number of either attribute provides the minimum number of objects for a population (Bradley 2000:126).

5. Daily Life in the Asylum

Figure 5.4: Matchbox from tobacconist Thomas Saywell of Park Street in Sydney (UF4286; P. Davies 2008).

Figure 5.5: Matchbox from Swedish manufacturer Björneborgs Tändsticksfabricks (UF17635; P. Crook 2003).

1880s and 1890s, including the Star of Erin and the Empire Palace (O'Donnell 1987:156). This pipe may thus date from the judicial phase at the Hyde Park Barracks in the late 19th century. The paucity of

Figure 5.6: Matchbox made in Lidkoping in Sweden between 1880 and 1890. The original design dates from 1851–1860 and was made in Finland by Lemminkainen (pers. comm. Jerry Bell 26 October 2010; UF17636; P. Crook 2004).

Irish-style pipes from the Barracks may reflect the intention of the Matron or the Asylum's Board not to supply pipes with national affiliations.

There were also thousands of matches and several hundred matchboxes in the collection. Safety matches were readily available by the 1860s, and typically cost only a penny a box. Most of the matches were wooden, square-cut sticks, although there are also round wooden examples, and 13 matches made from wax-hardened string (**Figure 5.2**). Complete examples were typically either 1¾ inch (44 mm) or 2 inch (51 mm) long. Matchbox trays and covers were also recovered in large quantities. These were mostly made from folded wood panels with printed paper labels. Box-making machines for cutting, folding and assembling small packages were readily available by this period, making and filling thousands of boxes each day (Cadbury 2010:108). Both labels and striking panels

Manufacturer	Place	Date range	Quantity
Bell & Black	London	1849–1881	1
Björneborgs Tändsticksfabricks	Stockholm	1866–	5
Bryant & May	London	1852–	1
Ellbo	Gothenburg	1867–1895	1
Lemminkainen[23]	Finland/Sweden	1880–1890	17
H. Nathan & Co	London	1876–1877	12
T. Saywell	Sydney	1865–1905	2
S. N. H.	London	1876–1877	1
Strängnäs Tändsticksfabricks Aktiebolag	Stockholm	1874–1881	1
Wexiö Tändsticksfabricks	Sweden	1868–1887	1

Table 5.6: Matchbox brands recovered from underfloor spaces.

---

[23] The Lemminkainen matchboxes were made at Lidkoping in Sweden during the 1880s, based on an original design from Finland dating from 1851 to 1860 (J. Bell pers comm. 30 October 2010).

5. Daily Life in the Asylum

Mouthpieces	Brown	Brown/yellow	Red	Yellow	Unglazed	Total
Level 2	7	13	4	3	60	87
Level 3	14	34	7	4	89	148
Total	*21*	*47*	*11*	*7*	*149*	*235*

Table 5.7: Glazed clay pipe mouthpiece colours from Levels 2 and 3.

	No staining	Light staining	Heavy staining	Total
Level 1	4 (9%)	38 (88%)	1 (2%)	43
Level 3	4 (5%)	27 (31%)	56 (64%)	87

Table 5.8: Staining and discoloration on clay pipe bowls from Levels 1 and 3.

(invented by 1855) were often preserved intact, while one example of a pipe bowl (UF3132) featured a match strike in the shape of a heart (**Figure 5.3**; Shaw-Smith 2003:206). The high representation of Swedish match makers reflects the dominance of Scandinavian manufacture and exports in the fire-lighting market in the 19th century, which was largely replaced by tariff-protected Australian production after Federation (Bell 2008; **Figures 5.4, 5.5, 5.6**; **Table 5.6**).

The largest concentration of clay pipes on Level 2 was in the south-east dormitory, where 168 clay pipe fragments (MNV 38) were recovered. There were also 958 wooden matches, with most found within a few metres of the fireplace at the western end of the room. The light and warmth of the hearth was clearly a place for the women to congregate. Some of this material, of course, may have derived from the Asylum women, who often occupied Level 2 when numbers of immigrant women were low. Pipe fragments, recovered in small numbers from the Hicks' family quarters, may relate to the private smoking of John Applewhaite, William Hicks (or any of the Applewhaite-Hicks women for that matter), or to the use of this area for Asylum wards after 1882.[24]

The main concentration of smoking, however, was clearly on the landing at the top of the stairs on Level 3. Among the 541 fragments found in the underfloor spaces from this area, were at least 43 complete or near-complete bowls. Women congregated at the top of the stairs and lost, discarded or stashed their pipes for later use. Over time, the pipes placed below the floorboards may have been forgotten (unsurprising given that many inmates probably suffered from memory loss and some were known to have senile dementia), or became obscured beneath later rubbish. Some elderly women died. The move to the new asylum at Newington in 1886 was abrupt, and small personal items, especially clay pipes hidden under the floor, may have been accidentally left behind. The popularity of smoking on the Level 3 landing is also evident from the 1,041 matches found in its underfloor spaces, along with 272 matchbox trays and covers.

The rear yard at the eastern end of the Barracks was enclosed in the 1860s to provide separate space for the Asylum women, with a kitchen, bathrooms and laundries. Of the manufacturers identified from 98 pipe fragments excavated in this area, only one was securely dateable to the convict period. The remainder dated broadly from the second half of the 19th century. It seems from the evidence of these artefacts that the Asylum women used the yard as a place to escape the confines of the dormitories and to spend time in the fresh air.

Many of the pipe mouthpieces showed evidence of glazing, applied during the manufacturing process, which kept the smoker's lips from sticking to the pipe (**Table 5.7**). This involved dipping the pipe end into a glaze before firing, to produce a smooth finish over the porous clay surface (Bradley 2000:109). Brownish-yellow glazes were the most commonly recorded pipe mouthpiece colour at the Barracks, while examples using red sealing wax, common to the later 19th century, were also identified. No examples of green glazes, however, were recorded in the assemblage.

The intensity of pipe use can also be measured by comparing degrees of tobacco staining recorded on complete bowls from Level 3 and Level 1 (**Table 5.8**). Dark discoloration is caused by the tobacco oils and tars being absorbed by the clay during smoking. Bradley (2000:127) notes that on very heavily smoked pipes, the outer rim of the bowl can become black with use, and Stocks (2008:41) has recently noted the presence of badly stained (torrefied) pipes at Parramatta from the early 19th century. Burial in certain soil conditions, however, can also remove smoking stains (Nebergall 1996), while burning pipes in a fire can whiten them as well. On both Level 1 and Level 3, a small number of pipes were discarded with no evidence of staining, and thus little, or no apparent, use. The majority of bowls

---

[24] Only one of the pipes from this area was datable: a Duncan McDougall pipe (UF3442) which could have been produced between 1846 and 1891.

5. Daily Life in the Asylum

Figure 5.7: Heavily stained stem fragment ground down to form new mouthpiece, with tooth marks (UF14388; P. Crook 2003).

Figure 5.8: Shortened and reworked stem with tooth marks around new mouthpiece (UF3216; P. Crook 2003).

from Level 1 (88%), occupied initially by convicts, and later by visitors to the Immigration Depot, showed signs of light staining and thus moderate use. A large proportion of pipe bowls (64%) from Level 3, however, showed signs of blackening and discoloration on both the interior and exterior of the bowl (**Figure 5.1**). This suggests that the Asylum inmates used their pipes frequently and carefully, having limited access to replacement pipes in the event of loss or breakage. Alternatively, short, heavily blackened pipes have been considered a symbol of identification with the working classes in colonial Sydney in the mid-19th-century, and the inmates may have followed this preference (Gojak and Stuart 1999:40). A plain black pipe bowl (UF3247) from Level 3 appears to have been manufactured from ball clay with the addition of red clay which turned black after firing (K. Courtney pers. comm. 18 March 2011).

Some of the clay pipes provide evidence of modification and reuse. At least 20 stem fragments from Level 3, and 4 from Level 2, have been shortened and re-ground. Several of these examples also have heavy tooth marks on the shortened stem (**Figures 5.7 and 5.8**). A common pattern was for the original pipe stem to have been broken, either accidentally or deliberately, leaving a very short stem attached to the bowl. The tip was then ground smooth to form a new mouthpiece, with either a rounded or straight finish. These short stems are generally less than 40 mm in length, which meant holding and smoking the pipe fairly close to the face, or possibly gripping the shortened stem with the teeth to free the hands while working. The short pipe stem also increased the 'hit' of nicotine.

In addition there are 4 examples of repaired clay pipes with bandaged stems consisting of coarse thread wrapped around a layer of paper, cardboard or resin (UF175, UF176, UF177 and UF178; **Figures 5.9, 5.10, 5.11, 5.12**). Two of the pipes (UF176 and UF178) that came from under the floor boards of the landing on Level 3, may derive from convict phase of occupation, rather than from the later Asylum phase. In addition, 2 pipe stem fragments from the rear yard (UG3631 and UG3632) were reground leaving facets around one end of the stem (**Figure 5.13**). Wilson (1999:325) identified similar examples from the Cumberland/Gloucester Streets site, in The Rocks, and suggests that they may have been used as a durable kind of chalk, used for marking masonry or brickwork. Unusual examples of pipes include one with a curved stem and copper-alloy ferrule (UF3171; **Figure 5.14**), similar to an example found at the Victoria Hotel in Auckland (Brassey 1991:29) and the bone screw mouthpiece of a composite pipe (UF3360). A small piece of uncut tobacco (UF3960) from under the Level 3 landing suggests that tobacco may occasionally have been chewed as well.

The popularity of tobacco smoking in colonial Australia, especially among men, is well documented (Cunningham 1966[1827]:132; Gojak and Stuart 1999; Walker 1984). Among women, however, smoking seems to have been a habit primarily of convict and Aboriginal women, and this may have largely ceased by the second half of the 19th century, especially in the cities (Tyrrell 1999:6). Casella has used pipe fragments from the solitary cells at the Ross Female Factory in Tasmania, to identify the use of illicit tobacco among convict women within the Crime Class section of the institution in the early 1850s (Casella 2001a:33). It is probably that, for inmates at the Hyde Park Asylum, tobacco was a simple indulgence and comfort, a way of dulling the daily tedium.

The crowded conditions in the Asylum meant that personal space and privacy were very limited. It is uncertain whether the women kept boxes, bags or chests to hold their few personal possessions. Small items such as clay pipes and tobacco may have been kept in bedding, in an apron pocket, or even hidden under the floorboards as a way of tucking them out of sight and maintaining ownership of them. However, the smaller numbers of pipes recovered from the Depot on Level 2, may suggest that immigrant women, generally from a higher social class, brought with them an awareness of emerging notions of respectability and gentility, which increasingly frowned on female smoking. They may also not have been in the Depot long enough to break and lose tobacco pipes.

Matron Hicks and the Government Asylums Board not only tolerated, but also facilitated, smoking among the inmates by providing tobacco as part of their rations. Freedom to smoke at other institutions, however, varied considerably. Smoking was forbidden at the Sydney Benevolent Asylum, the

5. Daily Life in the Asylum

Figure 5.9: Fluted bowl with bandaged stem of dark woven fabric (UF175; P. Crook 2003).

Figure 5.10: Short pipe stem with bandage of coarse thread over hardened gum or resin (UF176; P. Crook 2003).

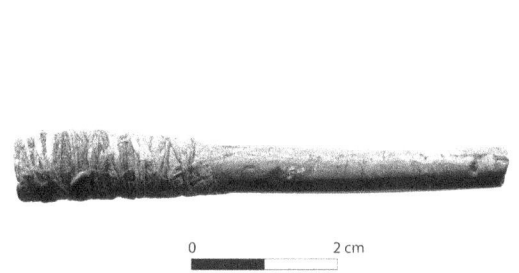

Figure 5.11: Pipe stem with bandage of coarse thread over cardboard (UF177; P. Crook 2003).

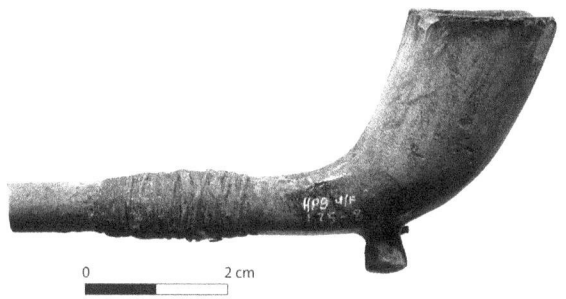

Figure 5.12: Stained pipe with bandaged stem (UF178; P. Crook 2003).

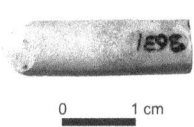

Figure 5.13: Clay pipe stem modified into possible chalk stick (UF3631; P. Crook 2003).

Figure 5.14: Curved pipe stem made by B. Jacobs of London, with mouthpiece edged with metal band (UF3171; P. Crook 2003).

predecessor of the Hyde Park Barracks institution (Cummins 1971:14). At the Melbourne Benevolent Asylum in the 1870s, a journalist noted that while smoking was forbidden inside, there was great consumption of tobacco in the garden outside (James 1969:157; Kehoe 1998:76). Permission to smoke at the Hyde Park Barracks helped with the smooth running of the Asylum. There is little to suggest that tobacco usage was linked to the personal morality of the inmates. Instead, it was made available as a simple indulgence, to comfort the lives of women beset by old age and infirmity. Tobacco provided relief from boredom, and a distraction for hands and minds. Sometimes it also served as a way of trading favours. Congregating in the stairwell or yard, or around the fireplace, or huddling in bed over a pipe, were probably opportunities for gossip and friendship for women who had few other comforts in their lives.

Sewing, Craft and Fancy Work

Sewing tools and equipment, such as buttons, thimbles, needles and pins, are another substantial component of the archaeological assemblage that provides insights into the daily lives and activities of the Barracks' women. These items are common to many historical archaeological assemblages, and are often interpreted as significant evidence of women's work in the domestic sphere (Beaudry 2006; Lydon 1993; Parker 1984). The scale of the Barracks sewing-related assemblage, and the survival and analysis of so many textile pieces, provides an excellent opportunity to expand this area of research.

A total of 4,899 items in the underfloor collection can be directly linked to sewing activities, comprising 6.1% of the collection as a whole (**Table 5.9**). This includes over 4,700 pins, as well as dozens of needles, cotton reels and other needlework tools. In addition, 10,002 fabric scraps have been recorded, mainly comprising cotton, wool and linen offcuts, along with a number of more or less complete clothing items. These are discussed further in 'Textiles' and 'Clothing' (below). While most of the sewing was done by hand, the Asylum acquired a second-hand treadle sewing machine in 1878 and another in 1880 (Hughes 2004:84).

Most pins were straight, copper-alloy forms with a simple conical head, ranging in length from 21 to 40 mm. Almost 500 pins were lost beneath the floor of the rooms occupied by the Matron and her family on Level 2, suggesting that Lucy Hicks' daughters

5. Daily Life in the Asylum

Item	Level 1 (UG)	Level 2 (UF)	Level 3 (UF)	Total
Pins	2,820	1,937	2,779	7,536
Needles	2	26	14	42
Pin cushion	–	–	2	2
Packets	–	4	3	7
Knitting needles	–	3	–	3
Cotton reels and labels	4	20	72	96
Thimbles	9	2	10	21
Scissors	4	1	4	9
Needlework tools (Bobbins, crochet hooks, etc)	15	12	10	37
Total	*2,854*	*2,005*	*2,894*	*7,753*

Table 5.9: Sewing equipment from all three levels of the main Barracks building (fragment count).

spent considerable time on needlework, while Hicks herself may have used the rooms for 'cutting out' when she lost access to the lockable room below the stairs. Although pins in historical contexts are normally associated with sewing, and thus women's work, Mary Beaudry notes that they have also been used to fix hairstyles and secure hats, to fasten nappies, and as 'poor man's buttons'. She also points out that pins were rarely used by professional tailors and dressmakers, but they were common in domestic contexts (Beaudry 2006:10–15). During the legal phase of occupation at the Barracks, pins may have been used to fasten papers together. The frequent use (and apparently careless loss) of large quantities of pins at Hyde Park Barracks coincided with the mass-production of pins from the 1830s onwards, especially in England, which reduced the cost of a pound of pins (containing about 10,000 pins) to only one or two shillings (Beaudry 2006:21; Petroski 1993:54–57).

Thimbles from the Asylum were mostly made of plain copper-alloy with a rolled rim — one example was marked 'FROM A FRIEND' (UF8919; **Figure 5.15**). Two finer thimbles were recovered from the Depot, one decorated with a floral motif (UF11168) and another which was silver plated (UF76).

Needles were another common item found, including a paper packet containing 22 needles manufactured by H. Milward & Sons (**Figure 5.16**). There was also a single needle pinned to a small piece of cloth, which survived under the floor for at least a century after it had been put down following the day's work. Two hand-sewn pin-cushions were also found under the floor in the Asylum on Level 3 (**Figure 5.17**).

Dozens of wooden cotton reels with paper labels were also recovered from the Depot and Asylum deposits. Several are preserved with skeins of thread, usually coloured black, red or brown. Surviving paper labels indicate that the most common thread manufacturer represented in the Barracks material is J. Brook and Sons of Meltham Mills in West

Figure 5.15: Small copper alloy thimble inscribed 'FROM A FRIEND' (UF8919; P. Crook 2003).

Figure 5.16: Needle packet from H. Milward & Sons (UF75; P. Davies 2010).

5. Daily Life in the Asylum

Figure 5.17: Handmade pin cushion (UF10763; P. Davies 2010).

Yorkshire (n=14). Other makers include I. and W. Taylor of Leicester, Griffith and Son of London and Clark and Co. of Paisley/Glasgow, along with Geary, Carlile, Alexander, and Clapperton. The number of Brook reels reflects the prominence of the firm among Yorkshire thread makers in the 19th century (Giles and Goodall 1992:176). Most reels contained either 100 or 200 yards of thread, with yarns of various grades or weights. Cotton thread was generally thicker than lace thread, twisted from three or more yarns into one (Ure 1970[1836]:226–227; **Figures 5.18** and **5.19**).

Figure 5.18: Three wooden cotton reels from the northern dormitory on Level 3 (UF8285; P. Davies 2010).

Figure 5.19: Wooden cotton reel with remnant brown thread (UF193; P. Crook 2003).

The bone lid from a cotton barrel (UF8842) was also recovered from the Asylum level (**Figure 5.20**). Prior to the mass-production of wooden cotton reels, from the 1840s onwards, cotton thread was wound on a reel attached to a spindle, and placed in a hollow container. A flat screw-on lid had a central hole through which the top of the spindle protruded. The cotton thread was drawn out through a small hole in the side of the barrel, and was wound back by turning the spindle (Groves 1973:33; Taunton 1997:85). When the barrel was empty the lid was unscrewed and the spindle was sent back to the makers for refilling. Cotton barrels were extremely practical devices, as the enclosed thread was kept clear and clean and did not get tangled up with other objects in the sewing box. The presence of such an item in the Barracks material, among all the conventional wooden reels, suggests that this object may have been a special tool, possibly part of one of the immigrant women's sewing boxes.

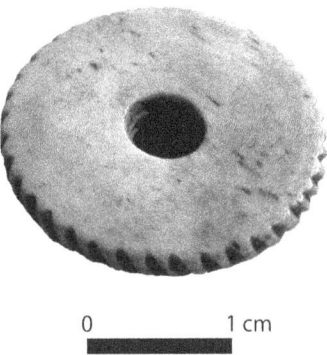

Figure 5.20: Lid from bone cotton barrel (UF8842; P. Davies 2009).

However, other familiar sewing items were much less common in the assemblage. For example, the remains of only 4 pairs of scissors were found in the Asylum level, which may relate to their greater cost, since scissors' mass-production did not begin until late in the 19th century (Beaudry 2006:122). Only 3 knitting needles were found, and all from Matron Hicks' quarters on Level 2. This is surprising given that hand knitting is an ancient craft practice which would be consistent with the kinds of 'women's work' normally done in the Asylum. The inmates did a great deal of sewing, but the archaeological evidence suggests they did little, or no, hand knitting.

Fancy Work

Along with the pins, needles and cotton reels associated with practical, everyday sewing, there were also items in the collection that demonstrate more specialised needlework. These include 19 bone bobbins, 2 bodkins, 2 crochet hooks and 7 unidentified bone tools probably associated with needlework (**Figure 5.21**; **Table 5.10**).

57

5. Daily Life in the Asylum

	Level 1	Level 2	Level 3	Total
Bodkins	2	–	–	2
Lace Bobbins	3	8	8	19
Crochet hooks	–	1	1	2
Tatting shuttles	–	2	–	2
Unidentified bone tools	5	1	1	7

Table 5.10: Needlework tools.

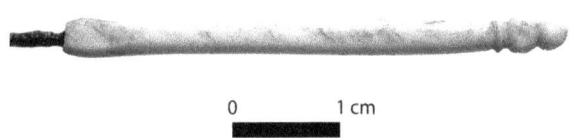

Figure 5.21: Bone handle of needlework tool (UF66; P. Crook 2003).

Bobbins were associated with lace-making, an ancient craft that had become a popular drawing room pastime by the late 18th century. Most lace produced in domestic settings was known as bobbin or pillow-lace. This kind of work involved the use of a pattern drawn on paper affixed to a pillow, along with pins, long threads and bobbins made of wood or bone. Simple lace patterns required up to 50 threads, while complex designs needed hundreds of threads, each attached to a pin and bobbin (Groves 1973:115). English bobbins often had a loop of wire strung with glass or stone beads to provide weight and maintain the necessary tension, a decoration known as a spangle (Deagan 2002:210–211). The pillow allowed the work to be rested on the lap.

During the 19th century the manufacture, display and wearing of fine or fancy needlework pieces by women in Australian colonial society (and elsewhere) helped to distinguish their social class, and degree of gentility within it. The fact that these women had not only the inclination, but also the time, to do such delicate and fine needlework, and consequently employ servants to do the everyday and hard manual work around the house, defined them as middle class. Such pursuits were part of a wider suite of middle-class and aspiring middle-class behaviours and ideology, that were often expressed through material possessions, such as table settings (linen, glass, silver, china) and domestic furnishings and clothing details etc. Lace-making was also, however, a cottage industry in Britain that kept large numbers of women and children working in arduous conditions (Beaudry 2006:151–152; Spenceley 1976). Historians and archaeologists have identified numerous examples of middle-class women engaged in fine needlework to decorate their homes and clothes, and to keep their hands busy (e.g. Beaudry 2006:45, 169–170; Corbin 2000:29–41; Fletcher 1989:3–9; Hayes 2008:318–320; Quirk 2007:184–186; Russell 1994:97–98; Young 2003:73), while convict women were often equipped with patchwork and quilting materials to keep them busy on the long sea voyage (Gero 2008:14–17). Immigrant women were also equipped with sewing materials on the voyage out to Australia (Gothard 2001:119), which they were encouraged to work on further in the Depot. The Hyde Park Barracks Daily Report of Wednesday 3 February 1864 noted:

> The work box belonging to the *Serocco* was opened today the work which was exceedingly good was distributed.

Asylum women appear to have undertaken little in the way of fancy sewing, lacemaking or embroidery, and they were not allowed to undertake paid or contract sewing outside of the institution because the demands of routine sewing for Asylum needs were considered too great (Q2368, Public Charities

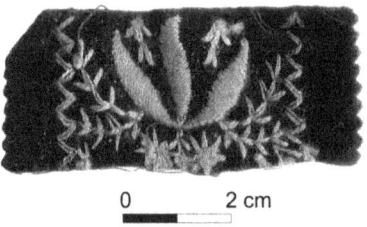

Figure 5.22: Brown velvet embroidered with flower and leaf design (UF978; P. Davies 2009).

Figure 5.23: Plain cotton fragment decorated in broderie anglaise from the Hicks apartments on Level 2. This technique was widely used for baby clothes, dolls' clothes and underwear in the 19th century (UF18059; P. Davies 2009).

Commission 1873:76). Examples of fine needlework (**Figures 5.22** and **5.23**) were confined to Level 2, and are one of the few archaeological patterns where class-based differences are apparent between the Asylum-occupied Level 3 and the predominantly Depot-occupied Level 2.

Hat-Making

Another task performed at times by the women was hat-making. There is no historical record of this work and the only evidence available derives from the archaeological material. At least 114 strands of plaited straw have been identified in the underfloor collection, including 24 pieces from Level 2 and 90 from Level 3 (**Figure 5.24**). A palm leaf shredding tool (UF11648) was also found beneath the floor of the Asylum. It features eight small metal teeth inserted into a wooden handle, and was used to slice fibre into strips which were woven into plaits for hat or basket-making.

Figure 5.24: Band of plaited palm fibre (UF11636; P. Davies 2010).

Hat-making from the leaves of the cabbage-tree palm *Livistonia australis* probably began among convicts during the early settlement of Sydney (Ritchie 1971 [1]:16). By the mid-19th century hats had become very popular among both men and women, especially in urban areas, and fine examples could cost up to 10 shillings each (Maynard 1994:170). Straw strips were plaited into narrow braids, and doubled over at each side, creating a serrated edge along each side of the braids. These were sewn into hats with a flat brim up to 15 cm wide (Ollif and Crosthwaite 1977:35). The work was fairly simple and required few tools and inexpensive materials, and it became a cottage industry as well as a common form of institutional labour in the 19th century (Rathbone 1994:33). There is no evidence that the hats were made for sale outside the Asylum and it appears from the location of the remains on Levels 2 and 3 that the work provided hats (and repairs to hats) for women in both the Asylum and Immigration Depot. Photographic evidence from the Newington Asylum around 1890 shows several women in the yard wearing straw hats (**Figure 5.43**).

Leather-Working and Shoe Repair

The underfloor collection also offers abundant evidence for leather-working and shoe repair in the

	Level 2	Level 3	Total
Shoe or slipper	1	3	4
Shoe lace	17	2	19
Heel	2	12	14
Sole	12	13	25
Welt	–	2	2
Upper	6	1	7
Unidentified offcuts	166	443	609
Total	*204*	*476*	*680*

Table 5.11: Shoe pieces and leather offcuts.

Asylum. While the women sewed their own clothing and bedding, boots and shoes were provided by outside contractors (Q2354–2355, Public Charities Commission 1874:76). Mary Applewhaite kept a stock book of such items given to each inmate 'lest they should require them a little too often' (Q2281, Public Charities Commission 1874:73). Evidence in the form of hundreds of shoe components and leather offcuts, suggests that in some cases the women themselves repaired shoes and boots (**Table 5.11**).

The boot trade was well established in Sydney by the 1870s, and it was a largely male-dominated industry, although historian Margaret Maynard notes that women in town and country areas commonly mended boots and shoes as well (Maynard 1994:127; *SMH* 1 October 1878, p.6; 8 October 1878, p.7). Evidence for shoe repair in the Barracks consists of numerous curved offcut scraps, along with heels and sole pieces (**Figure 5.25**). A rolled bundle of leather bound with a thong (UF7559) appears to be related to the repair or even manufacture of shoes (**Figure 5.26**). The leather is 1.5 mm thick and 139 mm (exactly 5½ inches) in width. A strip of leather hand-sewn into a simple loop (UF4374) may have functioned as a finger guard, while a roughly sewn leather knife sheath (UF17347; **Figure 5.33**)

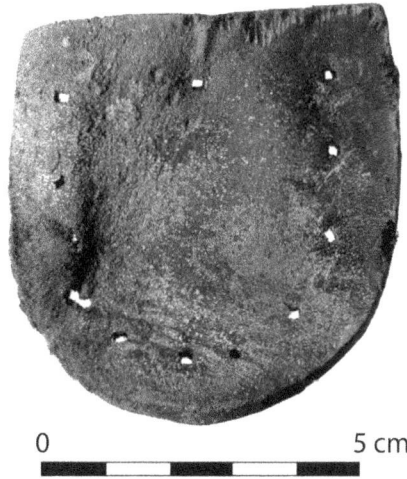

Figure 5.25: Leather shoe heel with square nail holes (UF7490; P. Crook 2003).

5. Daily Life in the Asylum

Figure 5.26: Roll of leather for shoe repair (UF7559; P. Davies 2009).

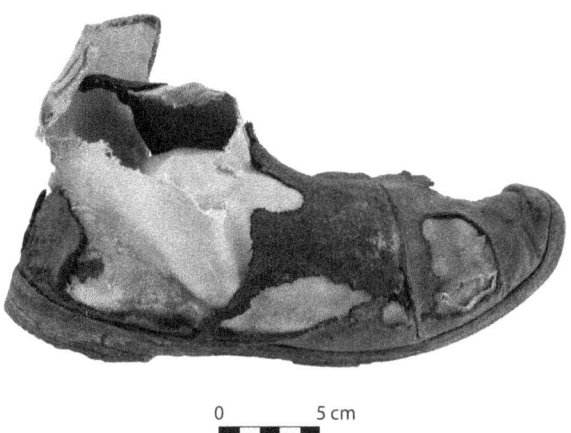

Figure 5.27: Shoe repaired with cotton insert (UF7568; P. Davies 2009).

may have been associated with leather working and shoe repair as well.

A well preserved leather shoe (UF7568) from the north-east dormitory on Level 3 reveals something of the style of footwear worn in the Asylum (**Figure 5.27**). The boot appears to have been rebuilt using a cotton canvas lining to re-attach the leather toe, the suede vamp (upper) and the leather back stay. It is not clear if this repair was done in the Asylum, or by a tradesman cobbler. Wear patterns at the toe indicate that the shoe was worn on the right foot. A hole has also been worn in the canvas lining at the toe, and part of the back stay has broken off. The shoe was fastened with 10 pairs of lace holes extending from the inside ankle to just above the sole. Each lace hole was reinforced with hand stitching, rather than with metal eyes.

Mending and Makeshift Tooling

Numerous artefacts were modified and reused by the Asylum women, evidence of their thrifty existence and the necessity of making-do in the institution. Textile offcuts, for example, provide insight into the processes of repairing and recycling clothes. Hundreds of pieces were cut or torn into specific shapes, presumably intended for re-sewing into a garment or other fabric item (see 'Textiles',

Shape	Level 2	Level 3	Total
Circular	–	5	5
Hexagonal	–	1	1
Irregular	40	1,742	1,782
Octagonal	–	1	1
Rectangular	47	647	694
Square	13	49	62
Triangular	16	32	48
Unidentified	2,491	4,702	7,193
Total textile offcuts	*2,607*	*7,179*	*9,786*

Table 5.12: Shape of textile offcuts from Levels 2 and 3.

below). These include at least 647 rectangular offcuts identified on Level 3 (**Table 5.12**). Several clothing items, including the remains of two plain cotton bodices or chemises (UF5534, UF18870) were hand-stitched in segments using these offcut pieces. In addition, a beautifully preserved purple floral bodice (UF52) was cut down to form a bodice with short calico sleeves (see 'Clothing').

In addition to these flat offcuts, at least 324 textile pieces were carefully cut or torn along the seams or hems of former garments to maximise the area of unstitched sheet fabric with which to make a new garment. As this process left behind only the spine or structure of the former garment, we have called them 'structural offcuts' (**Figure 5.28**). While they comprise just 3.3% of all fabric scraps, they are compelling evidence of the regular recycling of garments at the end of their life-cycle within the Asylum.

Further examples of 'making-do' are found with sewing tools and other domestic items. A tatting shuttle (UF33), for example, was crafted from wood-sheet covered with blue paper and joined with rough stitching (**Figure 5.29**). Temporary cotton reels were made by winding threads around a piece of bone (UF6965), paper (UF2775, UF4712; **Figure 5.30**), and a twist of newsprint (UF11305; **Figure 5.31**). A makeshift pin packet (UF4398) consisted of a rectangle of paper carefully torn and cut into

Figure 5.28: Plain cotton structural offcut hem (UF18778; P. Davies 2010).

5. Daily Life in the Asylum

Figure 5.29: Makeshift tatting shuttle, possibly crafted from a discarded matchbox (UF33; P. Crook 2003).

Figure 5.30: Makeshift thread reel made from piece of folded cardboard (UF4712; P. Davies 2010).

Figure 5.31: Makeshift thread reel made from folded newspaper (UF11305; P. Crook 2003).

Figure 5.32: Paper offcut used as pin packet (UF4398; P. Davies 2009).

Figure 5.33: Hand sewn leather knife sheath from the stair landing on Level 3 (UF17347; P. Davies 2010).

Figure 5.34: Roughly made wooden clothes peg (UF37; P. Crook 2003).

shape, with rust stains from the pins originally folded inside (**Figure 5.32**). Four roughly whittled wooden sticks with a point at one end were also found, which may have been used for splitting thick palm fronds into smaller pieces for hat-making. A complete circular pin cushion (UF10763; **Figure 5.17**) from the southern dormitory on Level 3 was hand made from fabric scraps which included several lines of illegible print.

Other items include a small pouch that was roughly made from cardboard backing stitched to a leather cover and protective flap (UF17347), possibly to hold a penknife or other tool (**Figure 5.33**). At least 2 clothes pegs were hand carved (UF37 and UF14414; **Figure 5.34**), along with 4 wooden stoppers (UF3485, UF4433, UF8998 and UF12576).

The inmates were not alone in their careful use of materials. Matron Hicks explained to the 1873 Inquiry that 'There are sheets to be patched — because when a sheet goes into holes I do not throw it away; I turn the sides to the middle, and make it do again' (Q2368, Public Charities Commission 1874:76). The Matron's additional comment, 'the old women are celebrated for patching', is demonstrated by numerous examples of patched clothes and darned stockings in the collection.

Additional evidence for thrift among the women is found in the repair of broken clay tobacco pipes (see 'Smoking') and the reuse of alcohol bottles to contain medicines (see 'Medicines').

Textiles

Textiles are a significant part of the Barracks assemblage, with 10,002 scraps and offcuts comprising 12.5% of the underfloor collection. The

Textile	Level 2	Level 3	Total
Composite	10	29	39
Cotton	1,789	5,056	6,845
Damask	1	–	1
Linen	35	302	337
Silk	61	89	150
Velvet	10	19	29
Wool	153	195	348
Unidentified/Mixed	823	1,430	2,253
Total	*2,882*	*7,120*	*10,002*

Table 5.13: Textile types from Levels 2 and 3.

majority of the fabrics were cotton pieces, with smaller quantities of linen, silk, wool and composite materials (**Table 5.13**). Textiles range in size from large offcuts torn from clothing to tiny scraps only a few millimetres wide. There were also dozens of clothing items and components identified in the collection, described further in 'Clothing'. The 'Unidentified/Mixed' category includes various pieces of thick, heavily woven wool, cotton and jute fibres probably used for furniture and floor coverings.

As textiles rarely survive in most archaeological contexts, we generally lack well developed methods of analysis and research for this class of artefact. Textiles do, however, have significant analytical potential, in terms of garments and clothing components versus cut pieces and rags; outer wear and underwear; women's and men's clothing; hand stitches and machine sewing; and changes in styles and fashion. In addition, textile manufacturing technologies, weave patterns, and dyes and colours are important expressions of changing industrial technologies and consumer behaviours (LaRoche and McGowan 2000:275; see also Barber 1991). We address a number of these issues below and in the following section on 'Clothing'.

The sheer quantity of textiles recovered from the Barracks has no known parallels in historical archaeology from around the world. A smaller assemblage, comprising around 1000 wool fragments, was recovered from cesspits at Block 160 in the Five Points site in New York City, and analysed in terms of textile technology and the beginnings of the garment industry in New York in the 19th century (LaRoche and McGowan 2000). Many of the pieces had been torn into strips, and were interpreted as evidence for domestic rug making. Cotton strips are also very common at the Barracks, but there is no evidence they were used in rugs, although they may have been used to stuff pillows and mattresses. Around 4000 textile fragments were recovered from sub-floor deposits in 3 adjoining houses in Kempten in southern Germany, dating between 1470 and 1530, representing a range of textiles and woven products (Atzbach 2013:266). Over 300 fragments of wool and cotton were also found on goldmining sites at Otago in New Zealand, probably representing European garments worn by Chinese miners (Ritchie 1986:551).

The Hyde Park Barracks collection includes more than 23 kg of textile and clothing fragments. Some textile offcuts were probably sold by weight to the ragmen who provided scrap fabric to the local paper industry,[25] but many smaller pieces were clearly swept under the floorboards. Some of these rags *may* have been used as sanitary napkins (e.g. UF11602) or as toilet paper, especially among bed-ridden old women. Rolls of toilet paper did not come into popular use until late in the 19th century, and until this time most people used cotton waste or old newspapers instead (Eveleigh 2002:136). Further examination and chemical analysis of stained textile fragments may be necessary to determine such uses.

The large amount of cotton in the collection reflects the dominant position this textile had secured in the international textile industry by the 19th century. While wool and linen were the traditional garment textiles of northern Europe, by the late 18th century cotton factories in England were producing huge quantities of cotton fabric, known generically as 'calicoes', using raw material imported from India, the United States and the West Indies (Yafa 2006:59). Small-scale textile production had occurred sporadically in Australia during the first half of the 19th century, but most operations lapsed due to lack of raw materials and skilled workers (Liston 2008; Maynard 1994:34–36; Stenning 1993). Historian Deborah Oxley (1996:16) noted that there were few textile workers among female convicts sent to New South Wales. Instead, most textiles for clothing were imported in bulk from Great Britain — a scrap of fine cotton from Level 2 was marked 'Thos. Hoyle & Sons; Manchester; British Cambric' (UF4713; **Figure 5.35**).

Silk pieces came in a range of colours, with black and brown the most common hues, along with shades of pink, green and purple. Silk clothing

Figure 5.35: Scrap of fine cotton with manufacturer's stamp in black ink (UF4713; P. Davies 2010).

---

[25] A paper mill was established on the Georges River near Liverpool in 1867. It used linen and cotton rags, recycled paper and imported pulp to produce newspaper and strong brown wrapping paper (Davies 2005:64; Sinclair 1990:36–37).

and accessories were associated with fashion and style in 19th-century Australia (Fletcher 1984:121–122; Maynard 1994:113), with working-class men and women's love of wearing silk clothing often making it difficult for new arrivals from England to distinguish between convicts, emancipists and free settlers (Elliott 1995). Most of the identifiable silk fragments from the Barracks were from ribbons, although there were also the remains of a silk scarf from below the landing on Level 3 (UF16754) and a brown silk sleeve cuff (UF10820) also from the Asylum.

When the Immigration Depot opened in 1848, the old convict hammocks were replaced with folding iron beds, which were later used by the Asylum women as well. Mattresses and pillows were generally made from 'ticking', a thick linen or cotton fabric usually woven in blue stripes or checks. Hundreds of pieces of this material were represented in the collection, and it may also have been used for bath towels and dishcloths, as looped cotton (terry towelling) only became used for bathing towards the end of the 19th century (Young 2003:98). In some cases this bedding material was used for garments as well, with the remains of an apron (UF18607) made from this fabric found on Level 3.

Cotton Prints

Cotton prints at the Barracks included a wide range of colours and patterns (**Table 5.14**). The most common print colours were blue and mauve or purple, generally used for clothing items. Undergarments in this period were normally white, rather than printed, as coloured underwear was considered slightly debauched (Baines 1966:254; Flanders 2003:270). In the 18th and 19th centuries whiteness was often associated with physical cleanliness and moral propriety, and the uncoloured remains of underclothing at the Barracks may reflect this preference, or else a simple concern with economy (Tarlow 2007:170). Outer clothes, however, along with drapery and furniture fabrics, were typically printed with colours and patterns. Women in both the Asylum and the Depot appear to have worn clothing from a variety of fabrics, designs and colours.

Cotton printing was used in India for several thousand years prior to the development of the industry in Europe in the 17th century. Prints were originally made with wood blocks, but the development of cylinder printing in the 1780s in England and France transformed the industry (Baines 1966:266). A polished copper cylinder was engraved with a pattern around its circumference and then rolled horizontally through a coloured dye. The excess was scraped off with a steel blade, leaving the colour only in the engraved pattern. The calico was rolled around the drum and drawn tightly over the engraved pattern, printing onto the cloth. By the early 19th century, multiple cylinders were used to print complex, multi-coloured pieces at high volume. By 1851 production had reached 600 million yards of printed textile, and by 1889 there were almost 2 billion yards printed annually, and brightly coloured cottons were cheaply available for mass-market consumption (Turnbull 1951:81, 114).

Dyes and mordants were also improved during this period. Until the middle of the 19th century, textile dyes were based on traditional plant and metallic substances. In 1856, however, the first commercially successful synthetic dye was accidentally discovered by 18-year-old William Henry Perkin at the Royal College of Chemistry (Tordoff 1984:20). His creation of a purple dye (known as mauveine) from coal tar prompted a rush of research into the manufacture of synthetic dyes, resulting in new, cheap colours for the textile industry (Garfield 2000:64–70).

Within a year of its discovery purple had become a highly fashionable colour for women's clothing, stimulated in part by the Empress Eugénie of France who wore it often. Technical refinements in the next few years improved printing on silk and cotton, and purple was all the rage until about 1861, when fashion moved on. Mauve soon shifted from the colour of fashion and display to a colour of mourning, when Queen Victoria graduated from black to mauve several years after the death of Prince Albert in 1861. By the late 1860s, mauve was all but forgotten as a fashionable colour.

Purple print designs at the Barracks were mostly two-tone mauve, stylised floral and foliate patterns, with simple lines and flattened colour (**Figure 5.36**). At least 76 different patterns in purple have been identified in the underfloor assemblage, along with others in red and blue. Such textiles became very common at the Asylum in the 1870s, just as the general price of printed calicoes in England steadily declined (Turnbull 1951:112). The women wore clothing made from a mix of cheap, colourful prints and plain, undecorated cottons.

Print Colour	Level 2	Level 3	Total
Aqua	–	10	10
Black	17	18	35
Blue	37	387	424
Brown	52	95	147
Composite	62	83	145
Green	2	6	8
Orange	–	2	2
Pink	6	13	19
Purple	112	212	324
Red	12	40	52
White/Cream	51	205	256
Yellow	1	5	6
Unidentified	1,437	3,980	5,417
Total	*1,789*	*5,056*	*6,845*

Table 5.14: Cotton textile print colours.

5. Daily Life in the Asylum

Figure 5.36: Purple cotton prints from Levels 2 and 3; *Row 1:* UF46430, UF9286, UF10818, UF11537; *Row 2:* UF11561, UF11656, UF18260, UF18268; *Row 3:* UF18341, UF18389, UF18399, UF18455; *Row 4:* UF18463, UF18473, UF18486, UF18496; *Row 5:* UF18497, UF18542, UF18548, UF18577; *Row 6:* UF18614, UF18711, UF18765, UF18768; *Row 7:* UF18830, UF18881, UF18899, UF18954 (P. Davies 2011).

Clothing

Fashionable dress and convict clothing in 19th-century Australia has been reasonably well documented over the years (e.g. Elliott 1995; Fletcher 1984; Flower 1968; Maynard 1987, 1994; Sanders 1992; Scandrett 1978; Whitty 2000; Young 1988). The clothing worn by working Australians, however, as well as the uniforms of those in institutions, is much less well known, as items were often worn until they were threadbare, and few survived to have found their way into museum collections. Numerous clothing pieces from the Hyde Park Barracks thus provide an important source of information about how the inmates dressed, the accessories they wore, and how uniforms functioned in a context of institutional refuge. Most of the women wore simple cotton or woollen garments, including petticoats, a chemise (shift or undershirt) and dress (bodice and skirt), along with an apron and bonnet, and a nightgown for bed.

Several items of clothing identified in the Barracks underfloor collection probably relate to convicts. The most notable example is a complete blue striped cotton shirt found on Level 3 (UF51). This neatly sewn garment includes a simple upright collar with two bone buttons, a narrow v-neck, and gathered cuffs on the sleeves. A small broad arrow stamp on the tail marks the garment as government property, although this style of shirt was worn by both convicts and free workers. Another patched and poorly preserved shirt (UF8114) was also found on Level 3, while a set of hand-sewn linen braces (UF53) includes remnants of yellow wool (Parramatta) cloth. This item may have been made from the lining of a convict jacket. Several historians have pointed out that convicts in Australia did not necessarily dress differently from other colonists, which, as we note above, often made it difficult for new arrivals from England to distinguish between convicts and other groups (Elliott 1995; Maynard 1994:14–23). Margaret Maynard (1994:21) has also argued that coarse yellow clothing was synonymous with convicts in the 1820s and 1830s, and that the Hyde Park Barracks (HPB) shirt (UF51) could actually have belonged to a soldier.

Clothing was available from various suppliers in colonial Australia. Local tailors made garments for men, but they struggled to compete against cheaper imports from England. There was little in the way of readymade clothing for women and children, however, until the 1880s. Public auction and the second-hand market thus remained important sources of clothing for many people, while tailors and dressmakers made clothing to order (Maynard 1994:39–40). Most women, however, made their own clothing, as well as clothing for their husbands and children. From the 1850s onwards this became easier with the introduction of self-acting sewing machines, and the production of dress patterns and pattern books for use in the home (Arnold 1977:3; Godley 1996; Knox 1995:77–78).

Figure 5.37: Blue woollen sock (UF10760; P. Davies 2010).

Many of the Asylum women wore thick, machine-knitted stockings made from cotton or wool, either calf or knee length. Knitted fabric is more elastic than woven fabric because it is composed of interlocking loops made from one continuous piece of thread, providing a flexible, smooth fit for items worn close to the body such as socks or stockings (Palmer 1984:3). Numerous examples of stockings have been found in the underfloor collection, including one that bore the HPB laundry stamp (UF11734). Most of the stockings had been darned or repaired at some stage, with most wear at the toes and heels. A pair of pale blue, knee-high socks from Level 3 may have been worn in bed by invalids (UF10760; **Figure 5.37**), while an intact stocking made from silk and fine cotton featured an embroidered flower above the ankle (UF948). Two much-worn slippers were also found on Level 3, with leather soles and heels, chamois sides and cotton lining (UF127).

Pieces of fabric from garments for upper parts of the body, and bodices were also recovered from the Asylum rooms on Level 3, including hand-sewn sleeves made in segments from various plain cotton offcuts (UF5534, UF11629). Most sleeves were long (shoulder to hand) and several still had wrist buttons attached (**Figure 5.38**). A remarkably well preserved cotton bodice was found in the large southern dormitory of the Asylum. It was made from purple-printed cotton with short calico sleeves and metal hooks-and-eyes (UF52; **Figure 5.39**). The item features a shallow V-neck and pleats to gather the garment at the waist, and it has a HPB

Figure 5.38: Remains of cotton cuff and sleeve with blue geometric prints (UF11546; P. Davies 2010).

5. Daily Life in the Asylum

Figure 5.39: Cotton bodice in purple print and modified with plain calico sleeves (UF52; P. Davies 2010).

Figure 5.40: Cotton apron with hand-made lace trim; button and tie remnant preserved at waist (UF54; P. Davies 2010).

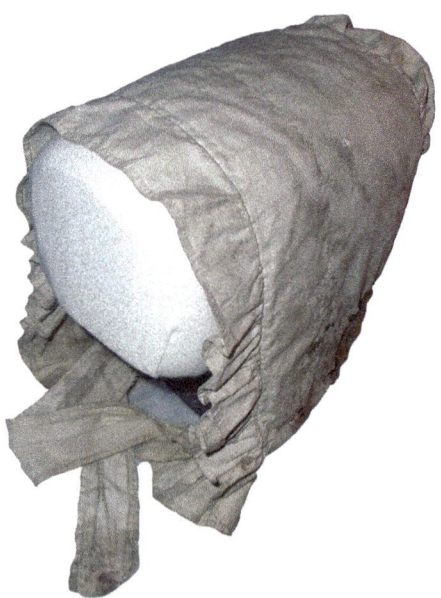

Figure 5.41: Hand sewn bonnet with ruffle around face (UF55; P. Davies 2010).

laundry stamp at the rear. The mix of fabrics used in the bodice is evidence of a highly individual manufacture or alteration, perhaps made by one of the Asylum women for herself or a friend. Another complete cotton bodice, for a child or infant, was found under the stair landing on Level 3 (UF930; See 'Children at the Hyde Park Barracks').

Other clothing items include the remains of 5 aprons from the Asylum, with examples in a brown and white check pattern (UF11638), red polka dots (UF9284), and blue and white stripes (UF18607; **Figure 5.40**). Aprons were important emblems of women's work, providing protection from dirt in manual labour and thus serving as visible signs of industry. They were commonly worn both in the home and in institutions (Cunningham 1974:148; De Marly 1986:118). Examples of headwear worn by the Asylum women were also found in the collection. These include the remains of 9 cotton bonnets, all found on Level 3. One was marked with the HPB laundry stamp and was sewn with a ruffle around the face and a cotton tape tie (**Figure 5.41**). Photographs of inmates in the dining room and the yard of the Newington Asylum, taken around 1890, show most of the women wearing aprons and head coverings such as bonnets (**Figures 5.42** and **5.43**).

Various clothing accessories were also identified in the collection (**Table 5.15**). These include the remains of 7 handkerchiefs from Level 3, including several examples in fine woven linen. There were also various leather belts and clothing buckles made from ferrous metal and copper alloy (**Figure 5.44**). The remains of gloves were also identified, including three complete cotton gloves from the Asylum (**Figure 5.45**) and 4 finger pieces from leather gloves in the Immigration Depot. Wearing

Clothing items	Level 2	Level 3	Total
Apron	1	5	6
Belt	1	6	7
Bodice	–	9	9
Bonnet	–	9	9
Braces	2	6	8
Buckle	6	13	19
Collar	2	3	5
Cuff	5	18	23
Glove	6	6	12
Handkerchief	–	7	7
Pocket	2	2	4
Ribbon	41	40	81
Skirt	–	2	2
Sleeve	–	8	8
Sock/Stocking	9	38	47
Total	75	172	247

Table 5.15: Garment remains, components and accessories recovered from the underfloor collection.

5. Daily Life in the Asylum

Figure 5.42: Dining room at Newington Women's Asylum, around 1890 (Small Picture File, Mitchell Library, State Library of NSW).

Figure 5.43: Inmates in yard at Newington Women's Asylum, around 1890 (Small Picture File, Mitchell Library, State Library of NSW).

kid leather gloves denoted affluence and class in the 19th century, marking the divide between those who worked and those who did not. Gloves were often worn very tight, restricting the manual activity of the wearer (Levitt 1986:130). The fragments of leather gloves derive mostly from Level 2, occupied at various times, both by the immigrant women, who came to Australia to work in domestic service, and by the Applewhaite-Hicks daughters and their friends. Even among the Asylum women, however, there were a few who kept the cheaper cotton gloves as a sign of personal respectability, even though cotton gloves were considered vulgar in some quarters (Beaujot 2012:44; Flanders 2003:256).

There were also dozens of ribbons and ribbon fragments in silk and silk-like fabrics, in a variety of colours (**Figure 5.46**). These were often used as dress accessories to update and refresh an old outfit (Fletcher 1984:120–121). Ribbons were found in almost the same quantities in the Asylum as in the Depot, and suggest that the inmates may have taken the opportunity to trim their clothing or bonnets with a little colour.

Clothing fasteners were also found in large numbers in the underfloor spaces. These included 193 buttons from Level 2 and 396 from Level 3, along with 750 ferrous and copper alloy hooks-and-eyes (**Figure 5.47**). Button materials included shell, bone, copper alloy and rolled iron, along with smaller numbers of horn, wood and glass. Button styles included sew-through examples with one, two, three, four and five holes, along with various shanked and cloth-covered (dorset) types. Bone buttons with a single hole were used either with a pinshank or as a blank for thread or fabric-covered buttons (Lindbergh 1999:51). Button manufacturers identified include Harris & Son, McGowan, and Boggett & Co, all of London.

Buttons and hooks were used to fasten various items of clothing, including bodices and sleeve cuffs (Lindbergh 1999:51). They were distributed fairly evenly throughout the underfloor spaces on both levels, suggesting that the sewing of buttons on clothing, and their accidental loss, were widespread in the Asylum and Immigration Depot. The large numbers reinforce the amount of sewing and

Figure 5.44: Copper alloy belt buckle with central lozenge and four leaf motif (UF67; P. Davies 2010).

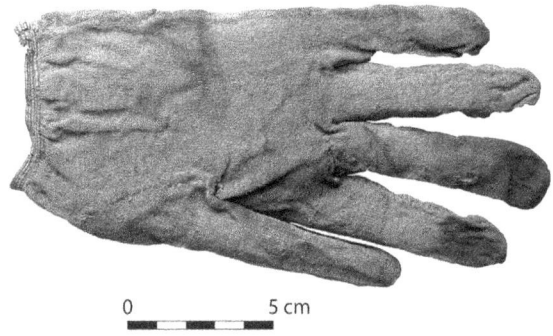

Figure 5.45: Plain cotton glove with elastic wrist band (UF10793; P. Davies 2010).

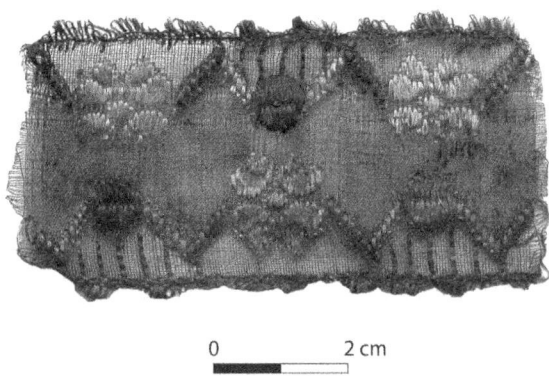

Figure 5.46: Open weave brown ribbon with blue loops on selvage and hand sewn floral motif (UF11521; P. Davies 2010).

Figure 5.47: Card backing for a packet of hooks-and-eyes (UF17508; P. Crook 2003).

5. Daily Life in the Asylum

	Bone	Composite	Copper	Ferrous	Glass	Horn	Plastic	Shell	Wood	Unid	Total
1-hole	9	1	–	–	–	–	–	–	2	–	12
2-hole	3	2	3	–	1	10	1	9	1	1	31
3-hole	10	–	2	–	–	–	1	2	–	–	15
4-hole	14	1	14	4	7	5	–	18	–	2	65
5-hole	3	–	–	–	–	–	–	–	–	–	3
Shanked/cloth	–	1	14	17	8	–	–	2	–	19	61
Unidentified	–	–	–	–	–	–	1	–	–	5	6
Total	*39*	*5*	*33*	*21*	*16*	*15*	*3*	*31*	*3*	*27*	*193*

Table 5.16: Button forms and materials from Level 2.

	Bone	Composite	Copper	Ferrous	Glass	Horn	Plastic	Shell	Wood	Unid	Total
1-hole	40	–	–	–	–	1	–	–	1	–	42
2-hole	–	1	2	1	2	–	1	7	–	1	15
3-hole	17	–	–	–	1	1	–	–	–	–	19
4-hole	56	–	34	21	7	41	3	35	–	11	208
5-hole	5	–	–	–	–	1	–	–	–	1	7
Shanked/cloth	–	7	35	6	1	–	1	2	–	30	82
Unidentified	–	–	3	9	2	–	1	–	–	8	23
Total	*118*	*8*	*73*	*37*	*13*	*44*	*6*	*44*	*1*	*51*	*396*

Table 5.17: Button forms and materials from Level 3.

clothing repair that the women were engaged in, with most hooks and buttons small enough to fall between the floorboards. The buttons were not, however, a standard type, as might be expected in an institutional context. Instead, the collection is distinctive for the sheer diversity of forms and materials (**Tables 5.16** and **5.17**). Buttons entered the Barracks on many different garments and were then reused before their eventual discard or loss.

Women at the Hyde Park Asylum each wore a similar set of garments, issued to them on their arrival. These generally comprised a long-sleeved cotton chemise or undershirt, one or more petticoats of plain or printed calico, a cotton or wincey[26] dress (skirt and bodice), and machine-knit cotton or wool stockings. In addition they wore cotton aprons of various colours and patterns, leather shoes or slippers, and a bonnet or woven-straw hat for outside use. This was very similar to the clothing worn by women at the Port Macquarie Asylum in the 1860s. Frederic King, Secretary of the Government Asylums Board, reported that the women were provided with 'one dress, one shawl, one apron, one flannel petticoat, one chemise, one cap, one pair shoes, and one pair plain woollen stockings' (Government Asylums Board 1867:108).

King also noted that the recent establishment of the Port Macquarie Asylum (in 1866) meant that there was little in the way of old clothing to supplement supplies and keep the women warm in winter. At Hyde Park, in contrast, the women were in the habit of wearing second-hand skirts as warm petticoats. The evidence thus suggests that the inmates wore lighter cotton prints in the warmer months and wool blends in the winter.[27] This echoes historian Margaret Maynard's view that climate and environmental conditions in Australia had an important impact on the way people dressed, and that most people made practical choices in what to wear, rather than slavishly following English cool-weather models (Maynard 1994:151).

The clothing and textile remains also indicate considerable diversity in the cotton print patterns worn by the women. With more than 70 different purple prints identified in the collection, the fabric from which the women made their clothing was not identical and standardised but varied subtly according to the textiles available from local distributors, or from low cost purchase of end-of-line bolts of fabric, or from recut second hand clothing. While inmates generally wore the same array of garments, each woman's appearance varied slightly,

---

[26] Wincey [linsey-woolsey] was a plain durable cloth with a linen or cotton warp and woollen filling. In the United States it was known as 'Negro cloth' (K. Wilson 1979:264).

[27] Catherine Turner, a patient from the Sydney Infirmary, was admitted to Hyde Park Asylum on 18 August 1876. Wearing only 'a tattered nightgown, old tweed skirt, two petticoats and a scanty shawl', Lucy Hicks complained to Frederic King that it was too cold to discharge a patient in such weather (Godden 2006:258–259).

in terms of the different fabric patterns used in their clothing, and probably, in shapes and styles.

The unimportance of a strict institutional uniform at the Hyde Park Asylum is also evident in testimony given by Matron Hicks to the Public Charities Commission in 1873. She acknowledged that while the women dressed 'as nearly as possible' in a uniform, some preferred 'to keep their own clothing — for instance, if a woman is in mourning' (Q2359, Public Charities Commission 1874:76). Others were 'too proud' to wear a uniform and continued wearing their own clothes (Q618, Government Asylums Inquiry Board 1887:459). Hicks was flexible in her management of the inmates, recognising that the women were not prisoners but 'poor old creatures' for whom clothing was a matter of comfort and convenience rather than discipline and control.

Lucy Hicks was also involved in both the manufacture and the distribution of clothing. As noted, the Asylum received large bolts of cloth, such as 1000 yards of calico, supplied by tenders issued by the Government Asylums Board (Q2368, Public Charities Commission 1874:76). One thousand yards of calico provided fabric for up to several hundred chemises and night dresses (Government Asylums Inquiry Board 1887, Appendix C:51). Mrs Hicks used a room on Level 1 to cut the fabric into pieces for sewing into dresses and underclothing, although she appears to have lost the use of this room in 1871 when the Census office claimed it. Her willingness to undertake such work created financial savings for the institution, and ensured that she exercised considerable control over the work of the inmates and the basic form and size of garments that they made and wore.

Mrs Hicks kept a store of nightgowns, chemises and other garments sewn by the inmates, to be handed out as required. Old clothes that were beyond repair or recycling were taken away by the rag-man, or ended up beneath the floor (Q3215, Government Asylums Inquiry Board 1887:509). New clothes, including dresses and aprons, were also handed out on special occasions such as Christmas and the Queen's Birthday 'to those who wanted them' (Q3213, Government Asylums Inquiry Board 1887:508).

The sewing and repair of garments by the Asylum inmates is also significant in terms of variations to uniform clothing. The women spent their days sewing and patching, and were often in a position to sew or modify their own clothes, or the clothing of friends within the Asylum. They could also personalise garments in small ways, such as with buttons, and make clothes to fit the individual more comfortably. Numerous examples of hand sewing preserved in the collection indicate widely varying skill levels, from very fine and regular stitches to unevenly sewn hems, seams and patches, and the crude darning of stockings. Some of the work was made easier by 1878, when a second-hand treadle sewing machine was purchased, with another in 1880 (Hughes 2004:84). It is probable that the women exercised some control over the clothing they wore, and that they need not have been limited to wearing shapeless, poorly fitting institutional garments.

When inmates were discharged from the Hyde Park Barracks Asylum, or left of their own accord, they were permitted to retain the clothing they had worn within the institution. If they absconded in Asylum apparel, however, they could be prosecuted for theft (see 'Regulations'). Several garments in the collection, including a cotton bonnet and a stocking, are marked with the HPB laundry stamp. These items suggest that, officially at least, clothing ultimately belonged to the institution, rather than the individual inmates who sewed and wore it.

Women at the Hyde Park Asylum thus wore clothing that was more or less the same as that of other working women of the period. This included dresses, petticoats and chemises, along with aprons, bonnets and stockings. Inmates dressed according to their station in life, which was basically one of domestic service. Their work, and the clothing they wore, was familiar and respectable. Their humble, durable clothing emphasised thrift, modesty and morality.

There is no evidence, however, that the women's clothing was disciplinary or punitive, in the way, for example, that penitents of Magdalen Asylums in Ireland wore shapeless, sexless garments with strips of calico tied tightly across the breasts as part of their 'remorseless penance' (Finnegan 2004:81, 195–196). Instead, there was a closer parallel with the inmates of the Magdalen Asylum in Philadelphia in the 19th century, whose muslin petticoats, cotton stockings, caps and shoes emphasised neatness, modesty and economy (De Cunzo 1995:88). Archaeological and historical evidence from the Hyde Park Asylum suggests that the clothing worn by the inmates was a uniform of economy and convenience, rather than one intended to discipline and depersonalise the individual.

RELIGIOUS INSTRUCTION AND PRIVATE DEVOTION

One of the benefits of locating both the Immigration Depot and the Destitute Asylum at the Hyde Park Barracks was its proximity to St James' Anglican Church, St Mary's Catholic Cathedral and St Stephen's Presbyterian Church, and to the residences of the respective clergy, thereby helping to meet the needs of the inmates for moral and religious instruction. While this was important to ensure the moral integrity of vulnerable young women at the start of their new lives in Australia, it was also important to bring comfort to older women at the end of their lives and to other women unable to work and care for themselves due to illness.

Clergymen often held services within the main

Barracks building, and along with various evangelical societies, they also visited the women to bring them small comforts and read and pray with them. In his testimony to the 1873 Public Charities Commission, Stephen Robins, a Sydney City Missionary and regular visitor to the institution, said:

> ... I was there [at the Hyde Park Barracks] yesterday, and I have been in the habit of going there for eleven years. Now, I went in a different way yesterday (I go to read and pray with the sick and dying women, and then I go down stairs to hold service in the big room), but yesterday I went in a different way. I took a few tracts with me, and went to a few individuals — nearly all I could get access to — and I spoke to them. (Q2514, Public Charities Commission 1874:83)

He also noted that the Protestant and Roman Catholic inmates at the Hyde Park Barracks were segregated into separate wards:

> ... a great many ladies go in and give them [the inmates] a little tea and sugar, and speak kindly to them. The Protestant side stands better than the other. They are divided there — the Protestants from the Roman Catholics — and the Protestants get the best privileges, as there are more people to visit them. (Q2515, Public Charities Commission 1874:83)

When asked if they were unduly favoured, he replied:

> No, not at all; but the people seem to care more for them, and they are not allowed, you know, according to the rules of the institution, and the priests and that, to *go on the other side*. (Q2516, Public Charities Commission 1874:83, emphasis added)

This testimony provides a remarkable insight into the religious activities of the Asylum (and we will return to the issues of segregation and the distribution of tracts further on), but it also highlights the importance of these 'visitors' to the institution. They were more than just well intentioned visitors — they were political advocates. Not only did they have a substantial influence on the public inquiries (especially the 1886 Government Asylums Inquiry Board), they used the newspapers to criticise and challenge the management of the institution. During an outbreak of smallpox in 1881, Mrs Hicks, under direction from Mr King, Manager of the Government Asylums, quarantined the Hyde Park Barracks, halting all day leave for inmates and disallowing visits from outsiders for several months. Some inmates left the Asylum rather than be shut in and deprived of visits from their children and friends (Government Asylums Board 1881:1135). The Ladies Evangelical Association brought the situation to the attention of the general public in a brief note in the *Sydney Morning Herald* on 20 January 1882. Matron Hicks then issued a statement, via her husband (a journalist):

> When the smallpox first broke out, it was thought advisable that Hyde Park Barracks should be quarantined and an order was forwarded from the Colonial Secretary's Office that all liberty should be stopped to the inmates, and all visitors — Sisters of Mercy, Flower Mission Ladies — should be refused admission. This has been perfectly understood by these ladies, to whom the matter has been explained, and, as far as the Sisters of Mercy are concerned, cheerfully complied with; the order was forwarded in due course through the manager of asylums (Mr King) to Mrs Hicks, as matron superintendent of Hyde Park, and acted upon by her. As a matter of fact, Mrs Hicks has made applications to the Board of Health to free the institution from quarantine, and each time has met with a distinct and peremptory refusal. (*SMH* 1 February 1882, p.5)

An anonymous 'observer' wrote to the *Herald* two days later complaining that while the quarantine kept the old women in and visitors out, Matron Hicks and her family continued to come and go as they pleased (*SMH* 3 February 1882, p.7).

Disapproval of Matron Hicks seems to have been widespread among the evangelical visitors. While it was not unleashed in full until the 1886 Inquiry (when the Matron was accused of being a drunkard, of bribing inmates, impersonating Lady Martin and using Asylum produce for her family's benefit), evidence of it can be seen in Stephen Robin's testimony to the Public Charities Commission (Q2521–2524, 1 October 1873). When asked whether he was 'satisfied' with all he had seen at the Hyde Park Barracks over the 11 years of his visiting, i.e., 'the mode in which it is conducted — and what [he had] seen of the inmates', he replied 'I would not like to say all I think sometimes, but I think that there is a good deal of [sectarian] partiality shown there'. When reminded by the President of the Inquiry that his evidence would be recorded and printed, he responded 'Then I shall say nothing more' (Q2521–2524, Public Charities Commission 1874:83).

Advice to the Dejected: Religious Tracts at the Hyde Park Barracks

In addition to their political efforts to safeguard the good management of the Asylum, visitors were also responsible for bringing into the Barracks one of the most intriguing groups of artefacts found under the floorboards: religious tracts. At least 42 and probably 112 fragments from 19th-century tracts

5. Daily Life in the Asylum

survive in the archaeological collection, in addition to other religious material such as pages from the Bible, prayer books and periodicals.

Religious tracts are a phenomenon of the early 19th-century, an outcome of the growing evangelical movement throughout the Western world that coincided with innovations in printing-press production. Sermons, theological debates and prayer books were soon supplemented by fables, Bible stories, advice books, and even tracts on current events and world history. They were deliberately non-denominational to appeal to a broad range of Christian sentiments, and ranged from four- and eight-page pamphlets to bound volumes of 100 or 200 pages (Howsam 1991). Stories for children with a moral or religious message were also produced in large numbers (Butts and Garrett 2006:3; Cillin 1913), but only one of these was identified in the Barracks collection (UF14432). Tracts were also read on the migrant ships to Australia to sustain the spiritual health of those on board (Haines 2006:95–96).

Tracts were not, however, respected literary devices of their time. William Thackeray lamented that, while in days gone by, it 'required some learning ... to write a book',

> ... now, in the age of the duodecimos, the system is reformed altogether: a male or female controversialist draws upon his imagination, and not his learning; makes a story instead of an argument, and, in the course of 150 pages (where the preacher has it all his own way) will prove or disprove you anything. And, to our shame be it said, we Protestants have set the example of this kind of proselytism — those detestable mixtures of truth, lies, false sentiment, false reasoning, bad grammar, correct and genuine philanthropy and piety — I mean our religious tracts, which any woman or man, be he ever so silly, can take upon himself to write, and sell for a penny, as if religious instruction were the easiest thing in the world. We have set the example in this kind of composition, and all the sects of the earth will, doubtless, speedily follow it. (Thackeray 1840)

The Religious Tract Society (RTS) was founded in London in 1799 to publish and promote Christian literature. It was one of several evangelical organisations to emerge in this period with the aim of spreading the message of salvation. In Australia the British and Foreign Bible Society was represented by the Auxiliary Bible Society of NSW, founded in 1817, while the Sydney Diocesan Committee was the local branch of the Society for Promoting Christian Knowledge. The latter had a book depository at St. James' Church, directly across the road from the Hyde Park Barracks. The Australian Religious Tract Society was established in Sydney in 1823 as an auxiliary of the English organisation. Its objective was to 'inculcate evangelic sentiments', by providing the means of:

> ... cheap, useful, and pious Reading; that the poorer Classes of the Community, and the young People more especially, who may be able to read, may obtain some of the most instructive and important Lessons of Life at a very small Expence. (*Sydney Gazette* 9 October 1823, p.3)

Tracts were first published in Australia in 1836 'for the dissemination of moral, domestic and patriotic feelings' (*Sydney Gazette* 19 March 1836, p.4). In later years, the Religious Tract and Book Society Depot was located only a few blocks from the Barracks, on the corner of King and Pitt Streets. There was also a Wesleyan Book and Tract Depot nearby at 95 King Street in the early 1870s (see **Figure 1.2**). The Australian RTS alone distributed more than 600,000 publications locally between 1823 and 1851 (Australian Religious Tract Society 1851:8). It is easy to imagine clergymen and visitors from the Ladies Evangelical Association picking up a bundle of cheap tracts for distribution among the Asylum inmates from one of the four religious book depots only a short walk away.

The above mentioned Stephen Robins, from the Sydney City Mission, was a likely source of tracts. The Mission was founded in 1862, and included Anglicans, Methodists, and Presbyterians on its ruling committee, but no Catholics (Owen 1987:20). The work of Robins and other missionaries involved making house-to-house visits to spread the message of the gospels, and visiting hospitals, gaols and the Destitute Asylum to conduct religious services and distribute tracts. The Mission had a bookstall nearby at the head of Sussex Street. Robins was a regular visitor to the Barracks, and often brought 'a few tracts' with him when he came to hold services for the women (Q2514, Public Charities Commission 1873:83).

William Hicks, second husband of the Matron was another likely source of tracts entering the Barracks. Although he worked in Sydney as a journalist, in a former life he had been ordained as an Anglican priest (Hughes 2004:160–161). Hicks was the author of *A Concise View of the Doctrine of the Baptismal Regeneration*, published in London in 1856, and he published numerous other tracts (Venn 1947:360). He worked with John Ferguson, owner of Ferguson's Book Depot at 387 George Street, throughout the 1870s on a number of benevolent committees and fundraisers (including Sydney's first spelling bee; *SMH* 7 September 1875, p.8). Hicks' Cambridge education, parish experience, evangelical background and pastoral work suggest that he had a genuine concern for the spiritual welfare of the Asylum inmates.

Many of the pages of the religious books were

5. Daily Life in the Asylum

incomplete or single-leaf, providing no evidence of whether they were stitch-bound in a book, or stapled, pinned or tied in a pamphlet. Most of the books were small, around 4.5 inches (114 mm) tall, reflecting their 'pocket companion' nature. From the 240 torn pages, books and paper fragments containing religious or moral texts identified in the collection, the titles of at least 20 tracts could be identified. These included:

> *Advice to the Dejected*
> *Are You Afraid to Die?*
> *The Economy of Human Life* (by P. D. Stanhope)
> *James Gibbons* (published by the Religious Tract Society, London)
> *Matt the Idiot Boy*
> *Old Dinah*
> *Prayers for Morning*
> *Prayers of St Bridget*
> *Richard Weaver's Leaflets* (No. 16)
> *Self Help*
> *Strange Tales, from Humble Life* (by John Ashworth)
> *Sunday Rest*
> *Litany for the Sick*
> *The Believer's Pocket Companion* (by William Mason)
> *The Levites*
> *The Life of Havelock* (by Rev Thomas Smith)
> *The Portuguese Convert* (Gosse's Gospel Tracts)
> *The Prison Death-Bed*
> *The Prodigal Son* (from *The British Workman*)
> *The Christian Herald and Signs of Our Times*

Some of these tracts, including *The Prison Death-Bed*, *Litany for the Sick*, and *Advice to the Dejected*, must have been confronting subjects for the aged and destitute women, many of them bedridden, but they were probably the target audience for tracts of this kind. One of the documents is a scrap of paper with the title *Are You Afraid to Die?* carefully torn from the original page. This item appears to have been important enough to one of the inmates to tear out and save (**Figure 5.48**). Other titles, such as *Self Help* and *Sunday Rest* stressed personal morality as keys to self-improvement. The title *Are you Hired?* (UF6977) was found on the stair landing on Level 3 and is likely to have been brought to the Barracks for the young women of the Immigrant Depot.

Smith's *Lecture of the Life of Havelock* (UF17529), printed in 1860 for the YMCA at St Barnabas in Sydney, celebrates the courage and religious strength of Sir Henry Havelock, the British soldier and hero of the Indian Mutiny in 1857. Havelock's deep religious faith, temperance and evangelical fervour made him a model of Christian militarism in the Victorian period.

At least one of the tracts, *The Believer's Pocket Companion*, has a name written on the inside of the cover: 'Ann Sarran [indeterminate]' (UF8226, L2-3 JG27 JS4). This small, leather-bound tract survived complete, although the majority of the pages have been eaten away. The identity of Ann Sarran is unknown. This edition is likely to have been printed in London between 1801 and 1816, so she may predate the Asylum records.

A page from the tract *Old Dinah* relates to the Old Testament story of Dinah, daughter of Leah and Jacob (Genesis 34). Dinah was raped by Shechem the Hivite, leading her brothers to make war as vengeance for her disgrace. The affair emphasises the importance of chastity and family honour, and the relationships between personal morality, household control, and involvement with outside groups (Frymer-Kensky 2002:179–198).

An intact book of moral instruction was found in the northern dormitory on Level 3, *The Economy of Human Life*, purporting to be 'translated from an Indian Manuscript, written by an Indian Brahmin' (UF2109; **Figure 5.49**). The book, in fact, was written by Philip Dormer Stanhope, 4th Earl of Chesterfield (1694–1773). Chesterfield is best remembered for his witty, shrewd and cynical letters to his illegitimate son Phillip Stanhope. The 'Economy' was originally published in 1751 and went through dozens of editions. It was translated

Figure 5.48: Heading carefully torn from religious tract (UF17368; P. Davies 2009).

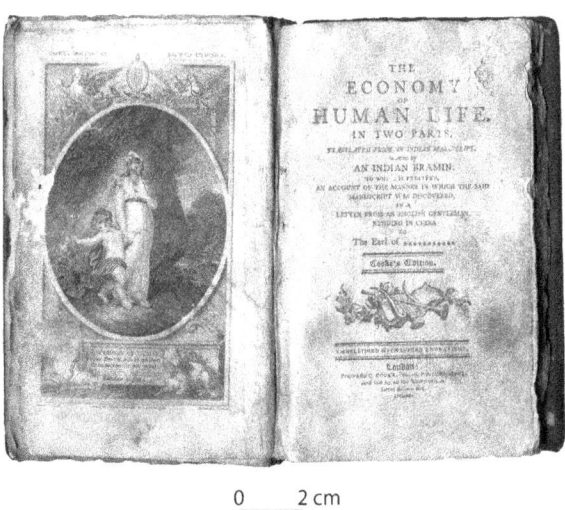

Figure 5.49: *The Economy of Human Life*, originally written by the 4th Earl of Chesterfield (UF2109; P. Davies 2009).

into Hebrew (1778) and German (1814), and this Cooke's edition was published in 1796. It is a book of moral instruction, advising the reader on such topics as Modesty, Prudence, Temperance and Chastity. It describes the moral duties of men and women, of masters and servants, and prescribes proper conduct with reference to a range of human conditions. As such, it is an example of the kind of reforming literature given to the Asylum women for their moral improvement, and functioned alongside Bibles and religious tracts as a guide to appropriate behaviour.

Official church literature was also discovered among the assemblage. In addition to 39 fragmented pages from Bibles, hymn books and prayer books recorded in the Level 3 stair landing, an intact leather-bound edition of the King James Bible, published by the British and Foreign Bible Society in 1830, also survived under the floorboards (UF28). A badly rat-chewed prayer book (UF17905) was found beneath the floor of the southern dormitory on Level 3. It was probably a Catholic missal, and included chapters on Indulgences, Devotions for the Sick, Litany of the Sacred Heart, and Litany for a Happy Death (**Figure 5.50**). Two small page fragments from a prayer book were also found, printed in English on one side and Latin on the reverse (UF18115, UF18116). While these probably derive from a Catholic missal, publications in Latin and English continued to be used in the Anglican tradition in the 19th century as well (Maskall 1846).

A fragment of the Scots-Gaelic Book of Common Prayer was also found beneath the floor of the Level 3 landing (**Figure 5.51**). Scottish Gaelic (or Erse) was widely spoken in the western highlands of Scotland and the Hebrides, and many women who migrated from the region to Australia in the 19th century spoke little or no English. Gaelic Bibles and psalm books were often provided on migrant ships to sustain the faith of, and give comfort to, passengers (Watson 1984:59–60). Although many Highlanders were Catholic, this book is likely to be a Presbyterian

Figure 5.51: Fragment from the Scots–Gaelic Book of Common Prayer (UF17513; P. Davies 2010).

Figure 5.52: Title page of moralizing tract, 'Self Help' (UF17558; P. Davies 2010).

item given the importance of private prayer books in the Protestant tradition. The book may have been kept by one of the inmates as a personal relic of her homeland and religious identity, or possibly because she could not read English.

Rosaries and Devotional Medals

Most of the religious and moral texts were brought into the Asylum from the outside, and expressed an evangelical response to the perceived needs of the inmates. There were items, however, that embody a more private religious identity, one that sustained the inmates in old age and infirmity. Most of these items derive from the Catholic tradition, and represent not only a personal religious sentiment among some of the women, but also the institutional expression of the sectarian divide (see below).

Catholics have traditionally engaged in a wide range of extra-liturgical devotions, related especially to the belief that the Virgin Mary and the saints can intercede with God on behalf of the faithful, a

Figure 5.50: Rat-chewed Catholic prayer book (UF17905; P. Davies 2010).

view long rejected by Protestant denominations. The rosary was the oldest and most popular of all Catholic devotions, having achieved widespread use in Europe by the 14th century (Lysaght 1989:10). Both as a prayer and set of beads, the rosary is an example of a 'sacramental' that can be used by the faithful for their spiritual benefit. Other popular sacramentals include crucifixes, holy cards, scapulars and religious medals with images of Christ, Mary or a saint.

All of the Catholic items were located in the underfloor spaces in the southern rooms of Level 3. These items include a number of rosary elements and devotional medals. The most remarkable example is a complete rosary with a gilt crucifix and red-painted dried berry beads, joined by a copper-alloy link chain and a Sacred Heart medal inscribed 'O MARIE CONÇUR SANS PECHE / SOUVENIR L'MISSION' (UF62). In addition there were two Sacred Heart medals with three-point attachments for use in a rosary (UF682, UF10932) and three lengths of chain with small remnant beads (UF9515, UF11377, UF7593).

Evidence of another type of rosary, in the form of 47 blue and five clear round beads strung on thick white cotton (UF61) was recovered. While most of the beads are now loose, one intact section has 10 blue beads between two clear beads, suggesting that it is the decade of rosary.

In addition to the rosaries were seven devotional medals, with inscriptions in English, French and Spanish (**Figure 5.53**). The five legible examples include:

UF17835 (Crucifixion)
'MERE DE DIEU PRIEZ POUR NOUS' (Mother of God pray for us)
Reverse: 'CHRIST AYEZ PITIE DE NOUS' (Christ have mercy upon us)

UF17834 (Mary)
'MERE DE DIEU PRIEZ POUR NOUS' (Mother of God pray for us)

UF10552 (Miraculous)
'MARIA CONCEVID / SIN PECADO PNEGA / POR NOS' / 'QUE. RECURRIMOS A. VOS' (O Mary conceived without sin, pray for us who have recourse to you)

UF10527 (St Bernard)
'SAINT BERNARD' and a depiction of a saint reading a book
Reverse: '... POUR NOUS' and a depiction of a saint with a crook

UF10020 (Miraculous)
'MARIE CONÇUR SANS PECHE PRIEZ POUR NOUS' / 'QUI AVONS RECOURS A VOUS' (O Mary conceived without sin, pray for us who have recourse to you)

Figure 5.53: Devotional medal, obverse and reverse (UF17835; P. Davies 2010).

Two of the medals (UF10020 and UF10552) are of the kind known as Miraculous Medals, part of the early 19th-century revival of the cult of the Immaculate Conception. In 1830 a French nun received a vision of the Virgin Mary with instructions to produce a medal that would bring graces to whomever wore it. The medal was first struck in 1832, with an obverse image of Mary and a reverse bearing the letter M surmounted by a cross, over the sacred hearts of Jesus and Mary. The medals were hugely popular, with as many as 30 million in circulation by 1875 (Deagan 2002:54). Similar examples were also recovered from three locations at the Cumberland and Gloucester Streets site in Sydney, where they have been interpreted as evidence for Catholic individuals or households (Iacono 1999:64–65).

In addition there were the likely remains of two Catholic scapulars from Level 3, one from the stair landing (UF18143) and one from the small southern room (UF11576). Scapulars are another example of Catholic devotionals (such as the rosary), worn as a private pledge and reminder of faith. The tradition emerged in the 17th century, with two small pieces of cloth connected by bands worn over the shoulders at back and front, each bearing images or verses from scripture. The two examples from the Barracks consist of a heavy cotton base with a worn-away patch or label.

While it is certainly possible that some of these devotional objects were given to the Asylum women as gifts, most were probably among the private possessions of Roman Catholic inmates. Regardless of how the items were acquired, they reveal aspects of personal faith and prayer in the Asylum. While the many tracts were brought into the institution (and were often read aloud to the women) these may also have facilitated genuine religious feeling among the Protestant inmates.

Sectarian Division

As noted previously, we know from historical records that Protestant and Roman Catholic inmates at the

Hyde Park Asylum were segregated in separate wards. The spatial distribution of Catholic items in the underfloor collection provides additional evidence of this separation. All these items were found in the southern rooms on Level 3 and in the common area of the stair landing. No Catholic items appear on the northern side of the building on Levels 2 or 3. Only one explicitly Protestant item was found in the southern wards, in addition to three 'evangelical' texts. These latter fragments relate to tracts for which the specific denomination could not be identified from the surviving text, and could represent either Protestant or Catholic, but are more likely the former given the greater numbers of Protestant tracts produced in the 19th century.

The artefact evidence that the southern wards were for Catholic inmates and the northern wards for women of the Protestant faith accords with the building's local setting. St James' Anglican Church, completed in 1820, stands directly across Macquarie Street from the Barracks, and although the inmates were only rarely allowed out, visiting clergymen and missionaries associated with the church had ready access to minister to the women.

St Mary's Catholic Cathedral stands about 200 metres south-east of the Barracks, and its location, within sight of the southern dormitories, may have given comfort to the Catholic inmates. The cathedral had been destroyed by fire in 1865, but a temporary wooden structure was quickly erected for church services until the northern section was rebuilt in 1882 (Moran 1896:474). For inmates with limited mobility or those who were bedridden, looking out the window may have been as close to a church of their faith as they could get. A concentration of rosaries and devotional medals in the southern sick room also suggests that the recitation of prayers, including the rosary for sick and dying inmates, was common.

Sectarian divisions continued in death as they did in life. The customs for the final farewell to departed were sightly different:

> ... the bodies of the Roman Catholics are prayed over and sprinkled by the nurses with holy water, before they are taken away; no prayers are said over the Protestants; ... (Deposition of Lucy Applewhaite, *SMH* 30 August 1866, p.5)

They were buried in Protestant or Roman Catholic burial grounds, according to the religion entered on their admission book.

> ... in the case of the burial of Ann Miller, the order was to bury her in the Church of England Cemetery; she came as a member of the Church of Scotland, but afterwards was attended by the Rev. Mr. Allworth, and died a Church of England woman ... (Deposition of Lucy Applewhaite, *SMH* 30 August 1866, p.5)

Religious Faith Among the Asylum Inmates

The underfloor material provides evidence for the expression of private beliefs at the Barracks, especially for Catholic devotions among the Asylum women. Archaeological evidence suggests that rosaries and medals belonged to inmates as examples of personal Catholic devotion, although it is unclear the extent to which the rosary was recited privately by individuals or by small groups. With constant over-crowding, lack of privacy and limited opportunities to attend Mass, especially by elderly and frail inmates, these objects may have had significant personal value, providing the opportunity to pray for intercession and a degree of spiritual solace. In these institutional circumstances, it is possible that such devotions were more important to the Catholic inmates than the practices of the official liturgy, including the Mass and the Sacraments.

The rosary was also useful as a form of prayer for those who could not read. Rosary beads were small and were probably kept in a pocket, although Irish women in the 19th century often wore the rosary around their necks (Lysaght 1989:57). The breakage and loss of these objects may have been distressing, especially if they were one of the few personal items the women could bring with them into the Asylum.

Books and tracts, however, were the most frequent items of religious devotion recovered from the underfloor spaces in the Barracks. The impact of such material on the spiritual lives of inmates depended on the women's ability to read the pages. Literacy levels among migrants from the United Kingdom to Australia in the 19th century were high, between 70% and 80%, boosted by mass education, the increasing association between literacy and respectability, and the mass-production of cheap books and other printed material (Hassam 1995:xvi; Oxley 1996:186). This degree of literacy was also observed among Irish arrivals (Haines 1998:54). One indication that literacy in the Hyde Park Asylum was reasonably common was the establishment and maintenance of a library in the institution since it opened in 1862.[28] Fat skimmed off the soup and cartloads of bones from the kitchen were sold and the proceeds used to buy books and periodicals for the inmates. The abundance of newspapers from metropolitan Sydney, country areas and from overseas, along with history books and advice manuals, also suggests that reading, both private and aloud to others, was common among the women. While poor eyesight and even blindness restricted access to written material for some, two examples

---

[28] There was also a small library in the Liverpool Asylum for men, mostly with bibles, prayer, and religious books. Tracts were also distributed weekly (Select Committee 1862:947).

5. Daily Life in the Asylum

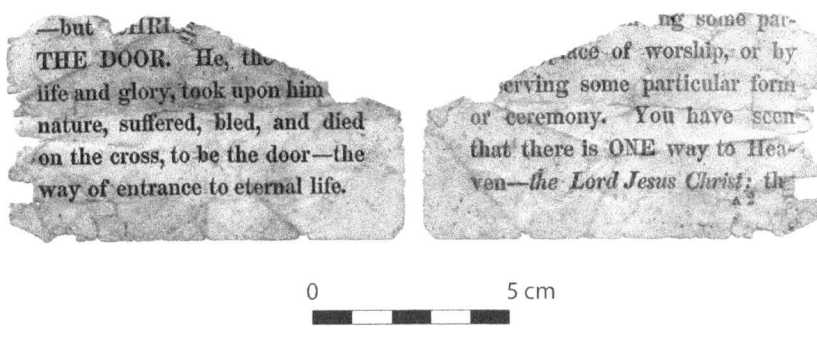

Figure 5.54: Large print religious tract from the Level 3 stair landing (UF17381; P. Crook 2003).

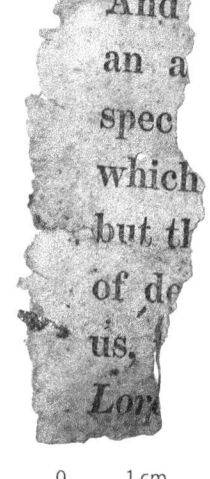

Figure 5.55: Fragment of large print religious text for the poorly sighted (UF17549; P. Davies 2010).

of tracts with large, widely spaced typefaces (UF17381, UF17549; **Figures 5.54** and **5.55**) were clearly intended for the aged and poorly sighted. After the installation of gaslights in the 1860s, one of the women's 'greatest comforts' was to have the newspapers read aloud at night (Hughes 2004:82).

In spite of the abundance of religious items from the Asylum, it is difficult to determine the impact of religious literature and other items on the spiritual lives of the inmates. All of the archaeological objects were, at some point, discarded or lost beneath the floorboards, no longer needed or wanted. Historians have argued that while a large minority of Australians expressed at least a nominal allegiance to religious faith during the 19th century, most were indifferent and lacked any religious conviction (Carey 1996:2). While some of the inmates may have been ignorant or disdainful of religion, many others retained some sense of spiritual faith, as a result of early upbringing and their exposure to books, tracts and other items available in the Asylum. The orderly structure of organised religion provided by prayers and visiting clergymen and missionaries may also have offered a sense of security in a world where the women had little else to call their own.

Printed Matter: Literature and Reading

In addition to the numerous religious and moral tracts found in the collection, there was a large array of other reading material, including newspapers, periodicals and other books. Fragments from at least 14 books or pamphlets without overt religious references were also recorded. These titles are both historical or non-fiction works, as well as advice manuals, and include:

The Matchmaker (UF17681 and UF17739)
Story of Lucknow, Great Mutiny in India (UF16159)
The Abkhasian Insurrection (UF17418)
Everybody's Garden (UF17519)
The World's Fair (UF133)
Newton Forster or, The Merchant Service (by Frederick Marryat, UF18863)
Chapters on Common Sense (UF17442)
For Young Children (UF14432)

Some of these titles may have been printed by the Religious Tract Society, or by other Christian publishers, as these organizations published thousands of books and pamphlets on a wide range of subjects. As we have noted, the newspapers and other reading material could have been brought into the Asylum by various means, including via visiting missionaries, by William Hicks, and by purchase for the Asylum library.

Another category of printed material is the newspaper assemblage, represented by at least 2,163 fragments of newsprint. Many of these are tiny pieces, only a few millimetres across, but others are more substantial, and from among them the following local, regional and European newspapers and periodicals can be identified:

Sydney Morning Herald daily by Charles Kemp and John Fairfax, 1842– (36 fragments, MNV: 15)
The Sydney Mail weekly by Fairfax, 1860–1938 (2 fragments, MNV: 1)
Town and Country Journal weekly by Frank and Christopher Bennett, Sydney, 1870–1919 (8 fragments, MNV: 4)
The Illustrated Sydney News by Walter George Mason, 1853–1872 (1 fragment, MNV: 1)
The Evening News by Samuel Bennett, Sydney, 1867–1931 (11 fragments, MNV: 9)
The Empire by Henry Parkes, Sydney, 28 December 1850 to 14 February 1875 (2 fragments, MNV: 1)
The Freeman's Journal, Sydney edition, 1850–1932 (tentative attribution: 1 fragment, MNV: 1)
The Cumberland Mercury (1868–1895), *The Parramatta Advertiser* (1844–) or *The Parramatta Chronicle and County of Cumberland Advertiser* (1859–1867) (1 fragment, MNV: 1)
Pastoral Times and Deniliquin Telegraph (tentative attribution: 1 fragment, MNV: 1)

5. Daily Life in the Asylum

Queensland Daily Guardian, Brisbane, April 1863 to June 1868 (2 fragments, MVN: 1)

The Tablet, weekly, London, 1840– (2 fragments, MNV: 2)

The Graphic: an illustrated weekly newspaper by Edward Joseph Mansfield, London, 4 December 1869 to 23 April 1932 (2 fragments, MNV: 2)

The British Workman, periodical to educate the Working Classes illustrated 4-page monthly by Thomas Bywater Smithies, 1855 [at least 1907] (5 fragments, MNV: 3)

Public Opinion (4 fragments)

The European Mail (5 fragments)

The Home News (1 fragment, MNV: 1)

The Country Gentlemen's [Journal?] (I fragment, MNV: 1)

The newspaper fragments are an invaluable means of dating the assemblage. By recording the small fragments of mastheads with the date of publication, or weather reports with the previous week's rainfall or shipping data with the next week's shipping news, very specific production dates could be identified. In other cases, dates or years could be gleaned from discussions of local or global events, made more closely dateable with the linking of Australia to the overseas telegraph in 1872 (Isaacs and Kirkpatrick 2003:9). A total of 280 newsprint fragments offered specific production dates or date ranges, and of these 90.3% date to the women's phase of occupation (1848–1886), and nearly three-quarters to the last 15 years of the Asylum and Depot's occupation (**Table 5.18**).

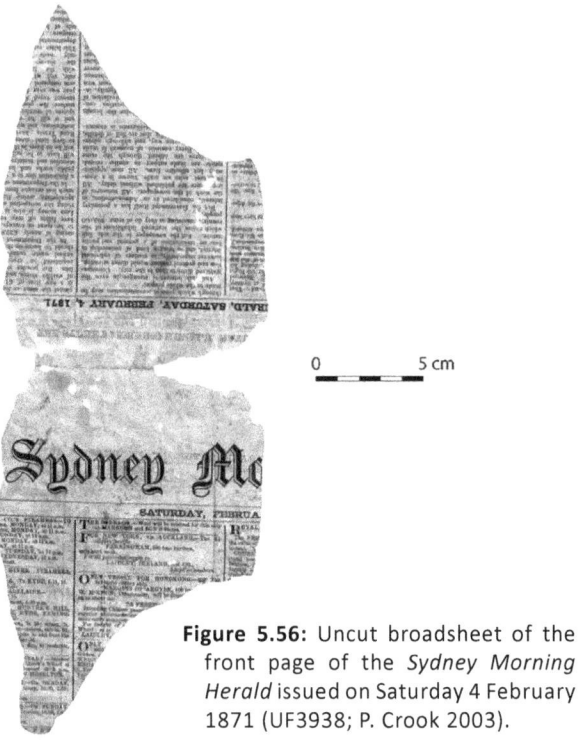

Figure 5.56: Uncut broadsheet of the front page of the *Sydney Morning Herald* issued on Saturday 4 February 1871 (UF3938; P. Crook 2003).

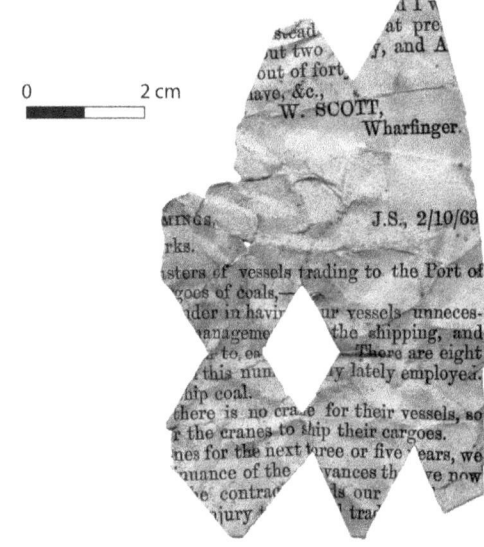

Figure 5.57: Sawtooth cuts on edge of newsprint (UF17499; P. Davies 2009).

Dates	Level 2	Level 3	Total
Pre-1848 (1839–1844)	0	2	2
1848–1886	139	114	253
1850s	0	1	1
1860s	13	34	47
1870s	57	78	135
1880s	70	3	73
1890s–1967	16	6	22
Total	*156*	*124*	*280*

Table 5.18: Fragments of dateable newsprint from Levels 2 and 3 of the main Barracks building.

The assemblage of newspaper fragments is intriguing for several other reasons. The quantity of reading material found in the under floor assemblage indicates that many of the Asylum women could read, and others enjoyed having books and newspapers read aloud to them. Some of the fragments are off-sheets, direct from the printers and not sold to the public (**Figure 5.56**). These may have been brought into the Barracks by the Matron's second husband, William Hicks, who was a journalist, and an editor of the *Sydney Punch* newspaper.

Several newspaper fragments have been cut with scissors into unusual patterns, including six pieces from the stair landing on Level 3 with diamond cut edges or mid-sections (**Figure 5.57**). While this may be a simple, purposeless activity done out of boredom, it could also represent attempts at decoration, where newspapers cut with saw tooth edges were used as temporary table or mantel placements or floor coverings. Other, undecorated fragments may have been deliberately placed under the floorboards to manage leaks, or used to cut out patterns for dresses — a task well suited to the large, uncut broadsheets.

6
PRIVATE LIVES

Along with the official history and material culture of the institutions occupying the Hyde Park Barracks there are the family histories, private lives and the ephemera of long-term residents and transient individuals who lived or sought refuge there. In this chapter we will examine the archaeological evidence for private or personal activities within the broad machinery of the institution. We begin with a brief biography of the rise and fall of the most significant individual associated with the Hyde Park Barracks during the women's phases of occupation: Matron Lucy Hicks. A great deal of research on the Applewhaite-Hicks family has been undertaken by Joy Hughes (2004:144–178) and we draw on that work here.

THE APPLEWHAITE-HICKS FAMILY

Matron Lucy Hannah Langdon, later Applewhaite and then Hicks, was born on 5 November 1833 in George Street North, The Rocks. She was the sixth child of English immigrants John and Mary Langdon (née Trinder), who had married in London c.1823 and migrated to New South Wales in 1828. They arrived with their three young sons, John and William (born in England) and Chadwick, born at sea on the voyage. Lucy was one of four children born in the colony; the others were Elizabeth (1831), Thomas (1832) and Emily Jane (1835) (Hughes 2004:144).

John Langdon was a merchant by trade and established a slaughterhouse on a grant of land at Darling Harbour. He also ran a butcher's shop in George Street. The business prospered, and in 1831 he obtained a 1280-acre grant of good grazing land in the County of Murray, along with assigned convicts to work it. Two years later he purchased 1280 acres at East Bargo, south of Camden, and was granted one more assigned convict (Hughes 2004:145).

John Langdon died in 1835 at the age of 37, when Lucy was two years old. Her mother remarried 18 months later, on 29 March 1837, wedding Thomas Holmes. Also a butcher, Holmes invested in Sydney property, with allotments in George Street, Glebe and Burwood, along with holdings near Auckland in New Zealand. He also set up the three Langdon sons in business — John and Chadwick as butchers, and William in his other enterprises. The three Langdon daughters — Elizabeth, Lucy and Emily — received a good education that included music lessons (Hughes 2004:145–146).

Thomas Holmes was also a founder of the FitzRoy Iron Mining Company, which established Australia's first blast-furnace for iron smelting near Mittagong (Jack and Cremin 1994:14–32). He sent specimens of iron to Bristol, where the iron was highly regarded (Askew 1857:312), for manufacture into knife-blades. One of his partners in the mining company was John Conrad Korff, who married the eldest Langdon daughter, Elizabeth, in 1847 (Hughes 2004:147).

At the age of 16, Lucy married the 30-year-old, Barbados-born English mariner, John Lithcot (also spelt Lythcote and Lythcot) Applewhaite on 12 September 1849, at the Anglican Christ Church St Laurence in George Street, Sydney. John Applewhaite was master of the *William Hyde*, a 532-ton barque built in 1841 that carried cargo and passengers. The couple spent the early years of their marriage at sea and in port in London and Adelaide, as well as in Lyttelton and New Plymouth in New Zealand. Their eldest daughter Mary was born aboard ship at Port Adelaide in 1850, and their son Phillip was also born on board in May 1852 (Hughes 2004:148; Askew 1857:310; NSW Death Certificate 1890/11629).

An account of one of their journeys from England to New Zealand was published in the *Lyttelton Times* by one of the passengers, and this gives a sense of what life was like for the family in the first years of their marriage:

> The *William Hyde* weighed anchor at Deal on the morning of Tuesday, October 21, 1851, and having a favourable wind went at once down the English Channel, and across that terror of English landsmen, the Bay of Biscay, where the wind and sea were both somewhat rough. On October 31 we passed Madeira at midnight, bearing S.E. by E. On November 8 we caught a shark, from which some excellent steaks were cut. On the 14th we sighted San Antonio (Cape Verde), bearing E. by S. and distant by about 40 miles. From thence to the Line the N.E. trades were very light, and it was not until November 25, thirty-five days from Plymouth that we passed the Equator ... From this point to about lat. S. 42.2 and E. long. 54.8 our course was slow and uninteresting, the S.E. trades entirely failing us. To beguile the time, however, the play of the "Merchant of Venice" was got up, and

performed before the passengers and crew ... On December 19, 47 days from Plymouth, we passed the meridian of Greenwich, lat. 34.19. On Xmas Day we were off the Cape, and the day was spent as nearly as possible after the Old English fashion. On New Year's Day the children of the cuddy and the forecabin had an entertainment in the cuddy, and the children of the steerage passengers were regaled with fruit, tarts, cakes and wine on the quarter deck. On Saturday, January 3, we made our best run during the voyage, having gone over 281 miles in twenty four hours, and from this time a good pace was kept up to Stewart Island, which we sighted on Saturday January 30, at break of day, lying N.E. by E., passing it so close as not to see the "Traps". At noon of the same day, we were off Otago where the wind headed us and kept us out till the 5th, when we safely anchored in Port Victoria, having accomplished our passage under the protection of a merciful Providence without a single casualty or serious disagreement and all in good health. (*Lyttelton Times* 14 February 1852, transcribed by Judy Clark; http://freepages. genealogy.rootsweb.ancestry.com/~nzbound/ wmhyde.htm, retrieved 12 April 2011)

Another account of a voyage aboard the *William Hyde* was written by John Askew, a steerage passenger from Newcastle (NSW) to New Zealand in 1853. Askew noted that Captain Applewhaite was 'a stout, broad-faced, good-looking Englishman, about 30 years of age, a thorough son of the sea, [and] as strong as two ordinary men'. He describes Lucy Applewhaite admiringly as:

> ... a pretty little woman, a native of Sydney, and about 22 years of age. She had in perfection the finely chiselled features so peculiar to the women of Sydney. Her hair was dark brown, and was shaded back in luxuriant tresses, fastened behind with a plain black ribbon. She generally wore a black satin dress, and a small white collar round her neck. Her name was Lucy, and she was as amiable as beautiful. (Askew 1857:311; see also Hughes 2004:148–149))

During heavy weather out of Auckland, pens for the sick sheep were set up in the ship's cuddy, where Lucy 'nursed them as carefully as ever Miss Nightingale nursed the wounded soldiers at Scutari; but all to no purpose, die they would and did, in spite of all her efforts to save them' (Askew 1857:318).

The *William Hyde* left Auckland on 22 April 1853, bound for Melbourne, but the ship ran aground when approaching The Bluff on New Zealand's south island. After a delay the ship docked in Melbourne on 28 May, but thereafter it disappears from shipping records for some years, suggesting that it had sustained sufficient damage to warrant substantial repairs. The Applewhaite family left the ship in Melbourne, and their lives at sea were now largely behind them (Hughes 2004:150). John continued to captain ships plying the inter-colonial trade and established an auctioneer's business which became insolvent in September 1854 (*The Argus* 14 September 1854, p.8).

Over the next year or two John and Lucy shuttled back and forth between Sydney and Melbourne. Their third child, Elizabeth, was born in Glebe, Sydney, in April 1855, followed by two more daughters: Lucy Holmes, who died soon after birth in 1857, and Emily, born in 1858.[29] By 1859, John and his brother Edward Applewhaite were keeping livery stables in Pitt Street when they were declared insolvent.[30] The register of assets at the stables included a mail phaeton (carriage), 2 horse harnesses, a chaff cutter and wheel barrow, all which were the property of Mr Holmes, Lucy's stepfather (Supreme Court, Insolvency Papers, SRNSW 4578; Hughes 2004:150).

When Lucy Applewhaite was appointed to the vacant position of Matron at the Hyde Park Immigration Depot in May 1861, with an annual salary of £70, it must have seemed like the best solution to the Applewhaite family's financial worries. Her appointment appears to have had the support of the Colonial Secretary, Charles Cowper, who knew the family through Lucy's stepfather, Thomas Holmes, and their shared interest in the FitzRoy Ironworks (Hughes 2004:151). The family moved into the Barracks, occupying quarters in the two western rooms on Level 2, overlooking the entrance on Macquarie Street. A few months later the family's fortunes improved further when John Applewhaite was appointed as an 'extra' clerk at the Immigration Agent's office at the Hyde Park Barracks, at a salary of 10 shillings per day (Hughes 2004:152).

The position of matron was one of the few 'respectable' options available to women of Lucy's background who wanted or needed to work. Such appointments tended to be reserved for middle-class women of respectable upbringing and credentials, which meant married women or widows were preferred (Alford 1984:184). Lucy was only 27 years old at the time, and the mother of four children. Although she had no experience as a matron, her

---

[29] The birth certificates of Clara and Helen Applewhaite have not been located. Their birth dates have been estimated from death and marriage records.

[30] Edward also held the license for the South Head Family Hotel in South Head (*SMH* 23 May 1859, p.3). It is unknown if John assisted him in this enterprise, but the assets of the hotel are listed in the insolvency register for both the Applewhaite brothers (Supreme Court, Insolvency Papers, SRNSW 4578).

years as a ship captain's wife had provided her with numerous challenges, including giving birth at sea, coping with extreme weather and emergencies, and living in cramped quarters, with small children, for extended periods. As a frequent visitor to foreign and British ports, she could empathise with the problems faced by young women migrating around the world to face the challenges of setting up a new life in Australia (Hughes 2004:152).

In February 1862 the government established an Asylum for Infirm and Destitute Women at the Barracks, appointing John Applewhaite as master of the new institution and Lucy as Matron — a position held in conjunction with her role in the Immigration Depot. The master's duties were mostly clerical and involved maintaining a register of inmates' admissions and discharges, and recording the receipt and issue of all stores including food, clothing and medical comforts (Hughes 2004:152). From 1863 he received an annual salary of £100 for the role.

As Matron, however, Lucy Applewhaite was responsible for the everyday operation of the Asylum and the management of at least 150 inmates. For the Asylum, she supervised the preparation of meals, the personal hygiene of the inmates, and the cleanliness of the premises and utensils, and enforced discipline. The only paid employees were the head laundress, Nancy Bell, and a nurse, Julia Williams (noted in the Switson trial, *SMH* 29–31 August 1866), each paid 12s a week. In August 1862 Lucy gave birth to her sixth child, John, who died the following year, all the while caring for her other young children and supervising shiploads of immigrant women as they arrived in the Depot.

With the benefit and security of government positions, as well as having living quarters within the Barracks, John and Lucy Applewhaite ostensibly had the income to maintain a middle-class standard of living for their family, an opportunity they may have lacked during the previous few years.

The family, however, appear to have been living beyond their means, as John Applewhaite faced a range of debts and financial disputes during this period. In 1865 a claim against his estate was upheld in the Supreme Court for non-payment of several promissory notes totalling £65 8s. 4d.[31] while in the following year the District Court granted writs against him totalling £36.

In January 1867, he filed for insolvency (his fourth in 13 years) with debts of over £500. His petition outlined the reason for his 'pecuniary embarrassment' as Hughes (2004:157) put it:

Firstly, when I originally obtained the Government Appointment which I now hold I was through previous business misfortunes in greatly involved circumstances and had then no immediate means of satisfying my Creditors. I was at time in the full belief that I was entitled to Considerable landed property at Canterbury in New Zealand of which I have since been fraudulently dispossessed and the value of which I estimated at between six and seven thousand pounds.

Secondly, From the date of such appointment until the present time I have been continually and unfortunately in the hands of money lenders to whom I was absolutely compelled to apply for loans at most exorbitant interest in order to satisfy their claims of the more clamorous of my old creditors beside which I have been put to very heavy law expenses both in the Supreme and District courts in causes arising from these claims.

Thirdly There are now several writs of Casa out against me and I am duly threatened that they will be put in force.

Fourthly I have had death and much sickness in my family and have been at great expenses arising from them.

It is quite impossible for me at this time simultaneously to pay off these pressing liability and I have no alternative but to sequestrate my estate and seek the protection of this honourable court.

J L Applewhaite

(4 January 1869, NSW Supreme Court, Insolvency Papers, SRNSW 2/9226, no. 8090)

Hughes (2004:156) notes that most of the debts on file were incurred since 1862, and reflect a relatively affluent consumption pattern appropriate for a middle-class family in a respectable position. Between 1861 and 1866 they spent £186 on childrens' boots and shoes, gloves, hats, silk braids and trimmings, and mourning clothes[32] from several Sydney retailers: David Jones, Thompson & Giles on George Street, McArthur's on York Street, Farmer's and Madame Ponder of Maison de Paris on George Street. This was alongside debts of £70 owed to grocers and butchers and £50 owed to a private doctor for medical attendance and Pinhey's pharmacy for medicines. The fact that the Applewhaites were able to continue to accumulate and sustain relatively large accounts may well be

---

[31] Applewhaite was subject to a compulsory sequestration in May 1865 filed by Thomas Gregan and Thomas Brown (NSW Supreme Court, Insolvency Papers, SRNSW 2/9147, no. 7116).

[32] The mourning clothes were needed for the deaths of their infant son John in 1863, Lucy's brother William Langdon and her stepfather Thomas Holmes in 1864, along with the death of their seven-year-old daughter Emily in 1865 (Hughes 2004:156).

[33] It is unknown how or by whom John was 'swindled' from such a large estate. His brother Edward died in 1864 (*SMH* 21 Jun 1864, p.9). Given Edward's diverse business interests, it is possible he owned land in New Zealand and it may be that John had expectations of inheritance.

an indicator of their public respectability, or their ability to reassure these shopkeepers that they had the means to meet their expenses. It may be that they were spending in the comforting expectation of £7,000 worth of property if John's claim of being defrauded of a Canterbury estate are to be believed.[33]

The Applewhaites had no landed property and their assets totalled a paltry £26 (£16 in furniture, £10 in wearing apparel). We know this from a poorly written inventory taken in evidence for the court, and conducted at the Applewhaites' quarters in the Barracks on 12 January 1867. The inventory lists a bird and cage, cruet stand, chiffonier and two dumb waiters, along with crockery and glassware. It identifies three rooms used by the family: one main 'Room', a Bedroom and Kitchen. It does not mention the children's bed furnishings. Hughes argues that the inventory is probably an inadequate record of the family's domestic possessions, and suggests that 'valuable items had been sold or perhaps spirited away to another part of the building' (2004:156). The taking of this inventory was part of the Applewhaites attempts at averting their own destitution. We will never know if the inmates of the Barracks were aware of the precarious financial position of the Master and Matron of their institution.

Applewhaite agreed to pay off his creditors at a monthly rate, but resisted and delayed payments until the matter disappears from the records (Hughes 2004:157). In 1868 Lucy gave birth to another son, William, and during the following year, on 27 May, John Applewhaite died of heart disease, at the age of 49, after almost 20 years of marriage to Lucy. His death certificate shows that he was suffering from 'syncope' (cardiac failure) and 'fatty degeneration of the heart' for a period of three months and that he was attended by the Asylum's dispenser, Dr George Walker. Like most of the inmates, he was buried promptly, on the following day, 28 May. He left Lucy with six children, aged between 18 years and 11 months.

The Government Asylums Board acknowledged 'the skill, energy, and tact, displayed by Mrs Applewhaite in the fulfilment of her duties', and recommended the abolition of the master's position. In June 1869, Lucy took charge of the Asylum as an independent matron, at a salary of £150 per annum, equal to the male masters in charge of the Liverpool and Parramatta asylums. This was offset by the reduction in salary for her duties as matron of the Immigration Depot, from £100 to £20, on account of the decline in immigrant arrivals (Hughes 2004:158).

Just over a year later, on 4 June 1870, Lucy married English-born William Henry Hicks at St James's Anglican Church, opposite the Asylum. Hicks was a family friend, and had assisted the Applewhaites during their financial difficulties in 1867 by providing £150 surety for one of their debts. Their last child, William Henry Applewhaite, appears to have been named in Hicks's honour (Hughes 2004:160).

William Hicks was born c.1827 in Caston, Norfolk, the son of John Raby Hicks. He described himself as a bachelor, but he had previously married a Charlotte Bailey in London around 1850 (Hughes 2004:159–160). In 1851 he was ordained a deacon at Salisbury and a priest the following year. From 1853 to 1855 he was curate of Ramsbury in Wiltshire. He graduated from Cambridge University in 1855 as Bachelor of Laws, and until 1864 served as vicar of Watton in Norfolk. Hicks was also the author of *A Concise View of the Doctrine of the Baptismal Regeneration* (1856) and numerous tracts (Hughes 2004:161; Venn 1947:360). Although his name appeared in the *Clergy List* until 1885, he migrated to Australia around 1861, and spent time in New Zealand on business. Hicks applied unsuccessfully for various government positions. In 1872, he embarked on a capitalist venture to operate a quartz-crushing operation on the goldfields of northwestern New South Wales, in Ironbarks (present-day Stuart Town), near Wellington (*SMH* 31 May 1872, p.5, 12 June 1872, p.7). He published reports about his trips there in the *Australian Town and Country Journal* in 1873, and in numerous letters to the Editor (e.g. *SMH* 22 June 1872, 21 August 1873).

Lucy was 37 at the time of her marriage to William, and together they had five children, only one of whom survived into old age: Lucy E. M. R. (b. Sydney 1871, d. 1892), John Raby (b. 1874, d. 1941), Claud A. R. (b. 1876, d. 1876), Kate R. (b. 1878, d. 1878) and Francis A. R. (b. 1879, d. 1896). All five were born at the Hyde Park Barracks while Lucy continued to run both the Asylum and Immigration Depot. She was 46 when she had her fourteenth and last child, Francis, in 1879. It was around this time that she may have begun employing a governess to look after the children so she could devote herself to the care of the Depot and Asylum (Hughes 2004:208).

On 1 January 1875, Lucy's 24-year-old daughter Mary Applewhaite, who worked as her mother's unpaid assistant, was appointed to the newly created position of sub-matron of the Asylum, with an annual salary of £50. There was discussion, at this time, about erecting new quarters for Matron Hicks and her growing family on the Macquarie Street frontage of the Barracks complex, but these plans did not eventuate. However, during 1882, the matron's quarters on Level 2 were given over to provide additional accommodation for the inmates (Government Asylums Board 1882:2). By 1883 the Hicks family was living at 143 Phillip Street, just a block from the Asylum, but it is unknown whether this was a private or government-sponsored arrangement.

Immigrant ships continued to arrive regularly: 13 vessels in 1878 and 12 in 1879. The *Australian Town and Country Journal* of 19 July 1879 described

Figure 6.1: Scenes from the Hiring Room at the Hyde Park Barracks Immigration Depot (*Town and Country Journal* 19 July 1879).

the crowded scene in the hiring room, where 'two hundred ladies in want of servants' sought to claim one of the 50 female immigrants from the *Nineveh*, a process that apparently took less than a quarter of an hour. Lucy Hicks was shown, fashionably dressed, behind the counter talking to an employer. A few months later, on hiring day on 31 October for the single women off the *Strathleven*, the *Evening News* recorded that Mrs Hicks 'was untiring in her exertions to satisfy all parties concerned'.

Earlier in 1879 Lucy's daughter, Helen Applewhaite had married Thomas William Garrett, a solicitor and prominent member of the Australian and New South Wales cricket teams. His father was Thomas Garrett, MLA for Camden, a former newspaper proprietor, who had been involved in Hicks' gold mining venture in Ironbarks (*SMH* 31 May 1872). Between 1878 and 1881 William Hicks was joint proprietor and editor of the satirical political *Sydney Punch* (Hughes 2004:171).

Mary Applewhaite, Lucy's daughter and the sub-matron, died of inflammation of the lungs on 21 September 1885, aged 34. She had spent the best part of 20 years — her entire working life — in the service of the Asylum and Depot. She never married or had children of her own, but instead answered to her mother as the matron, and to the needs of the inmates. While Matron Hicks received high praise during the peak of her own career, it is possible that much of the orderly management of the institution was due to Mary Applewhaite's untiring efforts. We will never know if she was satisfied with her duties or resented them, but her contribution to the efficient and economic management of the institutions was substantial. Frederic King, Manager of the Government Asylums Board, lamented that 'in her the inmates lost an ever kind and sympathising friend, and the Public Service has lost a most faithful and efficient officer' (Government Asylums Board 1885:1). The inmates contributed to a marble plaque in her memory that was placed in St James' Church where she worshipped. Memorials of this kind had been banned for many years, but one for Mary was permitted as a special case (*SMH* 7

December 1886, p.7). It reads:

> Mary Lucy Adelaide Applewhaite, who died 20th September, 1885, aged 34 years. Erected by the inmates of Hyde Park Asylum, in loving remembrance of their late sub-matron and sympathising friend. 'Inasmuch as ye have done it to one of the least of these, my brethren, ye have done it unto Me.' St. Matt. XXI., 40. (*SMH* 7 December 1886, p.7)

This suggests a different kind of relationship between staff and inmates than might be expected in an authoritarian institutional system. When Frederic King informed the Colonial Secretary of Mary's death, he added that Matron Hicks was dangerously ill and not expected to recover (Hughes 2004:174). However, within a week or so Lucy's health began to improve. She soon resumed her duties, and her daughter Clara took on the position of sub-matron.

The Hyde Park Asylum closed in February 1886. The inmates, together with Mrs Hicks and her family, moved to the new premises at Newington near Parramatta.

Hicks Family Quarters and Artefact Assemblage

Lucy Hicks and her family's quarters on Level 2 comprised two rooms, each measuring 19 by 35 feet, separated by the western end of the hallway. In 1865 the Colonial Architect installed ceiling boards in the quarters to prevent 'leakage' from the hospital wards above. In the following year he replaced the kitchen range, installed in 1848, that was also used by ships' matrons, and by female immigrants, when only a few were left in the Depot.[34]

The artefact assemblages in the underfloor spaces of the family's quarters differ in important ways from material in the other rooms of the Barracks. The large quantities of paper and textile offcuts, leather pieces, religious texts and clay tobacco pipes that characterise the spaces occupied by the Depot and Asylum are less evident in the Matron's quarters. The smaller quantities of discarded or lost items in the quarters may relate to the presence of floor carpets. In 1867, for example, Lucy requested a new carpet to be laid in her 'parlour', on the chance that she would receive a visit from Alfred, Duke of Edinburgh, who toured the Australian colonies in 1867–68 (McKinlay 1970). Henry Parkes, the Colonial Secretary, doubted the duke would visit Mrs Applewhaite's parlour, but agreed to the request if a carpet could be found (Hughes 2004:157). This new carpet was presumably intended to replace an older one.

The underfloor material in the matron's quarters included large numbers of small items such as beads, buttons and pins. The presence of 500 metal sewing pins, for example, indicates that the Applewhaite-Hicks daughters were frequently occupied with sewing and dress-making. Sixty-two buttons and more than 300 small glass beads in various colours were also found, especially in the southern room, which may relate to jewellery or clothing adornment. Slate pencils were also common, with 26 pencil fragments in the family's quarters and adjacent hallway comprising more than half the Barracks total (n=46).

Some of the artefacts in the Hyde Park Barracks assemblage can be linked to specific members of the Hicks family. A hand-written letter (UF3312) that seems to have been written to William Hicks describes a camp at Stony Creek[35] and concludes by wishing 'you [i.e. William Hicks,] Mrs Hicks and family all a M[erry] Christmas'. Unfortunately, the

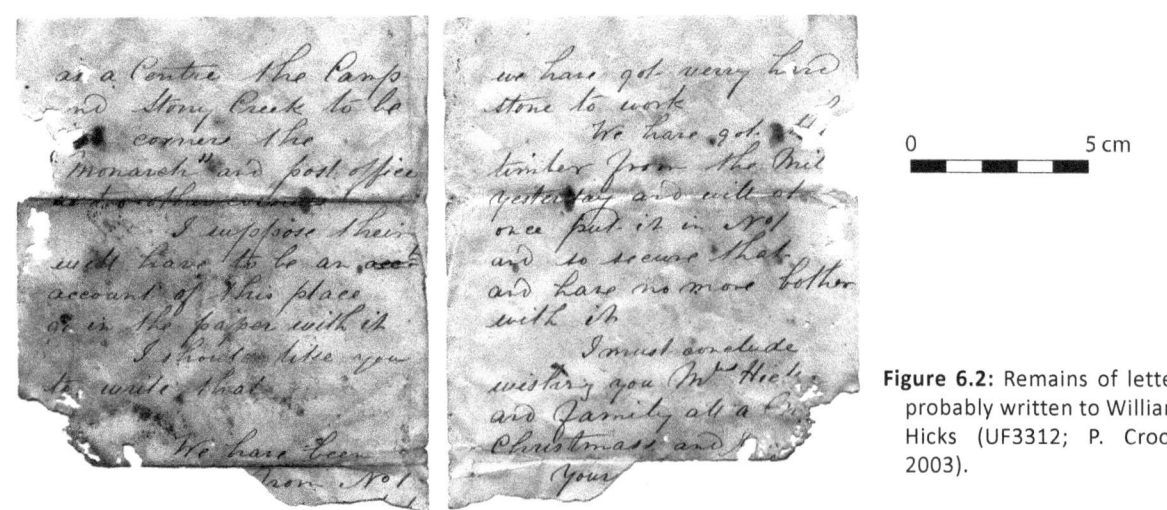

Figure 6.2: Remains of letter probably written to William Hicks (UF3312; P. Crook 2003).

---

[34] The Colonial Architect declined, however, to partition off one of three baths in the new bath house for the exclusive use of the Applewhaites, as it would substantially reduce the bathing facilities for the inmates (Hughes 2004:154).

[35] Crook and Murray mis-speculated the letter referred to Stony Creek in Victoria. Hughes' (2004:161) detailed investigation of Hicks's private letters revealed the publication of the settlement at Ironbarks described in this letter.

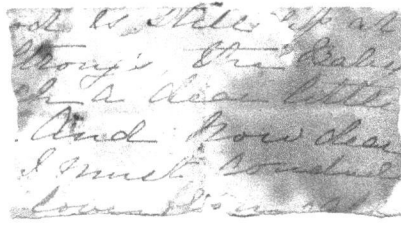

Figure 6.3: Remains of letter probably written by Lucy Hicks (UF17784; P. Crook 2003).

writer's name has been torn away, but the letter notes that an account of a place or building at Stony Creek 'should go in the paper' and probably relates to William Hicks's article on the goldfields settlement of Ironbarks (near Wellington in northwestern NSW) in 1873 (**Figure 6.2**). It was probably written by the mine manager, or another associate, in Hicks' quartz-crushing venture at Stony Creek.

Another, much smaller, scrap was probably written by Lucy herself (UF17784; **Figure 6.3**). While the bottom half of the signature has torn away, it resembles other documented examples of Lucy's handwriting. The sentences cannot be fully strung together, but some phrases are identifiable:

> ... your ... uld[have?] ...
> ...
> ... I must ask yo[ur] ...
> ... to excuse them ...
> ... I never ... which ...
> ... I have ... paper ...
>
> ... [ock?] is still up at ...
> ... Strony's [sic], the Baby ...
> ... [su]ch a dear little ...
> ... and how dear ...
> ... I must conclude ...
> ... love [l... H...ks]

The paper has been folded many times and may have been a note returned to her. It was recovered from the northern ward on Level 2, and while only a few phrases can be made out, it presents a softer, more personal side to the Matron whom we only know from parliamentary inquiries, day books and third-party accounts.

Lucy Hicks

It is difficult to establish just what kind of matron and a person Lucy Hicks was because there are several conflicting reports of her manner and managerial capabilities. Surviving records such as the Day Books for the most part are dry and official, noting requests for ash pits to be cleared, coal to be ordered and other tasks necessary for the management of the institutions. Few remarks offer any glimpse of the personality beyond that of the 'Matron'. Those that do, especially in her early years at the Barracks, suggest she had a staunch and judgemental attitude toward the women in her care. An entry in an 1862 Day Book by Matron Hicks regarding a sick child, John McMatton, reads:

> Mrs McMatton's child worse in consequence of the Mother's neglect. She is a most disobedient woman refusing to do everything she is told. Dr Allengbe has just been with it. Inform her that she will be sent away from the Depot if her conduct is again unfavourably noticed. (SRNSW 9/6181a HPB daily reports 1862)

The child died, aged 3 years and 3 months on 2 August 1862 and was buried at 3 pm the same day.

On the other hand, we can see the Matron as her employers did: a competent and energetic woman who was clearly able to respond to the unexpected, such as the arrival, in early 1862, of 150 infirm and destitute women from the Benevolent Asylum, with only a day's notice (Hughes 2004:152). She coped, it would seem, with her additional new role as matron, on top of her other responsibilities. We have no evidence of her personal response to the situation, but at the age of 29 or so she was capable of meeting the challenge.

The 1873 Inquiry presents Mrs Hicks as a competent, prudent and fair Matron, deftly managing the needs of the swelling numbers of inmates and, most importantly, keeping costs under tight control. While brisk and unsentimental, she also appears to have had some sympathy for 'the poor old creatures' under her care, recognising that sick, elderly women required special treatment, and that the increasingly crowded conditions were hardly conducive to the comfort of the inmates. When it was suggested that she was 'too tender' towards the women in her care, she responded 'I think that in a town like Sydney you must have such a place [as the Asylum]' (Q2382, Public Charities Commission 1874:77). Having been in the job for over a decade, and in full command of both the Depot and Asylum, she had the confidence to politely critique the decisions of the Board, in a manner appropriate to a woman in her position. She moralised about old women whose daughters were prostitutes and boasted about her efforts to prevent drunkards from drinking.

While Lucy Hicks was proudly middle-class, her colonial birth and lack of formal qualifications could have put her on her guard. When Lucy Osburn arrived to take up the position of Lady Superintendent at the Sydney Infirmary in 1868, her training at Florence Nightingale's school of nursing in London may have been seen as an oblique threat to Lucy Hicks, even though Osburn's salary was a little less than Hicks' (Hughes 2004:158). Lucy Hicks soon came to resent Osburn's assumption of superiority (Godden 2006:89; see also Barber and Shadbolt 1996:189).

A few years later, in 1878, Lucy Hicks still managed the controlled chaos of hiring days with vigour. Journalist John Stanley James noted '... the presiding genius was Mrs. Hicks, the matron, who bustled about directing everybody what to do' (*SMH* 24 May 1878, p.5). When single women from the *Samuel Plimsoll* arrived at the Depot in July the following year, the *Evening News* reported that 'no one ... could possibly come away without having admired the business-like style and kindliness displayed by the matron, Mrs. Hicks' (*Evening News* 3 July 1879). A few weeks later she was depicted by the *Australian Town and Country Journal* (19 July 1879; **Figure 6.1**) as firmly in command behind the counter during the chaos of a hiring day.

By 1886, however, a very different portrait of Matron Hicks was emerging. In January 1886, only a month or so before the move to Newington, a hiring day in the Immigration Depot was reported in the *Sydney Morning Herald*. Lady Carrington, wife of the Governor of New South Wales, had expressed a desire to witness the process, but she was initially dissuaded from attending by Mr Wise, the Immigration Agent, who feared she would be shocked by what she saw (*SMH* 21 January 1886, p.9). Matron Hicks was also accused by bystanders of favouring a politician with special treatment in securing a servant, while 400 members of the public fought to gain the services of 104 young women from the *Parthia*. In an 'exciting dialogue' with her accuser, Hicks responded that 'I hope I may drop dead if that's true' (*SMH* 21 January 1886, p.7). Explanations followed that presumably smoothed things over, but the image of government officials barely in control of a hiring process that had been occurring, by then for decades, did not reflect well on Hicks' capacity for managing the Depot.

Given her husband's connections with the Sydney press, it is difficult to ascertain whether the flattering accounts from the 1870s were possibly the view of a trusted friend (or even Hicks himself?) which overlooked any problems or preferential treatment on hiring days. With regard to later accounts, and criticisms of her behaviour, was Matron Hicks caught off-guard, or was there a genuine decline in standards?

A few months later, during hearings of the Government Asylums Inquiry Board, Lucy Hicks was subjected to further sustained criticism:

> There appears also ground for thinking that had the matron's attention been less occupied in her family concerns she would have been at liberty to better attend to her official duties; also, had she been supported by a more efficient sub-matron, many defects in matters of detail would have been forced on her notice, and might have been quickly rectified.
>
> Miss [Clara] Applewhaite, the daughter of Mrs. Hicks, occupies an unauthorised position in the Asylum, and her presence interferes with the responsibilities which properly fall on the matron and sub-matron. (Government Asylums Inquiry Board 1887:445–446).

Hicks was accused of numerous improprieties by some of the inmates, and by members of the Ladies Board. She was accused of withholding basic provisions — rice, sago, arrowroot and gruel — from sick inmates, and a patient insinuated that Hicks had sold hundreds of nightgowns, chemises and dresses belonging to the Asylum (Q2837, Government Asylums Inquiry Board 1887:501). In addition she was alleged to have fleeced dead inmates of their pocket change and savings, and to have impersonated one of the Ladies Board members, Lady Martin, to test the loyalty of the inmates or find out what their accusations against her would be (Q2786, Government Asylums Inquiry Board 1887:500). Most damagingly, she was also accused, not by the inmates but by the evangelical visitors, of being drunk.

To counter such reports by these 'stooges' or 'half-wits' as Matron Hicks called many of them, there were several accounts by witnesses of her devoted efforts, including Elizabeth Cross, inmate of 10 years: 'She is a good matron, God bless her!' (Q3050, p.505). Frederic King, Manager of Government Asylums and Lucy Hicks' superior, denied ever having seen her intoxicated, and generally endorsed her performance as matron:

> ... she is competent, especially from the aptitude with which she deals with those old women. It requires a peculiar person to deal with these old women, and although Mrs. Hicks might not be suitable in all respects for the position, her tact is valuable. (Q3643, p.519)

Hicks was also unconcerned that poisonous medicines — including morphia — stood on open shelves on wards, and that they were dispensed by inmates who could not read: 'You could not get educated people to do filthy dirty work' (p.528). She rarely accompanied the doctor on rounds, and she had no idea of the treatment individual women received or what he prescribed for them (Q3792–3796, pp.523–524). Nevertheless, her long-standing insistence on sanitation and hygiene had helped shield the inmates from the epidemics of scarlet fever, smallpox and typhoid that had swept Sydney from time to time.

The glowing approval of Mrs Hicks in 1873 seems genuine enough — just as legitimate as the criticisms brought against her 13 years later. Lucy Hicks may have been physically and emotionally worn out by the time she arrived at Newington. She was in her early fifties, had suffered an unknown illness in 1885 that brought her close to death, and in addition to giving birth to 14 children, she had endured the sadness of burying six of them, and a husband of 20 years, while at Hyde Park Barracks.

The death of her daughter, Mary Lucy Applewhaite, was not only a personal loss to Lucy, but also it would be a great loss to the Asylum. Mary had been sub-matron at the Asylum for at least seven years in an official capacity, but had been assisting her mother with its management for many years prior. It is likely that while Matron Hicks was on the stand answering questions during the first inquiry, it was in fact her daughter (or the efforts of all her older children) that had maintained the excellent state of the Asylum up until that time.

The emotional difficulty endured by Mrs Hicks at this time was also exacerbated by Supreme Court proceedings in 1885 concerning the distribution of her late step-father's estate. The following year, after the exhausting relocation to Newington, the last of her siblings, John Langdon, died. At Newington, in addition to six of her children in residence, she often cared for her three grandchildren and the son of her late sister (Hughes 2004:210).

At the Hyde Park Asylum, Lucy Hicks had the support of a diligent medical officer and her daughter Mary as a dedicated and competent sub-matron, but at Newington she had neither of these. The Board lambasted the efforts of the medical officer at Newington, Dr Rowling, as 'irregular, careless, perfunctory' (Government Asylums Inquiry Board 1887:430), while Clara Applewhaite seems to have lacked the competence of her late sister. At Hyde Park Barracks everyone was under the same roof (until 1883) and Mrs Hicks could maintain effective oversight, but at Newington the matron's quarters were too far removed from the wards and dormitories to ensure effective supervision.

Matron Lucy Hicks was also the victim of changing circumstances in public relief. The Hyde Park Asylum had been established as a temporary refuge for infirm and destitute women, but it evolved into a convalescent hospital where half the inmates were bedridden with a range of diseases and terminal illnesses requiring professional nursing care. The number of inmates increased inexorably over the years, as the condition of the building declined. The government ignored the changing nature of the Asylum, and it was thanks to Mrs Hicks and her family that the system kept going for as long as it did. It took the move to Newington and an official inquiry to make the collapse of the system publicly known.

In 1888, the Colonial Secretary, acting on the findings of the Government Asylums Inquiry Board, forcibly retired Lucy Hicks from her position as matron of the Newington Asylum. She received a substantial pension of £145 per annum in recognition of her long and devoted service. The family moved to Strathfield, where her husband, William Hicks, died in 1894 following months of illness. Lucy died on 14 July 1909, aged 75, survived by only five of her fourteen children (NSW Death Registration 1909/8648).

Marked Goods: Ownership and Identification

While Matron Hicks and her family had the most enduring impact on the Asylum and Immigration Depot, thousands of individual women passed through the doors of both institutions. As we discussed in 'The Inmates', we know the names of only one hundred or so of these women from historical records, and the archaeological record offers the names of a few more.

Artefacts marked with individuals' names are very rare finds in archaeological contexts. Two have been identified in the Cumberland and Gloucester Streets assemblage of 375,000 sherds in The Rocks (a name stamp for Charles Carlson [CUGL52811] and a tin measure owned by 'G. Briggs' [CUGL52720], see also Iacono 1999:85) and others are known (Crook 2008:228). More than a dozen examples were recovered from the underfloor assemblage at the Hyde Park Barracks (**Table 6.1**).

Names that appeared on medicinal vessels were noted previously, but other unique examples have also been identified. These include a name stamp marked 'T Brown' and a lace-edge handkerchief with 'M Probert' hand-written in ink on one corner. Owners' names were also hand-written on the inside of 3 religious pocket books, all of which were found close together in the north-eastern dormitory on Level 2 (UF28, UF8225 and UF8226). Two pre-date the establishment of the Asylum and these may represent second-hand donations or possessions brought into the institution, rather than representing the names of asylum or immigrant women. They may also have belonged to the institution's library of religious tracts.

A strip of wood from the landing on Level 2 adjacent to the Matron's quarters is marked with the handwritten name '… [indeterminate] Hicks' (UF4282), while another artefact marked with an individual's name is a luggage tag with the inscription 'Francis H[…re]ll'.

---

[36] An Alice Fry came to NSW as a bounty migrant in 1841 at the age of 28. She was listed as a cook who could read and write and a native of Liverpool. She was travelling with Ansom Fry, 24, a labourer native of County Cavan, Ireland. Both could read and write and both were Protestant. (SRNSW 4/4788 & 4/4863, Reels 2134, 1321, 07/08/1841 [NRS 5316, 5314]). This may be the same Alice Fry, future inmate of Hyde Park Asylum.

6. Private Lives

Item	Individual	Artefact	Context
UG1058	T Brown	Name stamp marked 'T Brown'.	L3
UF11500	M Probert	Lace edged handkerchief with 'M Probert' handwritten in ink on one corner.	L3-3: JG10 JS1
UF6624	F Cunningham	Pharmaceutical bottle marked: 'HYDE PARK ASYLUM / Name F Cunningham / Age [blank] / Date of Admission 21 May / The Lotion / ... Cunningham'.	L3-1: JG16 JS10
UF26	Alice Fry	Gin bottle re-used for medicinal purposes: 'Hyde Park Asylum / Name ... Alice Fry / Age ... [nil] / Date of Admission ... [nil / ... [unid]'.	L2-6: JG36 JS13
UF5479	Alice Peacock	Rectangular cotton fragment (52x38mm) with 'Alice Peacock' handwritten in cursive style. Possibly part of a name tag or a marker on a larger piece of fabric.	L2-2: JG51 JS3
UF8226	Ann Sarran	Small leather-bound, hard cover religious book, with brown cursive script on inside front cover 'Ann Sarran [indeterminate].	L2-3: JG27 JS4
UF8225	William and Betty Scott ?	Hardcover leather-bound pocket companion by the Society of Promoting Christian Knowledge, with lead pencil and ink on the lining of the back cover: 'William [surname indet]' & '[Betty Scott?]'; and dates 1830, 1836 [twice] and 1837.	L2-3: JG27 JS3
UF4372	Francis	Cardboard tag with handwritten script 'Francis H... [re?]ll'.	L3-5: JG3 JS2
UF6718	Hanna, Catherine, Alice	Scrap of blue paper with handwritten list of names, no surnames preserved.	L3-7: JG13 JS1
UF207	Cath[erine] Redmond, Isabella Lancashire	Printed form 'Surgeon's Requisition on the C[ap]tain for Stout, Wine, or Brandy / Date 6 August 1865 / [indet] Lucy / Hagan? [indet] / Redmond Cath[erine] / Hew? Robina / Lancashire Isabella / ...t Julia? / ... / G[riff]iths Jane / Miner M[ar]y / Hooper Honora ...'.	Unstrat.
UF28	Thomas Bagnall	Book with embossed leather cover from British and Foreign Bible Society, and handwritten on inside cover: 'Thomas Bagnalls Book 1837'.	L2-3: JG27 JS3
UF17391	Francis ? Grace Bishop	Two fragments of pale blue paper with handwritten brown ink: '... is Grace / Fl[?]ancis / ...ishop / Bishop.	L3-6: JG39 JS3
UF17601	Mrs Harris	Circular wooden disk with handwritten brown ink: 'The Ointment Mrs Harris'.	L3-6: JG39 JS4
UF17946	R D Ward	Printed form for rations to inmates, including arrowroot and sago, porter, wine, brandy, rum and milk, dated 1875, with handwritten 'yesterday' and signed by R D Ward (Surgeon).	L3-3: JG9 JS11
UF4282	... Hicks	Strip of wood with handwritten ink '[indeterminate] Hicks'.	L2-2: JG51 JS3
UF7405	Blanche Ellis	Scrap of paper with name and address on both sides: 'Miss Blanche Ellis / No 41 / Cedron / Regent St / Paddington'.	L2-1: JG22 JS10

Table 6.1: Artefacts marked with the names individual inmates, immigrants and other unknown persons.

Two of the women could be identified from medicinal bottles as inmates of the Asylum. Francis Cunningham is on the list of inmates transferred from the Benevolent Asylum in 1862, but no more is known of her life. Alice Fry was not recorded on any of the inmate lists, but her death certificate lists her address as Hyde Park Asylum. She died on 5 February 1868 of a uterine tumour, aged 56 years.[36]

The remains of several official blue forms reveal the names of a number of immigrant women who arrived on the *General Caulfield* in August 1865 (UF131, UF132 and UF207; **Figure 6.4**). The 'Surgeon's Requisition on the Captain for Stout,

6. Private Lives

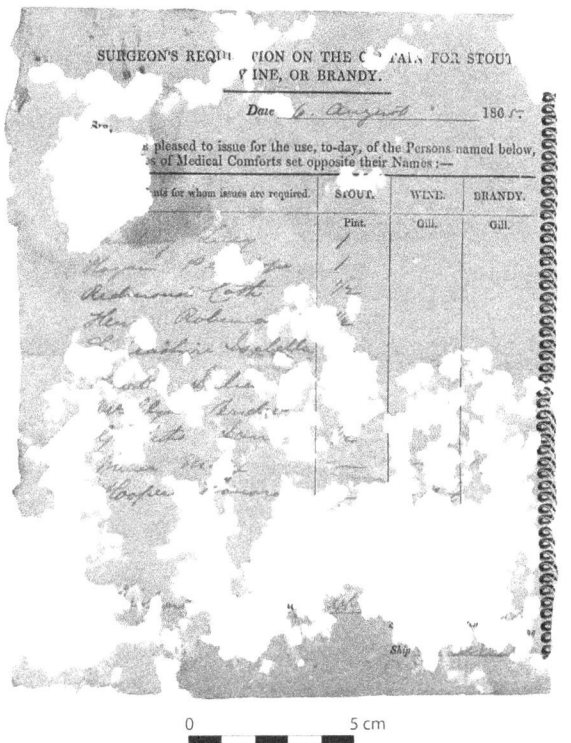

Figure 6.4: Government form regarding medical comforts to immigrants arriving on the *General Caulfield* in August 1865 (UF207; P. Crook 2003).

Wine, or Brandy' allowed for 1 pint or ½ pint of stout to women including Cath[erine] Redmond, Isabella Lancashire, Jane Griffiths, Mary Miner and Honora Hooper.

Ephemera and Keepsakes

In addition to evidence of the daily activities of the institution as a whole, a small number of artefacts from the Hyde Park Barracks assemblage provide insight into the private lives or personal mementoes of the inmates and immigrants. This class of artefacts goes beyond the typical classification of 'personal' artefacts in a regular archaeological assemblage — such as perfume bottles and hair care — although these were also present, and includes items revealing unique, individual behaviours.

The survival of paper and fabric from the assemblage has offered a number of extraordinary finds, objects discarded or lost and preserved as they were in use: a white square cotton handkerchief with an 1869 sixpence tied in one corner (UF160); a flask with a hemmed silk strap (UF4321; **Figure 6.5**); and a cherry liqueur bottle with a hessian stopper in place of a cork (UF6626).

It is unknown what precise function the coin tied in the hanky served. While it may have been used to weigh down a cover for a jar or bowl, the presence of only one weight suggests the purpose was probably to secure the coin, and then tie it, chatelaine-style, to a skirt or apron. Similarly, it is unknown who may have required a strap to carry the flask, but it too was probably tied to a skirt or worn around the wrist.

The Hessian-stoppered liqueur bottle presents another mystery. While initially made as a container for Danish liqueur and cordial maker, P. F. Heering, the bottle may well have been reused for medicinal tonics or lotions. However, the presence of a makeshift stopper in place of a cork — easily obtained from the Dispensary — and its survival under the floor boards alongside the window in the south-eastern ward on Level 3 (where repaired boards may have been easy to lift) does suggest deliberate concealment of contraband liquor. This area was also used to hide or store a cache of complete tobacco pipes.

Another remarkable item is the shellcraft cover of a pocket album, possibly of photographs or postcards (UF29; **Figure 6.6**), found beneath the floor of the northern dormitory on Level 2. The

Figure 6.5: Flask bottle with silk strap (UF4321; P. Davies 2009).

Figure 6.6: Shellcraft cover of a pocket album, possibly of photographs or postcards. The spine (UF3339) is marked 'FORGET ME NOT' (UF29; P. Crook 2004).

89

Figure 6.7: Remains of handwritten list, possibly a list of personal possessions (UF6716; P. Davies 2009).

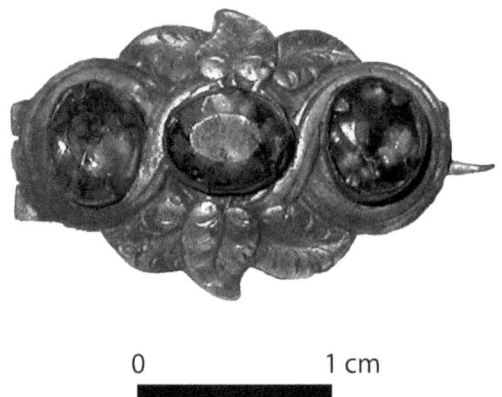

Figure 6.8: Gilt-brass brooch with three pink glass gems (UF64; P. Davies 2010).

spine is marked 'FORGET ME NOT', and the remains of the colour lithograph on the cover depict a park-like scene with strolling figures, bordered with a double row of shells. The item appears to be a keepsake in the Victorian sentimental tradition, and probably belonged to one of the young immigrant women.

There is also a paper fragment in the collection which appears to be a list of personal possessions (UF6716; **Figure 6.7**). The handwritten document includes some apparently phonetic spelling: 'Umbraler', probably meaning 'Umbrella' — particularly if pronounced in a broad Irish or Scots brogue. The '2 Punks' may be old terms for a shoemaker's punch or awl.

Small personal items and jewellery were also found in the underfloor spaces, including brooches (n=5) and gems (n=12). Costume jewellery was popular in the 19th century as a clothing accessory, as friendship mementoes and for mourning (Mezey 2005:30). Brooches from Level 3 include a copper alloy wire wound into an S-shaped double spiral (UF11544) and a gilt-brass brooch with three pink oval-facetted glass gems set within delicately incised leaves (UF64; **Figure 6.8**). From Level 2 there was a small decorative pin with a waratah-shaped shield (UF1608) and a leather brooch in the shape of a butterfly with flowers embroidered on each wing (UF17868). Imitation or paste gems were also found in small numbers on both Level 2 (n=5) and Level 3 (n=7).

There were large quantities of beads found on both Levels 2 and 3 (**Table 6.2**), which may have served as cheap jewellery items or decorative flourishes to clothing. Most beads were made of glass and represent a wide range of colours, but there are also examples in wood and ceramic. Some of the wooden beads appear to be modified seeds linked with ferrous chains, while others may derive from lace bobbins or rosaries (see 'Religious Instruction and Devotion').

CHILDREN AT THE HYDE PARK BARRACKS

Children were a small but constant presence in the Hyde Park Barracks over the years. The family of Matron Hicks lived in quarters on Level 2, and between 1849 and 1855 the Depot also housed the wives and children of convicts brought out to the colony to be reunited with their husbands and fathers. In addition, the female children of newly arrived immigrant families were often brought to the Barracks to provide relief from the crowded conditions on ship while their parents remained on board in Sydney Harbour (*SMH* 24 May 1878, p.5). The sojourn of these children in the Barracks, however, was unlikely to have been more than a few days. Several thousand Irish female orphans also passed through the Barracks between 1848 and 1852, but they were unlikely to have possessed much in the way of toys (see 'Charity and Immigration in 19th-Century NSW').

Lucy Hicks had 14 children between 1850 and 1879 (**Table 6.3**), five of whom died at young ages. The family lived at the Barracks from 1861 to 1882 before moving to premises nearby in Phillip Street. During the years of her tenure as Matron of the Depot and Asylum, the Applewhaite-Hicks children knew the Barracks as their home.

A small number of items from the underfloor collection can be directly related to children, including marbles, dolls, game pieces and other

Beads	Level 2	Level 3	Total
Bone	–	1	1
Carnelian	10	1	11
Ceramic	–	14	14
Copper alloy	1	1	2
Glass	413	264	677
Wood/seed	9	53	62
Unidentified	19	34	53
Total	*452*	*368*	*820*

Table 6.2: Bead materials.

Name	Born	Died	Age at death
Mary Lucy Adelaide Applewhaite	28 Oct. 1850	21 Sept. 1885	34 years
Philip L. Applewhaite	1852	1890	38 years
Elizabeth J. M. Applewhaite	1855	1931	76 years
Lucy Holmes Applewhaite	1857	1857	4 days
Emily A. Applewhaite	1858	1865	7 years
Helen Alice Maud Applewhaite	c. 1861	1944	83 years
John Charles Benyon Applewhaite	1862	14 Sept. 1863	18 months
Clara Ann Applewhaite	1865	1939	74 years
William H. Applewhaite	1868	1940	72 years
Lucy E. M. R. Hicks	1871	1892	20 years
John Raby Hicks	1874	1941	67 years
Claud Arthur Raby Hicks	15 Feb. 1876	16 Feb. 1876	1 day
Kate R. Hicks	19 Apr. 1878	20 Apr. 1878	1 day
Francis A. R. Hicks	1879	1896	19 years

Table 6.3: The children of Matron Lucy Hicks, formerly Lucy Applewhaite (Crook and Murray 2006:87–88; Hughes 2004:148–168; NSW Death registration 1909/8648).

	Level 1	Level 2	Level 3	Total
Dolls and tea sets	2	3	1	6
Marbles	23	20	12	55
Game pieces	6	13	2	21
Blocks	–	2	–	2
Dominoes	2	1	–	3
Cards	1	6	1	8
Toys	–	4	1	5
Unidentified	–	–	1	1
Total	*34*	*49*	*18*	*101*

Table 6.4: Child-related artefacts.

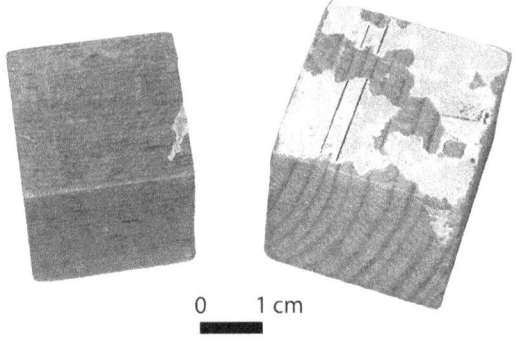

Figure 6.9: Wooden toy blocks with traces of illustrated paper (UF88; P. Davies 2010).

Figure 6.11: Printed cardboard toy figure (UF4285; P. Davies 2010).

Figure 6.10: Miniature pedestal fruit bowl from doll house set (UF10123; P. Davies 2010).

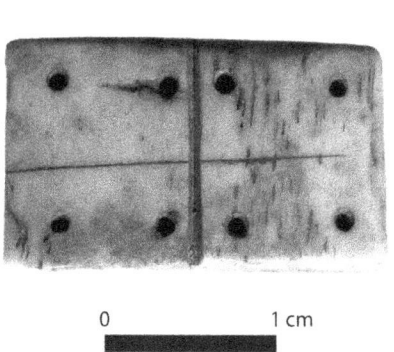

Figure 6.12: Small bone domino, probably handmade (UF89; P. Crook 2004).

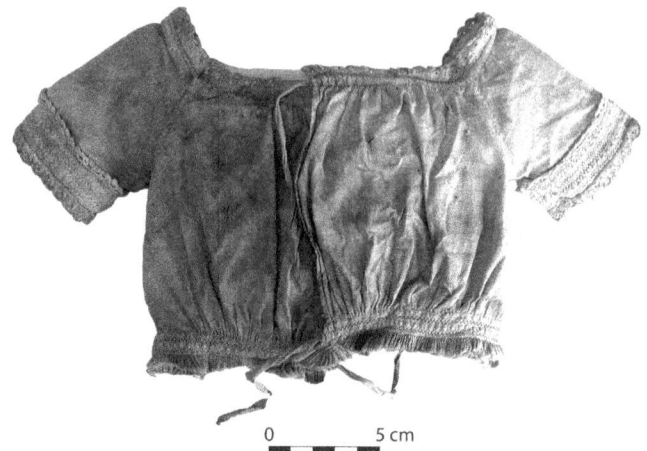

Figure 6.13: Infant cotton bodice with decorated bands at sleeves, waist and neck (UF930; P. Davies 2009).

	Level 1	Level 2	Level 3	Total
Slate boards	3	4	1	8
Slate pencils	19	40	8	67
Total	*22*	*44*	*9*	*75*

Table 6.5: Slate writing equipment.

objects (**Table 6.4**; **Figures 6.9, 6.10, 6.11, 6.12**). The most likely source of toys and child-related items is Matron Hicks' family. Eighteen of the 20 marbles from Level 2, for example, came from the short corridor between the family's rooms. All but one of the gaming tokens, however, came from the underground collection and may relate more to earlier convict activity.

A beautifully preserved infant's bodice was found beneath the Level 3 landing (UF930; **Figure 6.13**). The garment is hand-sewn in white cotton, with drawstrings at the waist and neck, and embroidered decoration at the neck, sleeves and waist. It may have been worn by several of the Applewhaite-Hicks children, although it is also about the right size for a large doll (White 1966:81–82).

Slates and slate pencils are also well represented in the underfloor collection. Although these items were used in a wide array of domestic, commercial and educational contexts through the 19th century and beyond, they are most often associated with children and schooling (Davies 2005; Davies and Ellis 2005). The distribution of slates includes 20 pencils and 2 slate board fragments from Matron Hicks' quarters, suggesting that the Applewhaite-Hicks children used and lost slates in the course of their lessons. It is unclear, however, if they attended a local school or if the older children taught the younger ones, although state elementary education was well established in New South Wales by the 1860s (Barcan 1965:142). Lucy Hicks also employed a governess in the early 1880s to help care for, and possibly teach, her younger children (Hughes 2004:208). Examples of slate pencils from the collection were mostly 4–5.5mm in diameter, typical of standard, mass-produced slate pencils of the period. Only 9 fragments were recovered from Level 3 (**Table 6.5**), supporting the hypothesis that in the Hyde Park Asylum, slate writing equipment was used by the children in educational activities, rather than writing or record keeping by or for the Asylum women.

7
THE ARCHAEOLOGY OF 19TH-CENTURY INSTITUTIONS

Historical archaeologists have been interested in the archaeology of institutions for a long time. These institutions range from missions and government outposts regulating the lives of indigenous people, to more mainstream entities such as hospitals, orphanages, asylums, workhouses, almshouses, schools, charitable institutions, or places of corrections such as gaols and juvenile homes. In recent years the nature of that interest has begun to change away from a focus on the institution *per se* to a consideration of the impact of institutions on the lives of their inmates (e.g. Beisaw and Gibb 2009). Thus what was already a highly varied field of investigation, due to the great range of institutions, the organisations responsible for their creation and management, and the diverse *purposes* of such institutions, has become even more complex. In some contexts institutions are the embodiments of ideologies, in others they are simply places where charity might be given or accepted, or where the sick can be made well or their passing eased. Thus our first point is very simple — the archaeology of institutions is no single pursuit, and the nature of our inquiries can intersect with a wide diversity of issues that in themselves might well demand a diversity of approaches.

Surveys of the field, such as De Cunzo's (2006, 2009) recent reviews, might be read as tending to argue the opposite. In her view the institutions that archaeologists need to focus on are those of reform, confinement and social change: 'Places of reform, surveillance, confinement, protection, control, ritual, punishment, resistance, inscription, segregation, labor, purification and discipline' (2006:167). For her the problematic of institutional archaeology is straightforward and linked with the archaeology of social institutions in the modernising world of the 18th century and afterwards:

> ... almshouses, poorhouses, prisons, asylums, hospitals, and schools. Material culture is used to accomplish and thwart institutional goals; as students of material culture archaeologists offer vital insights into the cultures and histories of institutions. (De Cunzo 2006:167)

and

> The material culture — architecture and landscape, furnishings, tools, dress, art, texts, food, all of it — is consciously as well as unconsciously planned to play a proactive role in accomplishing the institution's goals and purposes. (De Cunzo 2009:208)

Similar notions are at play in the idea of institutions as 'powered cultural landscapes', where physical spaces, modified by human activity, encode power relations (Spencer-Wood and Baugher 2010). In this model, institutions become sites of class tension and gender dynamics, power inequalities and heterarchy (Baugher 2010). In a similar way, archaeologies of internment focus on control and coercion in a variety of prison and labour camps (Myers and Moshenska 2011). Flowing from this is the notion of such places as 'total institutions' (Goffman 1961) and the connection of discourse about the design and operation of such places to more abstract notions of social control, discipline and behavioural modification (see Foucault 1973, 1977). Such an approach is strongly evident in Casella's (2007, 2009, 2011) recent work on the archaeology of institutions, with its emphasis on incarceration and confinement of 'the other', while Tarlow's recent review of the archaeology of workhouses in Britain stressed their role as 'coercive institutions of containment and reform' (Tarlow 2007:137). However, the archaeology of institutions also intersects with other discourses and bodies of knowledge, such as archaeologies of the body, and of sexuality, and 'queer' archaeology (e.g. Casella 2000a, 2000b, 2001c, 2002; De Cunzo 1995, 2001). Such archaeologies are based around the notion that total institutions act in totalising ways, that all such institutions serve such purposes, and that the primary goal of an archaeology of institutions is to map out the ways in which buildings and other items of material culture, when integrated with other documentary data, contribute to the ideological objectives of institutions.

While this is one legitimate reading of the goals of an archaeology of institutions, we argue that it contains overstatements that open the way for a less mechanistic (or perhaps nuanced) approach. The Panopticon or total-institution model overlooks, for example, many of the subtleties involved in the expression of relationships between authorities and inmates (Driver 1993:13). Goffman himself devotes much of his discussion in *Asylums* to considering the failures of surveillance and the ways inmates avoid regulation. Even De Cunzo (2009:207) has recently expressed uneasiness about such totalising views, where archaeological analysis serves simply to illustrate the workings of a pre-determined ideology.

We fully accept that managing the poor, the deviant, the sick, or the criminal generated technologies and processes of management that allowed for the treatment of individuals to occur at an industrial scale during the 19th century, but we do not see a logical distinction between institutions such as gaols and others such as factories or the military. In our reading one of the critical elements of modernity was the institutionalisation of many aspects of life 'outside' such totalising places. Flowing from this is the suspicion that institutions were generally far less successful in achieving their goals of punishment, modification, purification, etc. than they or their historians have claimed. Again we are presented with information that can be read as evidence of 'resistance' as distinct from evidence of corruption and ineptitude, or more simply, of a yawning gulf between the rhetoric of institutions and what actually transpired. Finally, in the bulk of cases archaeological analysis is focused more on buildings as items of material culture and on the analysis of written documents describing the purposes of such places, than on the material culture that is found on the sites. While there is no problem in drawing connections between the design of buildings and the totalising goals of the managers of such institutions, a limited recourse to other items of material culture, or in other cases simply a very limited array of material culture to work with, can lead to over interpretation of available evidence.

In the case of the Hyde Park Barracks many of these tenets of the archaeology of institutions are difficult to apply. On the one hand we have a built space that changes its purpose and its internal organisation over time. This is not a building designed in the modern way to discipline or punish, merely to accommodate people who had been punished by transportation, emigrants who were housed temporarily, and sick and destitute women who were in charitable care. After its closure as a convict barracks, the building was no longer associated with punishment or indeed with the modification of behaviour. While it is true that the inmates were offered pastoral as well as physical care, and there were 'regulations', we have noted many instances where authority was exercised in less rigid ways. The Hyde Park Barracks has an abundance of material culture that provides evidence that can elucidate aspects of life in this particular institution over some 40 years of its history.

The literature created by the archaeology of charitable care and reform is diverse and encompasses a range of institutions funded by government and church agencies, servicing the needs of diverse groups of disadvantaged and vulnerable members of the community. These include young 'fallen' women (De Cunzo 1995, 2001), indigenes (Birmingham 1992; Deetz 1963; Graham 1998; Lydon 2009; Middleton 2008; Sutton 2003), lepers (Prangnell 1999), the mentally ill (Piddock 2001a, 2007, 2009), orphans (Feister 2009; Godden Mackay 1997; Hughes 1992), dispossessed peasants and agricultural labourers (Fewer 2000), convicts and prisoners (Casella 2007; Casella and Fredericksen 2001; Egloff and Morrison 2001; Gibbs 2001, 2010; Gojak 2001; Jackman 2001; Karskens 2003; Kerr 1984; Morrison 2001; Nobles 2000; Oleksy 2008; Prentice and Prentice 2000; Starr 2001) and the poor (Baugher 2001; Baugher and Lenik 1997; Baugher and Spencer-Wood 2002; Divers 2004; Elia and Wesolowsky 1991; Huey 2001; Lucas 1999; Peña 2001; Piddock 2001b; Spencer-Wood 2001, 2009; Spencer-Wood and Baugher 2001).

Many of the studies of refuges for the poor focus on almshouses and poorhouses dating to the late 18th and early 19th centuries, and many have emphasised the labour of the workhouse inmates and its perceived redeeming qualities (e.g. Lucas 1999; McCartney 1987; Peña 2001). The only institution directly comparable in Australia to Hyde Park is the Adelaide Destitute Asylum (1849–1917), but the archaeological remains of these two institutions differ greatly (Piddock 2001b). The artefacts of the Adelaide Asylum were heavily culled and those that remain are largely unprovenanced (Megaw 1986; Szekeres 1987), whereas at the Hyde Park Barracks the artefacts can be traced to within a few metres of the point of their original recovery.[37] Consequently, Piddock's study concentrated on spatial analysis of the buildings of the Adelaide Asylum, and while it is of considerable interest in and of itself, it is not a comparable case study.

LIFE AT THE HYDE PARK BARRACKS

The Hyde Park Barracks does not readily conform to our conventional understanding of a 19th-century institution. It was divided between two different arms of the colonial government — one ushering in the workforce and life blood of a growing society; the other caring for the 'poor friendless old creatures', some the residue of past cultural structures now in decay. Its Matron of 24 years, Lucy Hicks, had a free hand to shape the daily routines of Asylum life and seemed to do so unaffected by the broader intellectual debates about workhouse control. Due to changes in its use, and in later 19th-century colonial politics, descriptions of the Barracks in the Sydney press plummeted from a well-run facility in the hands of a fair and competent mistress, to an establishment punctured with the neglect and

---

[37] While the joist spaces were narrow, items could move or be moved the full span of the room.

physical abuse of inmates, the abuse of property and privilege by the Matron and her family, and general disorder.

The archaeological assemblage from the Barracks offers a different perspective — a glimpse of daily life, not only of the institutional routine, but also of fleeting and probably private moments in the lives of the inmates, visitors and the matron's family, who shared the space. Trapped beneath the floorboards for over 100 years, the minutiae of beads, buttons, pins, newsprint, fabric and bottle glass offer a different means of interrogating the lives within the Asylum walls. Although the collection is small relative to the thousands of women (and their possessions) that passed through the corridors, it is significant. The collection has shed light on everyday practices such as the lighting of pipes, the dispensing of medicines, or mending of garments, that were occasionally mentioned in the 'official' account of daily life recorded by Commissions of Inquiry.

As a result the archaeological record of the Barracks provides an opportunity to create a less mechanistic view of almshouses as being institutions that were run on the same rigid lines and that were inevitably oppressive of their inmates. In this way a detailed archaeological record of the Barracks acts in the same way as the archaeology of 'slums' has promoted an understanding that the residential housing of working-class people was not inevitably the 'slum' portrayed in popular media (Mayne and Murray 2001).

Individuals used the institution strategically as one response to the related problems of poverty, illness, injury and infirmity. For their part the authorities, including Matron Hicks, members of the Asylums Board and visiting ladies, were not all-powerful and concerned only with reforming the inmates within the walls of the Asylum. Their responses to the women in their charge mixed prejudice and respectability with compassion and humanity. The infirm and destitute entered the institution, and negotiated its customs and boundaries for the days, weeks and even years in which they called the Asylum home.

Daily Labour

Women at the Hyde Park Asylum did nearly all the domestic work of the institution, including cooking, cleaning, sewing and washing. While most of the inmates were elderly and infirm, Matron Hicks retained a number who were strong enough to do the heavy work while earning a small daily gratuity. Sewing and patching were gentler, but still demanding tasks, which served a useful and practical function, as well as reinforcing the imperative of work in return for sustenance and the prevention of idleness. Some women sewed all day, sitting near the windows for light and the fireplaces for warmth, while others sewed in bed. Mary London explained that 'when I can sew, I sew; I do nothing but sewing' (Q3135, Government Asylums Inquiry Board 1887:507).

Sewing was, in fact, a common task in institutional settings during the 19th century. In the 1860s, men and women at the Melbourne Benevolent Asylum were employed in sewing, tailoring and cobbling boots, making most of the inmates' clothing on the premises (Kehoe 1998:32). Men and women at the New Norfolk Hospital for the Insane in Tasmania were also employed in making and repairing clothes and footwear (Piddock 2007:179). At the Beechworth Lunatic Asylum in Victoria, 200 female inmates repaired more than 50,000 clothing and bedding items during the year 1884, in what was clearly a large-scale commercial operation (Inspector of Lunatic Asylums 1885:56).

In one important respect, however, the Asylum differed from many contemporary charitable institutions — it did not have a commercial laundry to recover its costs. Many other refuges exploited their free labour force by selling their services into the marketplace, thereby making up the shortfall between private subscriptions and government contributions. The Sydney Female Refuge Society, for example, advertised 'Washing and Needlework Done at Reasonable Rates', which succeeded in defraying the expenses of the Society (Godden 1987:301; Sydney Female Refuge Society 1856:4). A central feature of the Geelong Female Refuge in the 1860s was its laundry, a 'sanctimonious sweatshop' and reliable money earner that made up for the scarcity in public donations (Swain 1985:15). The Convent of the Good Shepherd Magdalen Asylum in Melbourne operated one of the largest commercial laundries in the colony (Kovesi 2006:144–147), while at the Adelaide Destitute Asylum the laundry work was so strenuous that the women went on strike in 1888 (Geyer 1994:28). In this way the institutions efficiently combined economy of operation with the obligation for inmates to perform productive labour in the pursuit of moral training.

The work of those at the Hyde Park Asylum, on the other hand, was focused inward. Their cleaning and sewing was mutually self-supporting — all the inmates benefited from the work each woman performed. While much of the labour was undoubtedly tedious and tiring, it was also necessary and economical. The tasks were familiar and respectable, and more or less the same as those the women would have performed in private homes as domestic servants or in their own homes as daughters, wives and mothers. This was in stark contrast to the workhouses of England and Ireland, which, especially in the 1830s and 1840s, invoked a 'severe and repulsive' discipline (Thompson 1980:295) to ensure that arduous labour was not only a deterrent but even a punishment for the 'crime' of destitution. Workhouse labour was focused not only on self-sufficiency but also on profitability (Markus

1993:104). The work of picking oakum and grinding corn was directed outside the walls, with products sent away from the inmates who created them.

There is little evidence at the Hyde Park Barracks, however, of the worst excesses of the industrial workhouses of Britain, in spite of several historians' claim to the contrary (e.g. Jalland 2002:206; O'Brien 1988:52; Ramsland 1986:160). The architecture of the building, and the many government agencies competing for space in the complex, meant that punitive labour for several hundred mostly frail, sick and elderly inmates was never feasible, irrespective of whether it was ever desirable to parliamentarians of New South Wales. There were no cells for isolation and solitude, such as those at the Magdalen Asylum in Philadelphia (De Cunzo 1995:39), but open dormitories where the women were free to move around as they pleased. The original regulations drawn up for the management of the Asylum were long ignored by Matron Hicks. Instead, she exercised her own discretion, establishing routines that were sufficiently flexible and humane to accommodate the needs of the inmates.

'Making do': Institutional Consumption and Private Adaptation

The government outlay on destitute asylums rose from £8995 in 1862 when it took over many of the responsibilities of the Benevolent Society, to £26,885 in 1885, just prior to the second major overhaul of the administration of these institutions. The rate per inmate across the four asylums (Hyde Park, Macquarie Street Parramatta, George Street Parramatta and Liverpool) fluctuated between about £10 and £15 per annum, averaging £13 14s. 8¾d. over the period. Until the mid-1880s the Hyde Park Asylum was usually the most cost effective of the four, having the lowest cost per inmate: £11 2s. 5¼d. in 1871, £14 6s. 11¾d. in 1876, and £15 3s. 2d. in 1885 (Government Asylums Board 1872:406; 1875:928; 1885:720). This was a source of pride for Matron Hicks:

> When Sir Charles Cowper brought them [the old women] here he said that he wished the place to be as self supporting as possible, and that has been my great aim. (Q2353, Public Charities Commission 1874:76)

Most of the food consumed at the Barracks was supplied on contract under the direction of the Board, in consultation with the Matron. Bread, meat, vegetables, grains, dairy produce and fuel were supplied to the Asylum on a daily or weekly basis. Fabrics used for Asylum garb were ordered by the bolt from local wholesalers, under approval of the Board but in consultation with the matron (Q2356-2357, Public Charities Commission 1874:76). Kitchen, laundry and mess equipment were probably also ordered from local suppliers on the government books, and the purchase of substantial appliances such as stoves and boilers was arranged directly by the Colonial Secretary's office. Medical supplies and consumables were arranged by the Visiting Surgeon and Medical Attendant. Gifts, in the form of tea and sugar, flowers and reading matter were also brought on site by kind-hearted visitors.

In spite of this climate of wholesale, mess-hall consumption individuals experienced some degree of control over their material world. It is true that the female inmates were disrobed and bathed on admission to the Asylum and supplied with Asylum clothing, but they retained their own garments for visits away from the place. The archaeological evidence suggests that the clothes they wore inside were standardised but varied subtly according to print design and colour, and the ability of individuals to modify garments for fit and comfort — they were not necessarily restricted to wearing shapeless institutional garb.

It is also likely that the women were able to retain whatever personal possessions had survived the impoverished circumstances that led them to seek government assistance. The possession of too many personal effects, however, probably disqualified potential inmates from entry to the Asylum in the first place. While it is unlikely that they had bags or trunks in the Asylum, small pouches and pockets in aprons allowed the women to keep personal items close to hand, such as a pipe and tobacco, a few coins, or a prayer book or rosary. Taking advantage of loose floorboards to stash objects was another, perhaps riskier, way of hiding private possessions. Keeping objects out of sight may also have limited opportunities for theft, a common source of conflict in 19th-century benevolent asylums (Twomey 2002:68). Those who were able-bodied could earn small wages to purchase additional tea, sugar and tobacco from other inmates, and these funds could also be spent wherever they chose on their days of leave in the bustling markets of Sydney.

Tobacco also served as a means of small-scale institutional exchange. Mary Kennedy and Margaret Heggarty, who were inmates at the Asylum for more than 20 years, bought tobacco rations from those who did not smoke and sold them to those who did. Mary Wright, an elderly blind inmate, traded 'a box of matches or a bit of tobacco' for someone to 'lead her around' (Q2279, Q3185, Government Asylums Inquiry Board 1887:488, 508).

The Immigrant Depot women, too, had control over their goods and chattels, but within the confines of the Barracks those on short stays probably had limited access to their trunks, and only the Matron could unlock the fancy work they began onboard the ship.

Despite these limitations, the remains of many private possessions were recovered from under the boards. These include not only the items bearing the tags of ownership, such as the handkerchief and name stamp, but also those preserved in their *state of consumption* — the hessian stopper in the liqueur bottle, the silk strap around the bottle, and the sixpence tied in the hanky. Each bears the mark of a crafty, nameless individual making use of the limited resources available to perform tasks or behave in ways not catered for in the Asylum's operational budgets. Thrift is also apparent in the repair of broken clay pipes, cotton thread wrapped around a wedge of cardboard, and the many patches sewn onto holes in garments.

However, this 'making-do' strategy was not limited to the private customs of the inmates. The medical attendant or ward nurses were also 'making do' by using general purpose bottles and wooden discs when prescription bottles and labels were hard to come by.

While the practice of 'making do' is a phenomenon invariably associated with the poorer classes, or periods of extreme economic hardship (such as during the Great Depression), it is also frequently documented as being practised by pioneer settlers in remote regions, where distance from metropolitan retailers (and wholesalers) made supplies costly or uncertain. Rustic bush furniture, such as meat safes and pantries, buckets made from kerosene tins, bottles cut down into jars, and mattresses sewn from chaff bags, are iconic artefacts in this class (Isaacs 1990). The use of common newsprint cut into scalloped or saw tooth patterns to serve as mantelpiece lambrequins is also well documented (Lane and Serle 1990:248, 325; see also Praetzellis and Praetzellis 2004:162–166).

It is surprising then to discover an assemblage of makeshift material culture in the centre of a commercial hub such as Sydney in the 19th century. It demonstrates how those on the economic and social margins of society can be disengaged from the marketplace in their midst. Assemblages from institutional sites such as the Barracks also afford us an opportunity to study organised consumption on a large scale. While these artefacts represent only a small slice of the assemblage, they provide unique and remarkable insights into the management and utilitarian exploitation of material culture in the 19th century.

Improvement and Spirituality

The Hyde Park Barracks is a special case because it served both destitute and infirm women and arriving immigrants, and was never intended to be a vehicle of reform. It was instead a place of refuge, concerned more with the health of many of its inmates rather than with reforming their characters or exacting punishment for crimes, either of omission or commission. The Hyde Park Asylum was an institution that enclosed and confined a group of women based on their infirmity and destitution. The spartan meals, plain clothes and daily labour, however, were more about economy and convenience than control and discipline. The rapid, virtually overnight, creation of the institution in 1862 was an *ad hoc* response to a range of social, economic and political imperatives, rather than a carefully orchestrated plan of moral reform. It functioned as a workaday negotiation between its dedicated matron and the needs of several hundred women, circumscribed by the demands of thrift, hygiene and basic humanity. The complex was not hidden away on the edge of town like a prison, cemetery, abattoir or some other 'dirty' establishment, but was located right in the heart of a thriving metropolitan centre. In spite of attempts to separate the inmates from other users of the complex, the women moved about their allotted spaces freely, and instead of high walls they enjoyed attractive views over parklands and churches and busy streets outside.

The notion of 'improvement' has recently been explored by Tarlow (2007) to examine the processes of social and personal reform that occurred in Britain during the later 18th and early 19th centuries. Authorities established a range of institutions to support paupers, orphans and other marginal social groups, in the expectation that they would help to re-shape society and improve its moral and economic foundations. Asylums established in Australia during the 19th century often had similar 'improving' goals, expressed through such regimes as the 'moral treatment' of lunatic inmates in South Australia and Tasmania (Piddock 2001a, 2007, 2009). Material from the Hyde Park Asylum, especially in the form of religious tracts, provides evidence of attempts by clergymen, missionaries and other middle-class reformers, to enhance the moral, material and spiritual condition of a particular group of institutional inmates.

Tracts were a product of the evangelical revivals of the 18th and early-19th centuries. Evangelical doctrine promoted salvation by faith in Jesus Christ, a Puritan morality, and commitment to a life of holiness through prayer and Bible-reading. An important manifestation of this movement was the publication of thousands of cheap tracts for distribution to the poor, sick and desperate. Evangelical visitors brought large quantities of religious tracts into the Barracks and distributed them among the women. While it is unclear the extent to which the messages of such literature were read and absorbed by the women, the quantity of material reflects the efforts of outsiders to improve the moral condition of vulnerable inmates.

There are also items, especially from the Catholic tradition, that suggest a more personal spiritual practice. Rosaries and devotional medals were found exclusively on the southern rooms of Level 3, suggesting that this side of the building was for Catholic inmates, while the north side was for Protestants. This segregation reflects the wider sectarian division that characterised Australian society at this time.

Concluding Remarks

The historical archaeology of the Hyde Park Barracks is unique for a number of reasons. The preservation of such a large and diverse assemblage of paper, fabric and other materials in the dry cavity spaces under the floors is simply unparalleled in historical archaeology in Australia, and in the Anglophone world. The well documented history of the building provides a rare opportunity to directly link the artefact assemblages with particular phases of occupational history, specifically the Immigration Depot and Government Asylum for Infirm and Destitute Women. These institutions in themselves were unique in their time, and their management under the one Matron, Lucy Hicks, for 24 years makes them an exceptional example in the history of 19th-century institutions.

This remarkable case study gives cause to reflect on the attempts by the New South Wales Government to find a bed for every sick and indigent person in one of their four benevolent asylums, and their success as a bureaucracy in a political landscape of limited surveillance of publicly funded institutions. Within this meta-machinery of the institution lie the public and private histories of the Hyde Park Asylum itself, its inmates and governors. It is the story of private and public lives, and of a remarkable, if fallible woman, Lucy Hicks, whose family history is tightly interwoven with the history of the Asylum.

This Archaeology of Institutional Confinement merely touches upon the many facets of the world inside and outside the institution. The archaeological studies of medical care, religious comfort, clothing, bureaucracy and making-do at the Hyde Park Barracks provide incentives to foster this integration of archaeological and historical information.

Above all the historical archaeology of the Hyde Park Barracks demonstrates that an archaeology of institutions can do more than support or challenge the Dickensian view of Asylum life, or compare and contrast patterns in architectural typology. It can detect the provision of care and comfort within the broad processes of control and governance, it can explore the private and public facets of a diverse range of institutions, and it can elucidate the individual histories of the people who lived and worked inside the institution's walls.

Of course what we are left with is more than a set of oppositions between the power to dominate and control and the power to resist. Although there is little doubt that the archaeology of institutions can (and indeed does) allow us to explore the power of the state and its capacities to ensure discipline through surveillance and confinement, it is also true that not all institutions during this period existed to achieve such ends. At the Barracks there is abundant evidence of the complexity of such institutions where ambiguities in power relations were played out in the everyday world of lives being led in the expectation of a better life — either in this world or the next.

Appendix 1
Institutional occupants of the Hyde Park Barracks

(Source: Historic Houses Trust 2003:9)

1819–1848	Male government-assigned convicts
1819–1848	Deputy Superintendent of Convicts
c.1830–1848	Principal Superintendent of Convicts
1830–1848	Court of General Sessions
1831–1841	Board for the Assignment of Servants
1848–1886	Agent for Immigration
1848–1886	Female Immigration Depot
1848–1852	Irish Female Orphans
1848–1856	Government Printing Office
1856–1857	Stamp Office
1856–1859	Court of Requests
1856–1860	Department of the Chief Inspector of Distilleries
1857–1886	Vaccine Institute
1857	Department of the Agent for Church and School Estates
1858–1978	Sydney District Court
1861–1870	NSW Volunteer Rifle Corps
1862–1886	Government Asylum for Infirm and Destitute Women
1862–1907	City Coroner
1887–1951	Master in Lunacy Court and Offices/Protective Jurisdiction
1887–1896	Registrar of Copyright
1887	Registrar of Weights and Measures Office
1887–1970	Supreme Court Judges
1888–1898	Registrar of Patents Office
1888–1914	Master in Equity, Court and Offices
1888–1914	Bankruptcy Court
1888–1903, 1915–1961	Clerk of the Peace
1888–1913	Curator of Intestate Estates
1893–1915	Probate Court and Offices
1901–1938	Court of Review
1901–1979	Court of Marine Inquiry
1904–1910, 1919	Land Appeal Court
1905–1910	Patents Office and Library
1908–1911	Industrial Disputes Office
1908–1914	NSW Registrar, Commonwealth Conciliation and Arbitration Court
1911–1914	Industrial Court
1912–1927	Industrial Arbitration Court
1914	Office of the Undersecretary, Department of Labour and Industry
1915–1920	Necessary Commodities Control Commission
1915–1917	Wheat Acquisition Board
1917	Railway and Tramway Boardroom
1917	Public Trustee
1919–1944	Legal Aid Office
1921–1922	Profiteering Prevention Court
1922–1956, 1976–1979	Land and Valuation Court
1927–1977	Industrial Commission of NSW
1943	Chambers of the Public Defender
1944–1964	Court Reporting Branch
1979–1984	Department of Public Works Conservation
1984–2001	Parole Board/Offenders Review Board
1984–1990	Museum of Applied Arts and Sciences
1990–	Historic Houses Trust of New South Wales

Appendix 2
Inmates from the Destitute Asylum

(Sources: Government Asylums Inquiry Board 1887; Berry 2001; Hughes 2004:52–127))

Name	DoB	Birthplace	Admission	Years at HPB	Condition
Eliza Allen			1875	9	
Anne Ballard			1883	3	
Agnes Barr	1826		15.2.1862	24	Asylum's oldest inmate
Sarah Bath			1876	10	Bed-ridden; abdominal tumour
Bridget Belcher			1862		From Benevolent Asylum
Emma Bergin			1882	4	Sore leg
Mary Bradley			1866	20	
Eliza Brown	1779		1.3.1862		Transported in 1834 on *Numa*
Mary Burns			1882	4	
Ellen Burns			1862		From Benevolent Asylum
Eliza Burns			1867	19	
Mary Butler	1814		1866	20	
Elizabeth Carroll			1880		
Mary Ann Carter					
Ellen Clarke			1877		
Alice Clifton	1839		1862		Poor eyesight; prostitute
Eliza Clyde		England	15.2.1862		From Benevolent Asylum
Rose Collins			15.2.1862	4	Convict; transferred to Port Macquarie
Harriet Cook			1881	5	
Elizabeth Cross			1876	10	
Bridget Cullen	1814	Longford, Ireland	18.10.1884	2	Memory failing, blind & almost deaf
Francis Cunningham			1862		
Mary Dalley			1.1.1886		
?? Dawes					Very deaf
Hannah Dodd		Ireland	15.2.1862		Dementia, alcoholism
Honora Everard	c. 1830	Scotland			Blind; discharged for impertinence
Barbara Field			1883	3	
Mary Fitzpatrick	1804		Nov. 1864		Sound mind but destitute
Alice Fry	1812				Died 1868 from uterine tumour
Margaret Gannon			1880	6	

Name	DoB	Birthplace	Admission	Years at HPB	Condition
Kate Gilmore			1881	5	Suffered from 'fits'
Ann Griffiths			July 1876		Blind
Margaret Haggerty			1863	23	
Ellen Holmes			1881	5	
Ellen Howard	1850		1886		Paralysed
Amelia Howe	1841	England	1862		Husband in gaol
Johanna Hunt	1812		15.2.1862		Alcoholic; frequent gaol terms
Marjory Irwin			1862		From Benevolent Asylum
Margaret Jackson			1862	24	
Eliza Jenner					'Many times' in the Hyde Park Asylum
Mary Jones			July 1869		Violent, abusive, medically sane
Elizabeth Judson			1862		From Benevolent Asylum
Mary Ann Kennedy		Ireland	March 1862	24	Invalid, bed-ridden
Bridget Keys	1851	Yass, NSW	11.9.1868		Almost blind
Alice Kilpatrick	1860		5.11.1875		Partial paralysis; both parents dead
Louisa King	1838	England	1.3.1862		Epileptic
Ellen Lisbeth			1880	6	
Jane Lloyd		England	15.2.1862		
Mary London			1874	12	
Annie Mack			1886		
Jane Manuel			1885	1	
Margaret Marshall			1877	9	
Catherine McAnally			15.2.1862		Typhus fever in 1863
Bridget McCarthy			1884	2	
Margaret McDonald		Ireland	15.2.1862		
Elizabeth McLaughlin	1840		Aug. 1870		Paralysis
Elizabeth Mills	1836	NSW	15.2.1862	4	Paralysis
Clara Morris	1817		1872		Family neglect
Mary Murphy	1838		1881	5	
Mary Ann Murray	1810	Yorkshire	18.11.1880	6	Convict; blind; no relatives
Maria North					
Minnie Perks	1858	NSW	13.3.1874		Blind; Aboriginal
Margaret Pridmore			1877	9	Cared for Matron's chickens
Ellen Jane Purnell			1885	1	
Mary Rabey			1879		
Anna Read	1860		June 1876		Blind; epilepsy
Emma Redding			1871	15	Paralysed; bed-ridden

Name	DoB	Birthplace	Admission	Years at HPB	Condition
Ann Ritchie			April 1880	6	Wrote letters for inmates
Mary Rooney			1880	6	
Alice Sadlier			1881	5	
Sarah Saunders			1885	1	
Catherine Savage			1862		Blind; insane
Ann Sheldrick	1844	London	13.3.1862		Insane
Sophie Silkman			1885		
Anne Simpson			1883	3	
Jane Smith			1862		From Benevolent Asylum
Sarah Smith			1862		From Benevolent Asylum
Ann Stephenson			1883	3	Rheumatism
Emma Tait					
Amelia Thomas			1862		From Benevolent Asylum
Ellen Toole			Oct. 1864		
Mary Tracy					
Catherine Turner			18.8.1876		Paralysis; diarrhoea
Catherine Ward			1883	3	
Ann Welsh			1862		Senile dementia
Anne Wire	1816		1873	13	Chest and foot pain
Mary Wright			1882	4	Blind
Ellen Wright			15.2.1862	4	Transported *Hindostan* 1839
Caroline Wynn			1876	10	

Appendix 3
Artefact fragment counts from excavated deposits in Level 1 of the main building and peripheral areas

Item	South range	Rear yard	Entrance yard	North range	L1 NE room	L1 SE room	North Gatehouse	Total
Bead		1			21	50		72
Bone		1,369	42	1,012	2,631	3,453		8,507
Bottle glass	95	1,071	90	358	1,064	268	400	3,346
Building material	23	529	34	519	701	67		1,873
Bullet				17				17
Button	2	8	1	22	132	223		388
Ceramic (table)	177	616	99	87	248	569	73	1,869
Clay tobacco pipe	9	516	28	52	763	1,327	10	2,705
Clerical		8	4	44	79	55		190
Clothing accessory		1		3	11	17		32
Coin/token		2		4	8	21		35
Cutlery		30		2	93	42		167
Electrical		22	1	41	31	64		159
Furnishing		3	1	25	49	54	52	184
Game piece	3	3	2	7	16	12	9	52
Gunflint					13	3		16
Hardware	1	293	18	27	29	176	6	550
Hook and eye				7	25	792		824
Leather	1	11		18	82	217		329
Match				7		17		24
Nail	18	373	73	896	1,505	926	2	3,793
Other	13	32	2	28	68	61	78	282
Paper		1		26	3	20		50
Personal item		12		4	15	64	2	97
Pin	3	3	1	74	291	2,529	2	2,903
Printers' type				299				299
Seed	1			5	43	425		474
Sewing tool		3		2	11	25		41
Shell	46	103	1	110	283	102		645
Stoneware	14	121	18	7	54	33	78	325
Table glass	2	13	1	1	5	3	1	26
Textile		3		11	22	330		366
Tin can		5		3	37	156		201
Tool			2	3	10	3		18
Unidentified	5	243	18	240	249	564	1	1,320
Total	*413*	*5,395*	*436*	*3,961*	*8,592*	*12,668*	*714*	*32,179*

REFERENCES

Alford, Katrina 1984, *Production or Reproduction? An Economic History of Women in Australia, 1788–1850.* Oxford University Press, Melbourne.

Arnold, Janet 1977, *Patterns of Fashion 1: Englishwomen's Dresses and Their Construction c.1660–1860.* Macmillan, London.

Askew, John 1857, *A Voyage to Australia & New Zealand.* Simpkin, Marshall, & Co, London.

Atzbach, Rainer 2012, The Concealed Finds from the Mühlberg-Ensemble in Kempten (Southern Germany): Post-medieval Archaeology on the Second Floor. *Post-Medieval Archaeology* 46(2):252–280.

Austral/Godden Mackay 1997, *POW Project 1995: Randwick Destitute Children's Asylum Cemetery.* 4 volumes. Report submitted to Eastern Sydney Area Health Service, Heritage Council of NSW and the NSW Department of Health.

Australian Government 2008, *Australian Convict Sites: World Heritage Nomination.* Department of the Environment, Water, Heritage and the Arts, Canberra.

Australian Religious Tract Society 1851, Report of the Australian Religious Tract Society, for the Year Ended 31st December, 1851. Australian Religious Tract Society, Sydney.

Baines, Edward 1966, *History of the Cotton Manufacture in Great Britain.* Second edition, Frank Cass & Co, London.

Baker, Helen 1965, *Hyde Park Barracks.* Angus and Robertson in association with The State Planning Authority of New South Wales, Sydney.

Barber, Elizabeth J. W. 1991, *Prehistoric Textiles: The Development of Cloth in the Neolithic and Bronze Ages.* Princeton University Press, Princeton, New Jersey.

Barber, J. and A. Shadbolt 1996, Some Mutiny, Some Bounty: Psychohistory of Lucy Osburn. In *History, Heritage & Health: Proceedings of the Fourth Biennial Conference of the Australian Society of the History of Medicine,* edited by J. Covacevich, J. Pearn, D. Case, I. Chapple and G. Phillips, The Australian Society of the History of Medicine, Brisbane, pp. 187–192.

Barcan, Alan 1865, *A Short History of Education in New South Wales.* Martindale Press, Sydney.

Barnett, Samuel A. 1976, *The Rat: A Study in Behaviour.* Australian National University Press, Canberra.

Baugher, Sherene 2001, Visible Charity: The Archaeology, Material Culture, and Landscape Design of New York City's Municipal Almshouse Complex, 1736–1797. *International Journal of Historical Archaeology* 5(2):175–202.

Baugher, Sherene 2010, Landscapes of Power: Middle Class and Lower Class Power Dynamics in a New York Charitable Institution. *International Journal of Historical Archaeology* 14(4):475–497.

Baugher, Sherene and Edward J. Lenik 1997, Anatomy of an Almshouse Complex. *Northeast Historical Archaeology* 26:1–22.

Baugher, Sherene and Suzanne Spencer-Wood 2002, Almshouses. In *Encyclopedia of Historical Archaeology,* edited by Charles E. Orser, Routledge, London, pp. 15–17.

Beaujot, Ariel 2012, *Victorian Fashion Accessories.* Berg, London.

Beaudry, Mary C. 2006, *Findings: The Material Culture of Needlework and Sewing.* Yale University Press, New Haven, Connecticut.

Beisaw, April M. and James G. Gibb (eds.) 2009, *The Archaeology of Institutional Life.* The University of Alabama Press, Tuscaloosa.

Bell, Jerry 2008, *Lighting Up Australia: The Story of the Australian Match Manufacturing Industry 1843–2003.* Jerry Bell, Armadale, Victoria.

Benevolent Society of New South Wales 1820, *Annual Report of the Committee of the New South Wales Benevolent Society.* Sydney.

Bentham, Jeremy 1962, *Works, Published Under the Superintendence of His Executor, John Bowring.* 11 volumes, Russell and Russell, New York.

Berry, Bridget 2001, Government Asylum for Infirm and Destitute Women, unpublished research report held by the Historic Houses Trust of NSW.

Berry, Bridget 2005a, *Female Immigration Depot 1848–1886.* Pamphlet, Historic Houses Trust of NSW, Sydney.

Berry, Bridget 2005b, *Hyde Park Asylum for Infirm and Destitute Women 1862–1886.* Pamphlet, Historic Houses Trust of NSW, Sydney.

Birmingham, Judy 1992, *Wybalenna: The Archaeology of Cultural Accommodation in Nineteenth-Century Tasmania.* Australasian Society for Historical Archaeology, Sydney.

Bogle, Michael 1999, *Convicts: Transportation & Australia.* Historic Houses Trust of NSW, Sydney.

References

Boow, James 1991, *Early Australian Commercial Glass*. The Heritage Council of NSW, Sydney.

Bradley, Charles S. 2000, Smoking Pipes for the Archaeologist. In *Studies in Material Culture Research*, edited by Karlis Karklins, The Society for Historical Archaeology, California University of Pennsylvania, California, Pennsylvania, pp. 104–133.

Brassey, Robert 1991, Clay Tobacco Pipes from the Site of the Victoria Hotel, Auckland, New Zealand. *The Australian Journal of Historical Archaeology* 9:27–30.

Broadbent, James and Joy Hughes 1997, *Francis Greenway Architect*. Historic Houses Trust of NSW, Sydney.

Brodie, Allan, Jane Croom and James O. Davies 2002, *English Prisons: An Architectural History*. English Heritage, Swindon, United Kingdom.

Burritt, Patricia 1981, Royal Mint and Hyde Park Barracks Archaeological Investigation 1981. With nine appendices. Report submitted to the Heritage Council and the Public Works Department, Sydney.

Butts, Dennis and Pat Garrett 2006, A Short History of the Religious Tract Society. In *From the Dairyman's Daughter to Worrals of the WAAF: The Religious Tract Society, Lutterworth Press and Children's Literature*, edited by Dennis Butts and Pat Garrett, The Lutterworth Press, Cambridge, pp. 1–8.

Cable, K. J. 1981, Garrett, Thomas William (1858–1943), *Australian Dictionary of Biography* 8. Melbourne University Press, Melbourne, pp. 625–626.

Cadbury, Deborah 2010, *Chocolate Wars*. Harper Press, London.

Cage, R. A. 1992, *Poverty Abounding, Charity Aplenty: The Charity Network in Colonial Victoria*. Hale & Iremonger, Sydney.

Cannon, Michael 1988, *Life in the Cities*. Viking O'Neill, Melbourne.

Carey, Hilary M. 1996, *Believing in Australia: A Cultural History*. Allen & Unwin, Sydney.

Carney, Martin c.1991, Judge's Cottage Artefact Catalogue. Electronic resource, courtesy of M. Carney.

Carney, Martin and Matthew Kelly 1991, Excavation Area Reports: Judge's Cottage, 531 Kent Street, Sydney: April–July 1991. Unpublished report for Wendy Thorp.

Casella, Eleanor C. 2000a, Bulldaggers and Gentle Ladies: Archaeological Approaches to Female Homosexuality in Convict-Era Australia. In *Archaeologies of Sexuality*, edited by Robert A. Schmidt and Barbara L. Voss, Routledge, London, pp. 143–159.

Casella, Eleanor C. 2000b, Doing Trade: A Sexual Economy of 19th-century Australian Female Convict Prisons. *World Archaeology* 32(2): 209–221.

Casella, Eleanor C. 2001a, Every Procurable Object: A Functional Analysis of the Ross Female Factory Archaeological Collection. *Australasian Historical Archaeology* 19:25–38.

Casella, Eleanor C. 2001b, Landscapes of Punishment and Resistance: A Female Convict Settlement in Tasmania, Australia. In *Contested Landscapes: Movement, Exile and Place*, edited by Barbara Bender and Margot Winer, Berg, Oxford, pp. 103–120.

Casella, Eleanor C. 2001c, To Watch or Restrain: Female Convict Prisons in 19th Century Tasmania. *International Journal of Historical Archaeology* 5(1):45–72.

Casella, Eleanor C. 2002, *Archaeology of the Ross Female Factory: Female Incarceration in Van Diemen's Land, Australia*. Records of the Queen Victoria Museum No. 108, Launceston, Tasmania.

Casella, Eleanor C. 2007, *The Archaeology of Institutional Confinement*. University Press of Florida, Gainesville, Florida.

Casella, Eleanor C. 2009, On the Enigma of Incarceration: Philosophical Approaches to Confinement in the Modern Era. In *The Archaeology of Institutional Life*, edited by April M. Beisaw and James G. Gibb, The University of Alabama Press, Tuscaloosa, pp. 17–32.

Casella, Eleanor C. 2011, Lockdown: On the Materiality of Confinement. In *Archaeologies of Internment*, edited by Adrian Myers and Gabriel Moshenska, Springer, New York, pp. 285–295.

Casella, Eleanor C. and Clayton Fredericksen 2001, Introduction to the Archaeology of Confinement in Australia. *Australasian Historical Archaeology* 19:3–5.

Cassell's Household Guide c.1880, new and revised edition, London.

Chanin, Eileen 2011, *Book Life: The Life and Times of David Scott Mitchell*. Australian Scholarly Publishing, Melbourne.

Chilton, Lisa 2005, Single Female Immigration and Australia's Early National Identity. *Australian Studies* 20(1&2):209–231.

Chilton, Lisa 2007, *Agents of Empire: British Female Migration to Canada and Australia, 1860s–1930*. University of Toronto Press, Toronto.

Cillin, Maire Ni 1913, *Gill's Temperance Reader*. M. H. Gill & Son, Dublin.

Corbin, Annalies 2000, *The Material Culture of Steamboat Passengers: Archaeological Evidence from the Missouri River*. Kluwer Academic / Plenum Publishers, New York.

Courtney, Kris 1998, Piece Pipes: The Clay Tobacco Pipes from the Site of 'Little Lon', Melbourne, Australia. MA thesis, University of Melbourne, Melbourne.

Cozens, Charles 1848, *Adventures of a Guardsman*. Richard Bentley, London.

Crook, Penny 2008, "Superior Quality": Exploring the Nature of Cost, Quality and Value in Historical Archaeology', PhD Thesis, Archaeology Program, School of Historical & European Studies, Faculty of Humanities & Social Sciences, La Trobe University.

Crook, Penny, Laila Ellmoos and Tim Murray 2003, *Assessment of Historical and Archaeological Resources of the Hyde Park Barracks, Sydney*. Volume 4 of the Archaeology of the Modern City Series. Second edition, revised. Historic Houses Trust of New South Wales, Sydney.

Crook, Penny, Laila Ellmoos and Tim Murray 2006, *The EAMC Archaeology Database*. Volume 13 of the Archaeology of the Modern City Series. Historic Houses Trust of New South Wales, Sydney.

Crook, Penny and Tim Murray 2006, *An Archaeology of Institutional Refuge: The Material Culture of the Hyde Park Barracks, Sydney, 1848–1886*. Volume 12 of the Archaeology of the Modern City Series. Historic Houses Trust of New South Wales, Sydney.

Cummins, Cyril. J. 1971, *The Development of the Benevolent (Sydney) Asylum 1788–1855*. Department of Health, Sydney.

Cummins, Cyril. J. 2003, *A History of Medical Administration in NSW 1788–1973*. Second edition, NSW Department of Health.

Cunningham, Peter M. 1966 [1827], *Two Years in New South Wales*. Originally published by H. Colburn, London, Angus & Robertson, Sydney.

Cunningham, Phillis 1974, *Costume of Household Servants, From the Middle Ages to 1900*. Adam and Charles Black, London.

Damousi, Joy 1997, *Depraved and Disorderly: Female Convicts, Sexuality and Gender in Colonial Australia*. Cambridge University Press, Cambridge.

Davey, Peter (ed.) 1987, *The Archaeology of the Clay Tobacco Pipe*. BAR British Series 178, Oxford.

Davies, Martin 1990, Archaeological Report on the Hyde Park Barracks: Building Materials from the Underfloor Collection and Structural Features. Report submitted to the Historic Houses Trust of NSW, Sydney.

Davies, Martin 1993, Hyde Park Barracks Textiles — Primary Print Catalogue. Designs and Weaves: General Survey. Report submitted to the Historic Houses Trust of NSW, Sydney.

Davies, Peter 2005, Writing Slates and Schooling. *Australasian Historical Archaeology* 23:63–69.

Davies, Peter 2010, Women and Work at the Hyde Park Barracks Destitute Asylum, Sydney. *Australasian Historical Archaeology* 28:13–23.

Davies, Peter 2011, Destitute Women and Smoking at the Hyde Park Barracks, Sydney. *International Journal of Historical Archaeology* 15(1):82–101.

Davies, Peter and Adrienne Ellis 2005, The Archaeology of Childhood: Toys from Henry's Mill. *The Artefact* 28:15–22.

Davies, Peter and Jillian Garvey 2013, Early Zooarchaeological Evidence for Mus Musculus in Australia. *International Journal of Osteoarchaeology* 23(1):106–111.

Dawson, Joanna 2000, Crockery from Craiglockhart Poorhouse. Edinburgh. MA thesis, University of Glasgow.

Deagan, Kathleen 2002, *Artifacts of the Spanish Colonies of Florida and the Caribbean 1500–1800; Volume 2: Portable Personal Possessions*. Smithsonian Institution Press, Washington.

De Cunzo, Lu Ann 1995, Reform, Respite, Ritual: An Archaeology of Institutions; The Magdalen Society of Philadelphia, 1800–1850. *Historical Archaeology* 29(3):1–168.

De Cunzo, Lu Ann 2001, On Reforming the "Fallen" and Beyond: Transforming Continuity at the Magdalen Society of Philadelphia, 1845–1916. *International Journal of Historical Archaeology* 5(1):19–43.

De Cunzo, Lu Ann 2006, Exploring the Institution: Reform, Confinement, Social Change. In *Historical Archaeology*, edited by Martin Hall and Stephen Silliman, Blackwell, Malden, Massachusetts, pp. 167–189.

De Cunzo, Lu Ann 2009, The Future of the Archaeology of Institutions. In *The Archaeology of Institutional Life*, edited by April M. Beisaw and James G. Gibb, The University of Alabama Press, Tuscaloosa, pp. 206–213.

De Marly, Diana 1986, *Working Dress: A History of Occupational Clothing*. B. T. Batsford, London.

De Silvey, Caitlin 2006, Observed Decay: Telling Stories with Mutable Things. *Journal of Material Culture* 11(3):318–338.

Deetz, James 1963, Archaeological Investigations at La Purisima Mission. Annual Report of the Archaeological Survey, Department of Anthropology, University of California, Los Angeles, 1962/1963, pp. 161–241.

Dickey, Brian 1966, Charity in New South Wales, 1850–1914: Outdoor Relief to the Aged and the Destitute. *Journal of the Royal Australian Historical Society* 52(1):9–32.

Dickey, Brian 1973, The Sick Poor in N.S.W., 1840–1880: Colonial Practice in an Amateur Age. *Journal of the Royal Australian Historical Society* 59(1):16–30.

References

Dickey, Brian 1976, Hospital Services in New South Wales 1875–1900: Questions of Provisions, Entitlement and Responsibility. *Journal of the Royal Australian Historical Society* 62(1):35–56.

Dickey, Brian 1986, *Rations, Residence, Resources: A History of Social Welfare in South Australia since 1836*. Wakefield Press, Adelaide.

Dickey, Brian 1987, *No Charity There: A Short History of Social Welfare in Australia*. Allen & Unwin, Sydney.

Dickey, Brian 1992, Why Were There No Poor Laws in Australia? *Journal of Policy History* 4(2):111–133.

Dickey, Brian (ed.) 1994, *The Australian Dictionary of Evangelical Biography*. Evangelical History Association, Sydney.

Divers, D. 2004, Excavations at Deptford on the Site of the East India Company Dockyards and the Trinity House Almshouses, London. *Post-Medieval Archaeology* 38(1):17–132.

Driver, Felix 1993, *Power and Pauperism: The Workhouse System, 1834–1884*. Cambridge University Press, Cambridge.

Eggert, Paul 2009, *Securing the Past: Conservation in Art, Architecture and Literature*. Cambridge University Press, Cambridge.

Egloff, Brian and Richard Morrison 2001, 'Here Ends, I Trust Forever, My Acquaintance with Port Arthur': The Archaeology of William Smith O'Brien's Cottage. *Australasian Historical Archaeology* 19:14–24.

Elia, Ricardo J. and Al B. Wesolowsky (eds.) 1991, *Archaeological Excavations at the Uxbridge Almshouse Burial Ground in Uxbridge Massachusetts*. BAR International Series 564.

Elliott, Jane 1995, Was There a Convict Dandy? Convict Consumer Interests in Sydney, 1788–1815. *Australian Historical Studies* 26 (104):373–392.

Ellis, Malcolm. H. 1973, *Francis Greenway: His Life and Times*. Revised edition. Angus and Robertson, Sydney.

Emmett, Peter 1994, Convictism: Hyde Park Barracks and the antipodean gulag. *Historic Environment* 10(2&3):26–30.

Evans, Susanna 1983, *Historic Sydney as Seen By Its Early Artists*. Doubleday, Sydney.

Eveleigh, David J. 2002, *Bogs, Baths and Basins: The Story of Domestic Sanitation*. Sutton Publishing, Stroud, United Kingdom.

Feister, Lois M. 2009, The Orphanage at Scuyler Mansion. In *The Archaeology of Institutional Life*, edited by April M. Beisaw and James G. Gibb, University of Alabama Press, Tuscaloosa, pp. 105–116.

Fewer, Thomas G. 2000, The Archaeology of the Great Famine: Time for a Beginning? *The Internet Journal of Archaeology in Ireland* 1. Electronic document, http://www.ijai.supanet.com/vol1/vol1.htm. Retrieved 4 April 2008.

Finnegan, Frances 2004, *Do Penance or Perish: Magdalen Asylums in Ireland*. Oxford University Press, Oxford.

Fitzgerald Shirley 1987, *Rising Damp: Sydney 1870–90*. Oxford University Press, Melbourne.

Fitzpatrick, David 1995, *Oceans of Consolation: Personal Accounts of Irish Migration to Australia*. Melbourne University Press, Melbourne.

Flanders, Judith 2003, *The Victorian House: Domestic Life from Childbirth to Deathbed*. Harper Perennial, London.

Fletcher, Marion 1984, *Costume in Australia 1788–1901*. Oxford University Press, Melbourne.

Fletcher, Marion 1989, *Needlework in Australia: A History of the Development of Embroidery*. Oxford University Press, Melbourne.

Flower, Cedric 1968, *Duck & Cabbage Tree: A Pictorial History of Clothes in Australia 1788–1914*. Angus and Robertson, Sydney.

Foucault, Michel 1973, *The Birth of the Clinic: An Archaeology of Medical Perception*. Tavistock Publications, London.

Foucault, Michel 1977, *Discipline and Punish: The Birth of the Prison*. Translated by Alan Sheridan, Penguin Books, London.

Fowles, Joseph 1962 [1848], *Sydney in 1848*. Ure Smith, Sydney.

Freeland, John M. 1968, *Architecture in Australia: A History*. Cheshire, Melbourne.

Frymer-Kensky, Tivka 2002, *Reading the Women of the Bible*. Schocken Books, New York.

Gallagher, D. B. 1987, The 1900 List of the Pipe Makers' Society. In *The Archaeology of the Clay Tobacco Pipe*, edited by Peter Davey, BAR British Series 178, Oxford, pp. 142–163.

Garfield, Simon 2000, *Mauve*. Faber and Faber, London.

Garton, Stephen 1990, *Out of Luck: Poor Australians and Social Welfare*. Allen & Unwin, Sydney.

Gero, Annette 2008, *The Fabric of Society: Australia's Quilt Heritage from Convict Times to 1960*. The Beagle Press, Sydney.

Geyer, M. 1994, *Behind the Wall: The Women of the Destitute Asylum, Adelaide, 1852–1918*. Migration Museum, Adelaide.

Gibbs, Martin 2001, The Archaeology of the Convict System in Western Australia. *Australasian Historical Archaeology* 19:60–72.

Gibbs, Martin 2010, Landscapes of Redemption: Tracing the Path of a Convict Miner in Western Australia. *International Journal of Historical Archaeology* 14(4):593–613.

Giles, Colum and Ian H. Goodall 1992, *Yorkshire Textile Mills. The Buildings of the Yorkshire Textile Industry 1770–1930*. HMSO, London.

Gipps, Sir George 1925 [1844], Despatch to Lord Stanley (No.248), 28 November 1844, in *Historical Records of Australia*, Series I, Volume 24, The Library Committee of the Commonwealth Parliament, Sydney, pp.83–86.

Godden, Judith 1983, Philanthropy and the Women's Sphere, Sydney, 1870 – circa 1900. PhD thesis, Macquarie University, Sydney.

Godden, Judith 1987, Sectarianism and Purity Within the Woman's Sphere: Sydney Refuges During the Late Nineteenth Century. *Journal of Religious History* 14(3):291–306.

Godden, Judith 2004, Bathsheba Ghost, Matron of the Sydney Infirmary 1852–66: A Silenced Life. *Labour History* 87:49–63.

Godden, Judith 2006, *Lucy Osburn, a Lady Displaced: Florence Nightingale's Envoy to Australia*. Sydney University Press, Sydney.

Godden Mackay 1997, POW Project 1995, Randwick Destitute Children's Asylum Cemetery. Report submitted to South Eastern Sydney Area Health Service, Heritage Council of NSW and NSW Department of Health.

Godley. A. 1996, Singer in Britain: The Diffusion of Sewing Machine Technology and Its Impact on the Clothing Industry in the United Kingdom, 1860–1905. *Textile History* 27(1):59–76.

Goffman, Erving 1961, *Asylums: Essays on the Social Situations of Mental Patients and Other Inmates*. Doubleday, New York.

Gojak, Denis 1995, Clay Tobacco Pipes from Cadmans Cottage, Sydney, Australia. *Society for Clay Pipe Research Newsletter* 48:11–19.

Gojak, Denis 2001, Convict Archaeology in New South Wales: An Overview of the Investigation, Analysis and Conservation of Convict Heritage Sites. *Australasian Historical Archaeology* 19:73–83.

Gojak, Denis and Iain Stuart 1999, The Potential for Archaeological Studies of Clay Tobacco Pipes from Australian Sites. *Australasian Historical Archaeology* 17:38–49.

Gothard, Jan 2001, *Blue China: Single Female Migration to Colonial Australia*. Melbourne University Press, Melbourne.

Government Asylums Board 1867, Report of Visit to Port Macquarie Asylum for the Infirm and Destitute. *New South Wales Legislative Assembly, Votes and Proceedings* 1867–68, volume 4.

Government Asylums Board 1870, Annual Report. *New South Wales Legislative Assembly, Votes and Proceedings* 1870, volume 2, pp. 577–579.

Government Asylums Board 1871, Annual Report. *New South Wales Legislative Assembly, Votes and Proceedings* 1872. Volume 2, pp. 405–406.

Government Asylums Board 1873, Annual Report. *New South Wales Legislative Assembly, Votes and Proceedings* 1873–74, volume 5, pp. 221–223.

Government Asylums Board 1876, Annual Report. *New South Wales Legislative Assembly, Votes and Proceedings* 1876–77, volume 4, pp. 928–930.

Government Asylums Board 1881, Annual Report. *New South Wales Legislative Assembly, Votes and Proceedings* 1882, volume 2, pp. 1135–1140.

Government Asylums Board 1882, Annual Report. *New South Wales Legislative Assembly, Votes and Proceedings* 1883, volume 6, pp. 625–630.

Government Asylums Board 1883, Annual Report. *New South Wales Legislative Assembly, Votes and Proceedings* 1883–84, volume 6, pp. 631–636.

Government Asylums Board 1885, Annual Report. *New South Wales Legislative Assembly, Votes and Proceedings* 1885–86, volume 2, pp. 719–723.

Government Asylums Inquiry Board 1887, Report of the Government Asylums Inquiry Board; Together with Minutes of Evidence and Appendices. *New South Wales Legislative Assembly, Votes and Proceedings* 1887, volume 2, pp.403–566.

Graham, Elizabeth 1998, Mission Archaeology. *Annual Review of Anthropology* 27:25–62.

Graves, Rachelle P. 1994, Report on the Excavations in the Northeastern Courtyard of Hyde Park Barracks. Report submitted to the Historic Houses Trust of New South Wales.

Graves, Rachelle P. 1995, Report on the Excavations for the Installation of a Grease Trap. Report submitted to the Historic Houses Trust of New South Wales.

Groves, Sylvia 1973, *The History of Needlework Tools and Accessories*. David & Charles, Newton Abbot, Devon.

Haines, Gregory 1976, *The Grains and Threepennorths of Pharmacy: Pharmacy in New South Wales, 1788–1976*. Lowden Publishing, Kilmore, Vic.

Haines, Robin 1998, 'The Priest Made a Bother about It': The Travails of 'That Unhappy Sisterhood' Bound for Colonial Australia. In *Irish Women in Colonial Australia*, edited by Trevor McClaughlin, Allen & Unwin, Sydney, pp. 43–63.

Haines, Robin 2006, *Life and Death in the Age of Sail: The Passage to Australia*. National Maritime Museum, London.

References

Hamilton, Paula 2001, Irish Women Immigrants in the Nineteenth Century. In *The Australian People*, edited by James Jupp, Cambridge University Press, Cambridge, pp. 456–459.

Hammerton, A. James 1979, *Emigrant Gentlewomen: Genteel Poverty and Female Emigration, 1830–1914*. Croom Helm, London.

Hammerton, A. James 2004, Gender and Migration. In *Gender and Empire; The Oxford History of the British Empire*, edited by P. Levine, Oxford University Press, Oxford, pp. 156–180.

Hassam, Andrew 1995, No *Privacy for Writing: Shipboard Diaries 1852–1879*. Melbourne University Press, Melbourne.

Hayes, Sarah 2008, Being Middle Class: An Archaeology of Gentility in Nineteenth-Century Australia. PhD thesis, School of Historical and European Studies, La Trobe University, Melbourne.

Hendrickson, Robert 1983, *More Cunning Than Man: A Social History of Rats and Men*. Stein and Day, New York.

Higginbotham, Edward 1981, The Hyde Park Barracks: Notes on Level 2 and 3. Notebook held by the Historic Houses Trust of NSW, Sydney.

Higman, Brian W. 2002, *Domestic Service in Australia*. Melbourne University Press, Melbourne.

Hill, Rosamond and Florence Hill 1875, *What We Saw in Australia*. Macmillan & Co., London.

Himmelfarb, Gertrude 1984, *The Idea of Poverty: England in the Early Industrial Age*. Faber & Faber, London.

Hirst, John B. 1983, *Convict Society and Its Enemies*. George Allen & Unwin, Sydney.

Historic Houses Trust 2003, *Hyde Park Barracks Museum Guidebook*. Historic Houses Trust of New South Wales, Sydney.

Hoban, Mary 1973, *Fifty-One Pieces of Wedding Cake: A Biography of Caroline Chisholm*. Lowden, Kilmore, Vic.

Holt, Henry T. E. 1976, *A Court Rises: The Lives and Times of the Judges of the District Court of New South Wales (1859–1959)*. The Law Foundation of New South Wales, Sydney.

Horsburgh, Michael 1977, Government Policy and the Benevolent Society. *Journal of the Royal Australian Historical Society* 63(2):77–93.

Howsam, Leslie 1991, *Cheap Bibles: Nineteenth-Century Publishing and the British and Foreign Bible Society*. Cambridge University Press, Cambridge.

Huey, Paul R. 2001, The Almshouse in Dutch and English Colonial North America and Its Precedent in the Old World: Historical and Archaeological Evidence. *International Journal of Historical Archaeology* 5(2):123–154.

Hughes, Barry 1992, Infant Orphan Asylum Hall: Crockery from Eagle Pond, Snaresbrook. *London Archaeologist* 6(14):382–387.

Hughes, Joy N. 1994, Royal Birthdays: Glorious, Inglorious and Vainglorious. *Public History Review* 3:137–147.

Hughes, Joy N. 2004 Hyde Park Asylum for Infirm and Destitute Women, 1862–1886: An Historical Study of Government Welfare for Women in Need of Residential Care in New South Wales. MA (Honours) thesis, University of Western Sydney.

Iacono, Nadia 1999, Miscellaneous Artefacts Report. In *The Cumberland/Gloucester Streets Site, The Rocks. Archaeological Investigation Report, Volume 4, Part 2*. Godden Mackay Heritage Consultants. Report submitted to the Sydney Cove Authority, Sydney, pp. 11–118.

Ignatieff, Michael 1978, *A Just Measure of Pain: The Penitentiary in the Industrial Revolution, 1750–1850*. Macmillan, London.

Inspector of Lunatic Asylums 1885, Report of the Inspector of Lunatic Asylums on the Hospitals for the Insane for the Year ending 31st December 1884. *Papers Presented to Parliament (Victoria)*, volume 3, no. 57.

Inspector of Public Charities, Annual Report 1879, *New South Wales Legislative Assembly, Votes and Proceedings* 1879–80, volume 2, pp. 855–857.

Irving, Terry and Rohan Cahill 2010, *Radical Sydney: Places, Portraits and Unruly Episodes*. UNSW Press, Sydney.

Isaacs, Jennifer 1990, *Pioneer Women of the Bush and Outback*. Lansdowne, Sydney.

Isaacs, Victor and Rod Kirkpatrick 2003, *Two Hundred Years of Sydney Newspapers: A Short History*. North Richmond, NSW.

Jack, R. Ian and Aedeen Cremin 1994, *Australia's Age of Iron: History and Archaeology*. Oxford University Press/Sydney University Press, Melbourne.

Jackman, Greg 2001, Get Thee to Church: Hard Work, Godliness and Tourism at Australia's First Rural Reformatory. *Australasian Historical Archaeology* 19:6–13.

Jalland, Pat 2002, *Australian Ways of Death: A Social and Cultural History*. Oxford University Press, Melbourne.

James, John Stanley 1969 [1877–8], *The Vagabond Papers*. Melbourne University Press, Melbourne.

Karskens, Grace 1999, *Inside the Rocks: The Archaeology of a Neighbourhood*. Hale & Iremonger, Sydney.

Karskens, Grace 2003, Revisiting the Worldview: The Archaeology of Convict Households in Sydney's Rocks neighbourhood. *Historical*

Archaeology 37(1):34–55.

Kehoe, Mary 1998, *The Melbourne Benevolent Asylum: Hotham's Premier Building*. The Hotham History Project, North Melbourne.

Kelly, Max 1978, Picturesque and Pestilential: The Sydney Slum Observed 1860–1900. In *Nineteenth-Century Sydney: Essays in Urban History*, edited by Max Kelly, Sydney University Press, Sydney, pp. 66–80.

Kelso, J. 1995, 'Secure the Shadow': Anne Brennan and Anne Ferran, 28 August to 8 October 1995, Greenway Gallery, Hyde Park Barracks Museum. *Public History Review* 4:147–150.

Kerr, James S. 1984, *Design for Convicts*. Library of Australian History, Sydney.

Kerr, James S. 1988, *Out of Sight, Out of Mind: Australia's Places of Confinement 1788–1988*. S. H. Ervin Gallery in association with The Australian Bicentennial Authority, Sydney.

Kershaw, Roger and Janet Sacks 2008, *New Lives for Old: The Story of Britain's Child Migrants*. The National Archives, Surrey.

Kiddle, Margaret 1972, *Caroline Chisholm*. Melbourne University Press, Melbourne.

Kingston, Beverley 1988, *The Oxford History of Australia. Volume 3 1860–1900: Glad, Confident Morning*. Oxford University Press, Melbourne.

Kirshenblatt-Gimblett, Barbara 1988, *Destination Culture: Tourism, Museums and Heritage*. University of California Press, Berkeley.

Knox, William W. 1995, *Hanging by a Thread: The Scottish Cotton Industry c.1850–1914*. Preston, Lancashire.

Kovesi, Catherine 2006, *Pitch Your Tents on Distant Shores: A History of the Sisters of the Good Shepherd in Australia, Aotearoa/New Zealand and Tahiti*. Playright Publishing, NSW.

Lane, T. and J. Serle 1990, *Australians at Home: A Documentary History of Australian Domestic Interiors from 1788 to 1914*. Oxford University Press, Melbourne.

LaRoche, Cheryl J. and Gary S. McGowan 2000, "Material Culture": Conservation and Analysis of Textiles Recovered from Five Points. In *Tales of Five Points: Working-Class Life in Nineteenth-Century New York*, edited by Rebecca Yamin, John Milner Associates, New York, pp. 275–287.

Levitt, Sarah 1986, *Victorians Unbuttoned: Registered Designs for Clothing, Their Makers and Wearers, 1839–1900*. Allen and Unwin, London.

Lindbergh, Jennie 1999, Buttoning Down Archaeology. *Australasian Historical Archaeology* 17:50–57.

Liston, Carol 2008, Convict Women in the Female Factories of New South Wales. In *Women Transported: Life in Australia's Convict Female Factories*, edited by Gay Hendriksen and Carol Liston, Parramatta Heritage Centre, Parramatta, NSW, pp. 29–51.

Loren, Diana DiPaolo 2010, *The Archaeology of Clothing and Bodily Adornment in Colonial America*. University Press of Florida, Gainesville, Florida.

Lucas, Clive 1990, Hyde Park Barracks: Analysis of Physical Fabric. Report prepared for the Historic Houses Trust of NSW, by Clive Lucas, Stapleton & Partners, Sydney.

Lucas, Gavin 1999, The Archaeology of the Workhouse: The Changing Uses of the Workhouse Buildings at St Mary's, Southampton. In *The Familiar Past: Archaeologies of Later Historical Britain*, edited by Sarah Tarlow and Susie West, Routledge, London, pp. 125–139.

Lydon, Jane 1993, Task Differentiation in Historical Archaeology: Sewing as Material Culture. In *Women in Archaeology: A Feminist Critique*, edited by Hilary du Cros and Laurajane Smith, The Australian National University, Canberra, pp. 129–133.

Lydon, Jane 1996, Sites: Archaeology in Context. In *Sites: Nailing the Debate: Archaeology and Interpretation in Museums*, edited by Susan Hunt, Historic Houses Trust of New South Wales, Sydney, pp. 139–159.

Lydon, Jane 2009, *Fantastic Dreaming: The Archaeology of an Aboriginal Mission*. Alta Mira Press, Maryland.

Lysaght, Patricia 1989, Attitudes to the Rosary and Its Performance in Donegal in the Nineteenth and Twentieth Centuries, *Béaloideas* 66:9–58.

Mackaness, Caroline and Caroline Butler-Bowdon 2005, *Sydney Then and Now*. Thunder Bay Press, San Diego.

Macquarie, Governor Lachlan 1925 [1817], Despatch to Earl Bathurst, 12 December 1817. In *Historical Records of Australia*, Series I, Volume 9, Library Committee of the Commonwealth Parliament, Sydney, pp. 708–721.

Macquarie, Governor Lachlan 1925 [1822], Despatch to Earl Bathurst, 10 September 1822. In *Historical Records of Australia*, Series I, Volume 10, Library Committee of the Commonwealth Parliament, Sydney, pp. 671–701.

Markus, Thomas A. 1993, *Buildings and Power: Freedom and Control in the Origin of Modern Building Types*. Routledge, London.

Martin, A. W. 1969, Carrington, Charles Robert [Marquess of Lincolnshire] (1843–1928). In *Australian Dictionary of Biography* 3, pp. 358–359. Melbourne University Press, Melbourne.

Maskall, William 1846, *Monumenta Ritualia Ecclesiae Anglicanae, or Occasional Offices of the Church of England*. 2 volumes, William Pickering, London.

References

Mattick, Barbara E. 2010, *A Guide to Bone Toothbrushes of the 19th and Early 20th Centuries*. Xlibris, Bloomington, Indiana.

Maynard, Margaret 1987, A Form of Humiliation: Early Transportation Uniforms in Australia. *Costume* 21:57–66.

Maynard, Margaret 1994, *Fashioned From Penury: Dress as Cultural Practice in Colonial Australia*. Cambridge University Press, Cambridge.

Mayne, Alan J. C. 1982, *Fever, Squalor and Vice: Sanitation and Social Policy in Victorian Sydney*. University of Queensland Press, Brisbane.

Mayne, Alan J. C. and Tim Murray (eds.) 2001, *The Archaeology of Urban Landscapes: Explorations in Slumland*. New Directions in Archaeology, Cambridge University Press, Cambridge.

McCartney, M. W. 1987, Virginia's Workhouses for the Poor: Care for 'Divers Idle and Disorderly Persons'. *North American Archaeologist* 8:287–303.

McClaughlin, Trevor 1991, *Barefoot and Pregnant? Irish Famine Orphans in Australia*. The Genealogical Society of Victoria Inc., Melbourne.

McDonald, Travis 2005, Housing in Middle Virginia: The Diffusion of Everyday Life. *Perspectives in Vernacular Architecture* 10:169–184.

McIntyre, Perry 2011, *Free Passage: The Reunion of Irish Convicts and Their Families in Australia, 1788-1852*. Irish Academic Press, Dublin.

McKinlay, Brian 1970, *The First Royal Tour 1867–1868*. Rigby, Adelaide.

Megaw, Vincent 1986, Adelaide's Destitute Asylum: A Cautionary Tale of Rescue Archaeology and Confrontation Politics. In *Archaeology at ANZAAS Canberra*, edited by Graeme K. Ward, Canberra Archaeological Society, Canberra, pp. 64–73.

Mezey, Barney 2005, Reflections on Casselden Place Through Its Jewellery: A Comprehensive Study of Beads and Jewellery Items Recovered from Casselden Place During the 2002 Excavation. BA (Honours) thesis, La Trobe University, Melbourne.

Middleton, Angela 2008, *Te Puna — A New Zealand Mission Station: Historical Archaeology in New Zealand*. Springer, New York.

Mider, Dana 1996, Archaeological Investigations at the Hyde Park Barracks, Sydney: Inventory of Underfloor Deposits. 6 volumes. Report submitted to the Historic Houses Trust of NSW, Sydney.

Molesworth, Sir William 1967 [1838], *Report from the Select Committee of the House of Commons on Transportation*. Facsimile edition, Libraries Board of South Australia, Adelaide.

Moorhouse, Geoffrey 1999, *Sydney*. Allen & Unwin, Sydney.

Moran, Patrick Francis 1896, *History of the Catholic Church in Australasia*. The Oceanic Publishing Company, Sydney.

Morrison, Richard 2001, The Military Prison, Anglesea Parracks, Hobart. *Australasian Historical Archaeology* 19:97–106.

Myers, Adrian and Gabriel Moshenska (eds.) 2011, *Archaeologies of Internment*. Springer, New York.

Nebergall, P. J. 1996, Pipe Deposition Behaviour. *Journal of World Anthropology* 1(4) http://wings.buffalo.edu/research/anthrogis/JWA/V1N4/pipes-art.txt. Retrieved 22 February 2011.

Nobles, Connie A. 2000, Gazing Upon the Invisible: Women and Children at the Old Baton Rouge Penitentiary. *American Antiquity* 65:5–14.

O'Brien, Anne 1988, *Poverty's Prison: The Poor in New South Wales 1880–1918*. Melbourne University Press, Melbourne.

O'Brien, Anne 2008, Kitchen Fragments and Garden Stuff: Poor Law Discourse and Indigenous People in Early Colonial New South Wales. *Australian Historical Studies* 39(2):150–166.

O'Connor, J. 1995, *The Workhouses of Ireland: The Fate of Ireland's Poor*. Anvil Books, Dublin.

O'Donnell, Edward E. 1987, *The Annals of Dublin, Fair City*. Wolfhound Press, Dublin.

O'Farrell, Patrick 1987, *The Irish in Australia*. University of New South Wales Press, Sydney.

Oleksy, Victoria 2008, Conformity and Resistance in the Victorian Penal System: Archaeological Investigations at Parliament House, Edinburgh. *Post-Medieval Archaeology* 42(2):276–303.

Ollif, Lorna and Walter Crosthwaite 1977, *Early Australian Crafts and Tools*. Rigby, Adelaide.

Owen, June 1987, *The Heart of the City: The First 125 Years of the Sydney City Mission*. Kangaroo Press, Sydney.

Oxley, Deborah 1996, *Convict Maids: The Forced Migration of Women to Australia*. Cambridge University Press, Cambridge.

Palmer, Marilyn 1984, *Framework Knitting*. Shire Publications, Aylesbury, United Kingdom.

Parker, Rozsika 1984, *The Subversive Stitch: Embroidery and the Making of the Feminine*. Women's Press, London.

Parkes, Sir Henry 1892, *Fifty Years in the Making of Australian History*. 2 volumes. Longmans, Green and Co, London.

Peña, Elizabeth S. 2001, The Role of Wampum Production at the Albany Almshouse. *International Journal of Historical Archaeology* 5(2):155–174.

Pescod, Ken 2003, *A Place to Lay My Head*. Australian Scholarly Publishing, Melbourne.

Petroski, Henry 1993, *The Evolution of Useful Things*. Pavilion, London.

Peyser, Dora 1939, A Study of the History of Welfare Work in Sydney from 1788 till about 1900. *Journal and Proceedings. Royal Australian Historical Society* 35:89–130, 169–212.

Piddock, Susan 2001a, Convicts and the Free: Nineteenth-Century Lunatic Asylums in South Australia and Tasmania. *Australasian Historical Archaeology* 19:84–96.

Piddock, Susan 2001b, 'An Irregular and Inconvenient Pile of Buildings': The Destitute Asylum of Adelaide, South Australia and the English Workhouse. *International Journal of Historical Archaeology* 5(1):73–95.

Piddock, Susan 2007, *A Space of Their Own: The Archaeology of Nineteenth Century Lunatic Asylums in Britain, South Australia and Tasmania*. Springer, New York.

Piddock, Susan 2009, John Conolly's 'Ideal' Asylum and Provisions for the Insane in Nineteenth-Century South Australia and Tasmania. In *The Archaeology of Institutional Life*, edited by April M. Beisaw and James G. Gibb, University of Alabama Press, Tuscaloosa, pp. 187–205.

Pinder, Elizabeth c.1983, Archaeological Monitoring: Royal Mint and the Hyde Park Barracks, Macquarie Street, Sydney — November 1981 to July 1982 and January 1983 to June 1983. Unpublished report prepared by the Department of Anthropology, University of Sydney.

Potter, Meryl (ed.) 1981, Historical Archaeology at the Sydney Mint and the Hyde Park Barracks 1980–1981: Excavation Report. Report submitted to the NSW Department of Environment and Planning and the NSW Department of Public Works.

Powell, Alan 1977, *Patrician Democrat: The Political Life of Charles Cowper, 1843–1870*. Melbourne University Press, Melbourne.

Praetzellis, Adrian and Mary Praetzellis 2004, *Putting the 'There' There: Historical Archaeologies of West Oakland, I-880 Cypress Freeway Replacement Project*. Anthropological Studies Center, Sonoma State University, California.

Prangnell, Jonathon 1999, 'Intended Solely for Their Greater Comfort and Happiness': Historical Archaeology, Paternalism and the Peel Island Lazaret. Unpublished PhD dissertation, Department of Anthropology and Sociology, University of Queensland, Brisbane.

Prentice, Guy and Marie C. Prentice 2000, Far from the Battlefield: Archaeology at Andersonville Prison. In *Archaeological Perspectives on the American Civil War*, edited by C. R. Geier and S. R. Potter, University Press of Florida, Gainesville, pp. 166–187.

Proust, Katrina 1996, Historical Research: Demolished Structures at the Hyde Park Barracks. Report submitted to the Historic Houses Trust of New South Wales, Sydney.

Public Charities Commission 1874, Second report of the Public Charities Commission (Benevolent Asylums), *Votes and Proceedings of the New South Wales Legislative Assembly* 1873–74, volume 6.

Quirk, Kate 2007, The Victorians in 'Paradise': Gentility as Social Strategy in the Archaeology of Colonial Australia. PhD thesis, School of Social Science, University of Queensland.

Ramsland, John, 1986, *Children of the Back Lanes: Destitute and Neglected Children in Colonial New South Wales*. New South Wales University Press, Sydney.

Rathbone, Ron 1994, *A Very Present Help — Caring for Australians Since 1813: The History of the Benevolent Society of New South Wales*. State Library of New South Wales Press, Sydney.

Ritchie, John (ed.) 1971, *The Evidence to the Bigge Reports*. 2 volumes, Heinemann, Melbourne.

Ritchie, Neville 1986, Archaeology and History of the Chinese in Southern New Zealand During the Nineteenth Century: A Study of Acculturation, Adaptation and Change. PhD thesis, University of Otago, New Zealand.

Robbins, W. M. 2005, Spatial Escape and the Hyde Park Convict Barracks. *Journal of Australian Colonial History* 7:81–96.

Rushen, Elizabeth 2003, *Single and Free: Female Migration to Australia, 1833–1837*. Australian Scholarly Publications, Melbourne.

Russell, Penny 1994, *A Wish of Distinction: Colonial Gentility and Femininity*. Melbourne University Press, Melbourne.

Salt, Annette 1984, *These Outcast Women: The Parramatta Female Factory, 1821–1848*. Hale & Iremonger, Sydney.

Sanders, Jennifer 1992, Dress and Textiles. In *The Age of Macquarie*, edited by James Broadbent and Joy Hughes, Melbourne University Press in association with Historic Houses Trust of New South Wales, Melbourne, pp. 143–156.

Scandrett, Elizabeth 1978, *Breeches and Bustles: An Illustrated History of Clothes Worn in Australia 1788–1914*. Pioneer Design Studio, Lilydale, Vic.

Schiffer, Michael B. 1987, *Formation Processes of the Archaeological Record*. University of Utah Press, Salt Lake City.

Select Committee 1858, Report from the Select Committee on Irish Female Immigrants. *Votes and Proceedings of the New South Wales Legislative Assembly* 1858–59, volume 2.

Select Committee 1862, Report from the Select Committee on the Benevolent Asylum, Sydney. *New South Wales Legislative Assembly, Votes and Proceedings* 1861–62, volume 2.

Shaw, A. G. L. 1966, *Convicts and the Colonies:*

References

A Study of Penal Transportation from Great Britain and Ireland to Australia and Other Parts of the British Empire. Faber and Faber, London.

Shaw-Smith, David 2003, *Traditional Crafts of Ireland*. Thames & Hudson, London.

Sinclair, E. K. 1990, *The Spreading Tree: A History of APM and AMCOR 1844–1989*. Allen & Unwin, Sydney.

Smith, Babette 1988, *A Cargo of Women: Susannah Watson and the Convicts of the Princess Royal*. New South Wales University Press, Sydney.

Spenceley, G. F. R. 1976, The Health and Disciplining of Children in the Pillow Lace Industry in the Nineteenth Century. *Textile History* 7:154–171.

Spencer-Wood, Suzanne M. 2001, Introduction and Historical Context to the Archaeology of Seventeenth and Eighteenth Century Almshouses. *International Journal of Historical Archaeology* 5(2):115–122.

Spencer-Wood, Suzanne M. 2009, A Feminist Approach to European Ideologies of Poverty and the Institutionalization of the Poor in Falmouth, Massachusetts. In *The Archaeology of Institutional Life*, edited by April M. Beisaw and James G. Gibb, University of Alabama Press, Tuscaloosa, pp. 117–136.

Spencer-Wood, Suzanne M. and Sherene Baugher 2001, Introduction and Historical Context for the Archaeology of Institutions of Reform. Part I: Asylums. *International Journal of Historical Archaeology* 5(1):3–17.

Spencer-Wood, Suzanne M. And Sherene Baugher 2010, Introduction to the Historical Archaeology of Powered Cultural Landscapes. *International Journal of Historical Archaeology* 14(4):463–474.

Spiers, Sam 1995, Social Security: The Hyde Park Barracks and the Nature of Nineteenth Century Confinement. BA (Honours) thesis, La Trobe University, Melbourne.

Starr, Fiona 2001, Convict Artefacts from the Civil Hospital Privy on Norfolk Island. *Australasian Historical Archaeology* 19:39–47.

Stenning, Eve 1993, Nothing But Gum Trees: Textile Manufacturing in New South Wales, 1788–1850. *Australasian Historical Archaeology* 11:76–87.

Stocks, Robyn 2008, New Evidence for Local Manufacture of Artefacts at Parramatta, 1790–1830, *Australasian Historical Archaeology* 26:29–43.

Street, Sir Laurence, Sir Alexander Beattie and Rae Else-Mitchell 1993, *Unwritten Law: Reminiscences of Chancery Square*. CCH Australia, North Ryde, NSW and Hyde Park Barracks, Sydney.

Sutton, Mary-Jean. 2003, Re-Examining Total Institutions: A Case Study from Queensland. *Archaeology in Oceania* 38(2):78–88.

Swain, Shurlee 1985, *A Refuge at Kildare: The History of The Geelong Female Refuge and Bethany Babies' Home*. Bethany Child and Family Support, North Geelong, Vic.

Sydney Female Refuge Society 1856, The Report of the Sydney Female Refuge Society, for the Years 1853, 1854, and 1855. Sydney.

Szekeres, Viv 1987, Adelaide Destitute Asylum. *Heritage Australia* 6(3):29–31.

Tarlow, Sarah 2007, *The Archaeology of Improvement in Britain, 1750–1850*. Cambridge University Press, Cambridge, England, UK.

Tart, Mrs. Quong 1911, *The Life of Quong Tart or, How a Foreigner Succeeded in a British Community*. W. M. Maclardy, Sydney.

Taunton, Nerylla 1997, *Antique Needlework Tools and Embroideries*. Antique Collectors' Club, Woodbridge, Suffolk.

Thackeray, William Makepeace 1840, Madame Sand and the New Apocalypse. In *The Paris Sketch Book of Mr. M. A. Titmarsh*, reproduced by The University of Adelaide eBooks 2006. Retrieved 16 August 2010.

Thompson, E. P. 1980, *The Making of the English Working Class*. Penguin, London.

Thorp, Wendy 1980, Archival Report. Hyde Park Barracks, Macquarie Street, Sydney. 4 volumes.

Thorp, Wendy 1996, Review: Unstratified Artefacts, the Hyde Park Barracks Assemblage. Report submitted to the Historic Houses Trust of New South Wales.

Thorp, Wendy & Campbell Conservation Pty Ltd 1990, Progress Report #1: Artefact Analysis, the Hyde Park Barracks, Royal Mint Building and First Government House. Report submitted to the NSW Department of Planning.

Thorp, Wendy & Campbell Conservation Pty Ltd 1994, Management Programme and Assessment of Research Potential: Artefact Assemblages from the First Season, First Government House site, Sydney, Royal Mint Building, Sydney and the Hyde Park Barracks, Sydney. Report submitted to the NSW Department of Planning.

Tonkin, Peter J. 1997, The Hyde Park Barracks Archaeology Collection: Inventory of Catalogue. Report submitted to the Historic Houses Trust of New South Wales.

Tordoff, Maurine 1984, *The Servant of Colour: A History of the Society of Dyers and Colourists 1884–1984*. The Society of Dyers and Colourists, Bradford, West Yorkshire.

Townrow, Karen 1990, Lovely Linoleum. *Research Bulletin* 14. The Australian Society for Historical Archaeology, Sydney.

Turnbull, Geoffrey 1951, *A History of the Calico*

Printing Industry of Great Britain. John Sherratt and Son, Altringham, UK.

Twomey, Christina 2002, *Deserted and Destitute: Motherhood, Wife Desertion and Colonial Welfare*. Australian Scholarly Publishing, Melbourne.

Tyrell, Ian 1999, *Deadly Enemies: Tobacco and Its Opponents in Australia*. UNSW Press, Sydney.

Ure, A. 1970 [1836], *The Cotton Manufacture of Great Britain*. Johnson Reprint Corporation, New York, vol. II.

Vader, John and Brian Murray 1975, *Antique Bottle Collecting in Australia*. Ure Smith, Sydney.

Varman, R. V. J. 1981, Structural Report: The Hyde Park Barracks, Sydney: Report on the Internal Fabric. Report submitted to Historic Houses Trust of NSW, Sydney.

Varman, R. V. J. 1993, Hyde Park Barracks Stratigraphy. Report submitted to Historic Houses Trust of NSW, Sydney.

Venn, J. A. 1947, *Alumni Cantabrigienses: A Biographical List of all Known Students, Graduates and Holders of Office at the University of Cambridge, from the Earliest Times to 1900*. Part II, volume III, Cambridge University Press, Cambridge.

Victoria Barracks, Paddington (Proposed Conversion of, to Hospital Purposes), *New South Wales Legislative Assembly, Votes and Proceedings* 1870–71, volume 4, pp. 149–151.

Walker, Robin 1984, *Under Fire: A History of Tobacco Smoking in Australia*. Melbourne University Press, Melbourne.

Watson, Don 1984, *Caledonia Australis*. Collins, Sydney.

White, Gwen 1966, *European and American Dolls, and Their Marks and Patents*. Chancellor Press, London.

Whitty, Helen 2000, *Costume — Underwear*. Macmillan Education Australia, Melbourne.

Williamson, Chris 2004, Clay Pipes. In *Casselden Place (50 Lonsdale Street, Melbourne) Archaeological Excavations research Archive Report*. Godden Mackay Logan, La Trobe University and Austral Archaeology. Report submitted to Industry Superannuation Property Trust and Heritage Victoria. Volume 3(i):157–228.

Williamson, Chris 2006, Dating the Domestic Ceramics and Pipe Smoking Related Artifacts from Casselden Place, Melbourne, Australia. *International Journal of Historical Archaeology* 10(4):329–341.

Wilson, Andrew 1985, Artefact Analysis Report: The Mint and the Hyde Park Barracks Archaeological Investigation Stage 5.1. Report submitted to the Museum of Applied Arts and Sciences, Sydney.

Wilson, Andrew 1989, Artefact Analysis Report: The Mint and the Hyde Park Barracks Archaeological Investigation Stage 5.2. Report submitted to the Museum of Applied Arts and Sciences, Sydney.

Wilson, Graham, 1983, Archaeological Report, Hyde Park Barracks, September 1982 – January 1983. Report submitted to the Public Works Department of New South Wales, Sydney.

Wilson, Graham 1986, Archaeological Monitoring, Courtyard Clearance, Hyde Park Barracks, January – February 1984, Report submitted to the Public Works Department of New South Wales, Sydney.

Wilson, Graham 1999, Ceramics and Tobacco Pipes Artefact Report. In *The Cumberland/Gloucester Streets Site, The Rocks, Part 4 Volume 1*. Archaeological Investigation Report. Godden Mackay Heritage Consultants. Report submitted to Sydney Cove Authority. Volume 4(i):205–366.

Wilson, Graham and Peter Douglas 2005, *Castle Hill Heritage Park: Archaeological Excavation Report for the Stage 1 Redevelopment Area*. Archaeological and Heritage Management Solutions. Report submitted to Baulkham Hills Shire Council, New South Wales.

Wilson, Kay 1979, *A History of Textiles*. Westview Press, Boulder, Colorado.

Yafa, Stephen 2006, *Cotton: The Biography of a Revolutionary Fiber*. Penguin, London.

Young, Linda 1988, The Experiences of Convictism: Five Pieces of Convict Clothing from Western Australia. *Costume* 22:70–84.

Young, Linda 1992, Exhibition Review: Hyde Park Barracks. *Australian Historical Studies* 25(99):327–329.

Young, Linda 2003, *Middle-Class Culture in the Nineteenth Century: America, Australia and Britain*. Palgrave Macmillan, Basingstoke, Hampshire.

INDEX

Adelaide Destitute Asylum 48, 94–95
alcohol 36, 42, 61, 86, 89
ammunition 17
Applewhaite, Clara 32, 86–87, 91
Applewhaite, John 5, 31–32, 53, 79–82
Applewhaite, Lucy (see *Hicks, Lucy*)
Applewhaite, Mary 32, 59,82–83, 86, 91
Archaeology of Institutions 1, 33, 48, 70, 93–96
architecture 1, 6–9, 49
bathing 9, 35, 37, 40, 43, 45, 53, 63, 84, 96
beads (see also *Rosary*) 13, 17, 58, 75–76, 84, 90, 95, 103
Beechworth Lunatic Asylum, Vic. 95
Benevolent Asylum of N.S.W. 5, 10, 24–25, 29, 32–43, 54, 85
Benevolent Asylum, Melbourne 48, 55, 95
Bent Street 27
Bigge, Commissioner John Thomas 6, 8
blocks 63, 91
bone artefacts 17, 22, 39–40, 47, 69, 76, 103
bottles (see also *bottle glass*) 87–89, 97
bottle, reuse 89, 97
buckle 66, 68
bullets 103
buttons 13, 17, 55–56, 65, 68–70, 84, 95, 103
   pinshank 68
Capps, Mrs (Matron) 28, 32
cards 75, 91
Carters' Barracks 1, 24
Catholics 24, 71–72, 74, 76, 97
ceramic artefacts 13, 15, 17, 48, 90, 103
   stonewear 17, 103
Census, N.S.W. 1871 46, 70
Chancery Square 5
Charity Organisation Society 26
children 79–83, 86–87,90–92
Chisholm, Caroline 9, 27
clay tobacco pipes 17, 49–51, 53–55, 103
clerical (see also *writing equipment*) 17, 46, 81, 103
clothing (see also *footwear* and *hosiery*) 17, 36, 65–70, 103
   aprons 45, 66, 69–70, 96
   collar 65–66
   belt 66
   bodices 60, 65–66, 68, 92
   bonnets 66, 68, 70
   braces 65–66
   cuff 63, 65–66
   garments 17, 60, 63, 65–66, 69–70, 96–97
   gloves 66, 68, 81

hats 17, 36, 59, 61, 67, 69
   pocket 54, 66, 73, 76, 86–89, 96
   skirts 65–66, 69, 89
   sleeve 60, 63, 65–66, 68–69, 90, 92
coal 17, 85
coins 17, 89, 103
comb 17, 41
convicts 1–12, 19, 24–26, 33–34, 38–39, 49, 53–54, 58–59, 62–63, 65, 79, 90, 94, 99–101
convict family reunions 4, 90
copper artefacts 40, 55–56, 66, 68–69, 75, 90
Court of General Sessions 4, 99
Cowper, Sir Charles 10, 25, 32, 80, 96
cutlery 17, 36, 47–48, 103
death 26, 31–32, 34, 38–39, 43–44, 73, 76, 81–82, 84, 86–87, 91
Deputy Superintendent of Convicts 2, 99
devotional medals 74–76, 97
document 17, 46, 84–85, 88–90
dye 62–63
Female Immigrants' Home 26–27, 30
Female Refuge Society 24, 95
floor 4–8, 12–15
floorboard 11–14, 19
footwear 23, 28, 45, 59–60, 69–70, 81
   welt, shoe 59
   heel 59, 65
   slipper 59, 65, 69
   sole 59–60, 65
furnishing 17, 58, 84, 103
Garrett, Thomas William 83
Geelong Female Refuge, Vic. 95
George Street 1, 25, 40, 72, 79, 81, 96
glass 7–8, 15, 17, 41, 58, 103
   bottle glass 17, 95, 103
   table glass 17, 58, 82, 103
Government Asylums Board 10, 25–26, 35, 39, 70, 82
Government Asylums Inquiry Board 1886–87 10, 36, 86–87
Greenway, Francis 2, 6
gunflint 103
handkerchief 66, 87–89, 96
hardware 17, 103
Hicks, Lucy (née Applewhaite) viii, 5, 10, 19, 25, 29–30, 32, 40, 43, 48, 55–56, 69–70, 76, 79–87, 90–92, 94, 98
Hicks, William 10, 19, 45, 53, 72, 77–78, 82–84, 87
Hiring Room 4, 27, 29–30, 39, 82–83
Historic Houses Trust of N.S.W. xii, 1, 6, 21, 99
hooks-and-eyes 17, 68, 103

horn artefacts 69
hosiery 28, 61, 65–66, 69–70
    sock 65–66
    stockings 28, 61, 65–66, 69–70
House of the Good Shepherd 24
Hyde Park Asylum (see *Benevolent Asylum of N.S.W.*)
Hyde Park Barracks, building (see *architecture*)
Immigration Depot (see also *Hiring Room*) xiii, 1, 4–5, 8–9, 12, 26–27, 29–34, 39–40, 42, 44–47, 49, 51, 54, 56, 58–59, 63, 66, 68, 70, 72–73, 78, 80–87, 90, 96, 98–99
Immigration Office 4, 29–30, 32, 46, 80
Insolvency 8, 40, 80
Institutions, archaeology of (see *Archaeology of Institutions*)
Ireland 4, 26, 28, 33–34, 70, 87, 95, 100–101
Irish Female Orphans 27–28, 99
joist groups 11–16, 18
kitchens 2, 7–9, 23, 26, 29, 31, 40, 47, 53, 76, 82, 84, 96
lables 56
lamp 17, 49
landing, stair 8, 12, 14, 18–19, 49, 51, 53–54, 61, 63, 66, 73–74
laundry 31, 35–36, 40, 45, 53, 65–66, 70, 81, 95–96
leather 15, 17, 59–61, 65–66, 68–69, 73–74, 84, 88, 90, 103
legal period 9, 12–13, 18, 46, 56, 99
lighting (see also *matchboxes*) 8, 17, 49, 53, 77, 95
literacy (see also *reading*) 42, 72, 76
Macquarie, Governor Lachlan 1–2, 6–8, 23
Macquarie Street, Sydney 3, 27, 29, 33, 76, 80, 82
Macquarie Street, Parramatta 25, 96
Magdalen Asylum, Melbourne 35, 95
Magdalen Asylums of Ireland 70
Magdalen Society of Philadelphia 70, 96
makeshift tools 60–61
matchboxes 13–14, 15, 17, 18–19, 42, 49, 52–53, 61
matrons xiii, 4, 5, 10, 12, 28–33, 35–40, 44, 46–48, 54–55, 57, 61, 71–72, 79–87, 89–90, 94–98
mauve (see also *purple*) 63
meals 6, 26, 32, 36–37, 42, 45, 47–48, 81, 97
medals 74–76, 97
medicine 1, 17, 40–43, 61, 81, 86–89, 95
Melbourne Benevolent Asylum (see *Benevolent Asylum, Melbourne*)
mice (see also *rats*) 13–14
modified artefacts 54–55, 60–61, 89, 97
nails 8, 12–13, 15, 17, 44, 59, 103
New Norfolk Hospital for the Insane, Tas. 95
Norfolk Island Penal Station 4, 23
Newington Asylum, Parramatta 5, 10, 13, 26, 29, 32–36, 38, 44–46, 53, 59, 66–67, 84, 86–87
newspapers xiii, 10, 17, 19, 28, 46, 62, 71, 76–78, 83
newsprint 18, 49, 60, 77–78, 95, 97
Northern Range 4, 8, 20

N.S.W. Benevolent Asylum (see *Benevolent Asylum of N.S.W.*)
offcut, textile 1, 15, 18, 55, 60–62, 84
organic artefacts xiii, 11, 15, 17
Osburn, Lucy 85
packaging 17, 52
paper xiii, 1, 10–11, 13, 15, 17, 19, 21, 40–42, 46, 48–49, 52, 54, 56, 58, 60–62, 73, 84–85, 88–89, 91, 98, 103
paper clip 13, 46
Parramatta Female Factory 23
Parramatta Asylums 9, 25, 35, 38, 44–45, 48, 82, 96
patchwork 58, 61, 65, 70, 95, 97
Peacock, Alice 27, 88
personal items 1, 17, 53–54, 74, 76, 88–90, 96, 103
Port Macquarie Asylum 19, 25, 69, 100
Printing Office 5, 8, 99
printers' type 17, 103
Protestants 24, 43–44, 71
Public Charities Commission 1873–74 10, 25–26, 29–33, 35–38, 40, 47–48, 58–59, 61, 70–72, 85, 96
purple 60, 62–66, 69
rats 13–14, 40–41
reading 27, 42, 72, 76–78, 96–97
Regulations 26, 36–38, 46, 48, 70, 94, 96
religion 37, 70–77
religious instruction 4, 23–24, 27–28, 37, 70–74, 76–77, 90, 97
religious items (see also *devotional medals* and *Rosary*) 1, 17, 74–77
religious texts 17–18, 44, 71–74, 76–77, 84, 87–88, 90, 97
respectability 33, 54, 68, 70, 76, 80–81, 95
ribbons 46, 48, 63, 66, 68, 80
Rocks, The 3, 51, 54, 79, 87
Rosary 74–76, 90, 96–97
Ross Female Factory 54
St James' Church 3, 5, 29, 70, 72, 76, 82–83
St Mary's Cathedral 3, 29, 49, 70, 76
St Stephen's Church 70
sanitation 32, 38–41, 81, 86, 97
seeds 17, 22, 47, 90, 103
sewing artefacts (see also *buttons* and *textiles*) 1, 17, 27, 49, 55–58, 60, 62, 68, 70, 84, 95, 103
    bobbins 56–58, 90
    cotton reels 17, 55–57, 60–61
    crochet hook 56–58
    knitting needles 56
    needles, needlework 24, 28, 34–37, 55–59, 95
    pin cushion 56–57, 61
    pins 13, 17, 55–58, 60–61, 84, 90, 95, 103
    scissors 56–57, 78
    tatting shuttle 58, 60–61
    thimble 55–56
sewing machine 55, 62, 65, 70
shell artefacts 17, 22, 68–69, 103
shellcraft 89
shoes (see *footwear*)

Index

smoking (see *clay tobacco pipes*)
soap   17, 28, 40
stairwell   8, 18–19, 55
Stamp Office   99
string   17, 51–52
Sydney Female Refuge   24, 95
Sydney Infirmary   3, 26, 33–35, 45, 69, 85
Tart, Quong   45
textiles (see also *sewing artefacts*)   xiii, 1, 11, 13, 15, 17–18, 21–22, 49, 55, 60–64, 69, 84, 103
   calicoes   62–63
   cotton textiles   61–63
   cotton prints   63–64, 69
   jute   17, 62
   lace   58
   print, on fabric   63–66, 69, 96
tin can   103
Tinckam, Matron   32

tobacco (see *clay tobacco pipes*)
tools   17, 57–61, 93, 103
toys (see also *children*)
   doll   90–92
   dominoes   91–92
   game pieces   17, 90–91, 103
   teas set   91
tracts   44, 71–77, 82, 87, 97
unidentified artefacts   17, 58–59, 62, 69, 91, 103
uniforms (see *clothing*)
Walker, Dr George   13, 31, 39, 41, 82
workhouses   xiii, 1, 23–25, 28, 31, 93–96
Workhouse Act 1866   25
writing equipment
   slate board   17, 92
   slate pencil   17, 84, 92
   pen nibs   15, 17, 46
   pencils   17, 44, 84, 88, 92

www.ingramcontent.com/pod-product-compliance
Lightning Source LLC
Chambersburg PA
CBHW041358170426
43191CB00044B/2444